IF TREES COULD TALK

a memoir

MARGOT McMAHON

Margot McMahon Collection

AQUARIUS PRESS

Detroit, Michigan

If Trees Could Talk
© 2022 by Margot McMahon

978-1-7367677-2-6
Library of Congress Control Number: 2022938144

Editor: Lisa Allen

Disclaimer: This book is based, in part, upon actual events and persons. However, some characters and incidents portrayed herein are fictitious. Any similarity to any actual person, living or dead, or to any actual event is entirely coincidental and unintentional.

Cover art: (c) Franklin McMahon Estate

Credits: Franklin McMahon's recollections of WWII first appeared in *Mac & Irene: A WWII Saga* (2021) by Margot McMahon.

Margot McMahon Collection
AQUARIUS PRESS, www.AquariusPress.net

Printed in the United States of America

Contents

1997

"Why did we move to Spain?" I asked my mother the same day I noticed she was aging. I sat on the couch with Brie. Mom, in a blue-gray blouse matching her eyes, sat upright in a caned, press-back chair before a wall of windows. I sunk low in the couch by a limestone fireplace in a cotton collared shirt and blue jeans. Brie, her thirteenth grandchild, slept in my arms. A row of twenty silver-framed drawings with ink wash leaned in stacks on the fireplace seat. I barely noticed them—the living space was transformed into Dad's gallery regularly.

Dad entered and sat in his rotating leather chair where two walls of windows met. He said a museum was purchasing part of his collection, the Chicago Seven and Emmett Till Trials art, but not the complete Civil Rights Movement.

"I hoped they'd want more," he grumbled.

I looked at the flow of lines of open collared Till trial jurors slouched in short sleeves like they were on a front porch swing in sweltering Mississippi.

5

"When I think of the risk we took…" Mom said, looking to the ceiling for deliverance and shaking her head. "We never should never have attempted a year in Spain."

That's not an answer, I thought. We were sitting in their Keck and Keck mid-century living room. Full glass walls with wood frames and broad eaves kept the passive solar home cool. In winter, the low sun added warmth to the heat emanating from the parquet floors. A centralized fireplace and furnace added extra warmth to the open entrance, living room, den and dining area. Two expansive wings stretched to a studio, writing room, bath and kitchen one way and three bedrooms and two baths in the other. Long hallways had storage closets with drawers and an attic fan to draw in cool air at night. A chipmunk scurried past the dappled euonymus patch along the windowsill.

After Brie's birth, Mom stayed with us for the baby's first week. I noticed she had changed during that visit. She measured how much to help, was up at night, didn't climb the stairs more than once a day. That she said nothing was my first clue.

"Catholics were being called out by McCarthyism and dropping like flies," Dad said in a deliberately evasive syntactical inference. "Musicians, writers, and television working stiffs were blacklisted." I had to guess at his meaning. Smoke-filled rooms of self-important Washington guys stoked a communism alarm, hollering treason to creative folks. Reputations were destroyed by rumor, gossip and lies. Not much more than innuendo ended an artist's career. It was a widespread nuance of national betrayal pointed at creative types.

"While McCarthyism hysteria ran rampant," Mom said. "I had an endless routine of diapers, meals, errands and craved seeing Europe." I learned later that Franco's Spain in 1955 was a U.S. ally and was anti-Communist—they must have thought it would be easier for the family there at the time. From a packet of letters, I discovered Dad was commissioned to paint in Morocco. We all went. On the flight they lost one engine, which caused a rough landing and upchucking stomachs. Waiting in Madrid, their nine children (I'm the seventh) started to climb the pile of duffle bags in assorted striped and polka dot-colored clothing, playing King of the Hill. Our parents rented a British Hawk, and circus-like, our family trundled through Spain, conquering the impossible circus act of it all.

"We were a ragged band of wanderers, in the Hawk that wound through narrow streets filled with horns blowing incessantly!" Mom said. Dad's mysterious encaustic of a dusty European street with dark cloaks, helmeted guards, and narrow alleys hung on the living room wall. For the first time I focused on Dad's painting above the television console that showed Spanish faces in a crowd under arches on a street scene. Dad followed my gaze, and gave me a slight nod.

"Little boys pointed and laughed at us from the side of the road," Mom said. "The sights were European. The sounds were African. Chants sung in houses ended in high piercing wails." I remembered arriving at our rancho Villa Mar y Sol over-looking Malaga Bay. We tumbled out of the taxi, running through the rooms, shouting. It was 1957 and I was five months old.

Our one-story stucco rancho was across the street from an orphanage in one direction and a walled forty-foot drop to the bustling Torremelinos promenade and beach. Our backyard was the garden of Eden with banana trees, palms, flowering bushes and fruit trees; lemon, lime, olive, apple and pear. Hens tutted, roosters boasted, donkeys bellowed, dogs growled and cats purred. The girls had one room with a sink, three boys shared another room with its own bath and the oldest brother had his own room. I probably slept in Mom and Dad's room, leaving the fifth bedroom for Dad's studio. A second crib was in the seldom-used living room.

"You were called *Bonita Chicadina* by the help," Mom said. "I was relieved to be freed of the daily toil to spend more time with you kids."

"The Malaga maid especially liked you," Dad told me. She had carried me under the shade of the gnarly olive tree to sprinkle dried corn for the turkey and *pollos*. The older kids explored caves, had burros to ride and *el gallos* to chase. From the maid's arms, I watched them go. I waved goodbye when Dad and the older boys hiked a thousand-foot mountain. Meanwhile Mom worked out daily with the seventy-year-old German neighbor. My sisters dressed up and walked the evening promenade. I stopped crying when they didn't turn back. They told me about their trips to Tangiers, Casablanca, Fez and Morocco, Brussels, Paris and Lourdes while I helped sprinkle kitchen scraps for the *pollos*.

That year before Christmas, I cut my first tooth while Dad and my brother picked up the Volkswagen Microbus in Paris. Dad said driving a new stick shift car in Paris traffic was harrowing. The gears were stiff. They picked up Gramma's favorite Limoges perfume, visited the Prado and Gourdon's cave paintings, then, Gaudi's cathedral in Barcelona. The snow in the Sierra Nevadans caused them to be late by one day—Christmas afternoon. Our traditional holiday meal was a challenge. Mom and the cook modified the Spanish-style cooking on coal stoves using less olive oil. Our cook butchered the fattened turkey for our Christmas dinner. Malaga was one of the world's five major fishing ports. Local *pesce* preparations were *magnifico*, but wasted on kids who wouldn't eat fish. *Carne,* and anything canned, was very expensive, jellies costly, cookies, nonexistent. Custard was made from our eggs and powdered milk. The greens, tomatoes and peppers were from the rancho garden. I maybe ate it all mashed. Mom left the next morning for London's Boxing Day with the Australian neighbors who were returning home. I waved to her while sprinkling plate scrapings for the burro. Buena Dias Burro. Comida, Bebe Burro.

"With the Volkswagen, our world opened to monthly trips to Gibraltar for picnics and shopping," Dad recalled. "We were eating New Zealand burro, British jam, tea from London, Maxwell House coffee, peanut butter and canned ham. You were drinking Dutch *leche* and eating Heinz canned *bambina* food from the Chemist's shop. Your mother shopped at the Iron Mongers for kitchen items. Gibraltar English was different."

I learned to crawl, then stiff-legged step, stabilized by grabbing a table, then a couch while they went to bullfights, museums and Aix. If I started falling, I'd take a step to catch myself, and soon found I was walking confidently while they were in Bordeaux. At Easter, we celebrated my first birthday, and four family member's birthdays, with a chocolate cake from Brussels. I chased fluffy chicks, while Mom packed up the duffles for home. Besides the nine of us filing into the microbus, Mom fit a butter churn, a hand coffee grinder, sombreros, bullfight posters, striped and polka-dotted fabrics and dresses, red capes, girls' party dresses and boys' matador leggings and hats. Once I mastered toddling on the ship home from Spain, my mother picked me up from an afternoon nap. As it sometimes happens in our first year, I woke with an understanding of how to speak English.

"*Hola Mama.* How you?" I said

"*Bonita Chicadina, Bueno!*" she said.

"Go I," I ran off to where my sisters sat in a circle around Cat's Cradle being passed between their hands. The yarn was crisscrossed as were their knees.

"Speak me," I said. They looked at each other and dropped the yarn.

"No, no, no. You say, 'Talk to me.'" One looked into my face while holding both my hands. "In English you say, 'Talk to me.'" I didn't understand and pulled my hands away. I ran away and fell as the ship lurched with the waves. They restrung their yarn. The boys were rolling a ball that hit a toe and rolled away. I stumbled forward to the ball, but a brother got there first.

"*Por favor,*" I said. My brother laughed. They laughed and teased me.

"You say 'Please' in English." He walked away and they continued to play. After six brothers and sisters taught, teased, and taunted my first attempts of speaking English after a year of Spanish, I went silent and didn't speak for years.

"My first memory was staying on a farm in Wisconsin with Mrs. Anderson," I told my mother. "Why did I stay there?" With a jolt, Brie abruptly woke up and cried. I walked her around the living and dining room. As I bounced her, I looked more closely at the lyrical line-and-ink wash of Mose Wright pointing his quaking finger at the defendants, Bryant and Milam, during the Emmett Till trial. Those guys got away with murder. Look at Mrs. Bryant, trim in a dark dress, with makeup and coiffed hair. A pillar of society. What courage Dad had! The trial was in 1955 Mississippi. Mom reached for Brie from her chair to give me a break, which was not unusual. She loved hugging babies. Nothing seemed to calm Brie. I tried a pacifier, a bottle of water. Diaper changed, she started to calm down. Mom and Dad were still talking about the past, which was very unusual.

"You looked forward to going to Mrs. Anderson's farm when we drove the older children to the St. Lawrence Seaway and through upstate New York," Mom said.

"Until the moment came for you to leave the Volkswagen bus," Dad said. "We couldn't get you out from the back seat." I remember being picked up from the back corner of the third seat in a tight ball and handed out the sliding door. I remember feeling that I would never go home again. I learned Mrs. Anderson's patterns: Monday was baking day, Tuesday was for washing, Wednesday was tending the garden and so forth. Wash day included a large open tub swishing soapy clothes that were rubbed on a washboard, rinsed in a large stone sink, pressed through a roller that squeezed water into the sink. Baskets were full of damp cotton clothes pinned to lines outside. A grassy area was boxed in by tall vegetables. Wispy cotton candy fluffs streaked the blue sky over the corn field. Clouds blanketed the sun. Wind billowed and the white sheets flapped fiercely as a storm brewed in the west. We scurried to gather damp sheets and I picked up stray wooden pins. It was an early dinner, and early to bed as the rain poured down.

In a deep sleep, I was carried to the basement to huddle against an inside wall. A tornado whipped the landscape outside. The window wells filled with water. A frog swam by. Lightning flashed, thunder roared. The Andersons whispered about the roof, hugged me between them. We spent the night in the basement. I woke to sunlight in a bed upstairs. Otto had cleared the fallen trees and branches. A large box turtle had landed in the back yard. The wooden wishing well was gone.

When my family returned, the station wagon emptied of my older brothers and sisters. New words flowed into our cypress Greenbay Road home: Schenectady, Saratoga Springs, Seneca Falls and AuSable Forks-in-the-Adirondacks were chanted. Songs were sung. "Tippecanoe and Timbuctoo…" Black tri-pointed hats and tomahawks from Lake Champlain, snow globes with paddle boats and beaver skin hats entered the playroom.

As we sat recalling these old memories, I couldn't help but wonder if there was something I needed to know about the changes with Mom. *Is she starting to age?* It was almost like Mom's back hurt the way she flinched. Mom and Dad were sitting. Their stillness was unusual. Stories were not usually told, so this day was a gem. I knew to listen and not ask the questions that might cause them to stop speaking. Maybe there's a code here? Listen carefully.

"Why did I go to three kindergartens?" I asked. I'd gone too far as the look on Mom's face dropped with an unusual fatigue setting in.

"I've got to rest," she said. We said our goodbyes at the door.

I turned onto I-294 South. I checked the digital clock as I sped up the van, watching the speedometer. I was six weeks into a warning ticket for speeding. It was one of the ways I shaped time. I squished, squeezed, accordion folded and stretched time for my family, my art, my life. My mother was a master time-shaper who had tutored in a south side housing project while she raised nine children on Chicago's North Shore as a nationally-awarded travel writer. Of course! The Emmett Till Trial! The answer to "Why Spain?" Dad gave the clue of McCarthyism, but didn't tie it to his own qualms. After Dad had covered the Emmett Till Trial, he was at risk of McCarthyism. Mom's frustration with diapers and chores while yearning to travel was a catalyst for moving all of us. They wouldn't tell their children for fear they might say something at school. They probably planned to go in 1956, but waited until I was born. Spain was independent during WWII, not bombed, other than Guernica. Safe drinking water, good schools and groceries were available. By living in Spain, my parents would be certified non-Communists. That is why they moved us there. Why did that take a lifetime to figure out?

1955

A cold splash of water stung Mac's freshly shaved face. The first bird's shrill, sliding-whistle greeted the day, rhythmic, echoing and distant. "That's the early one that will get the worm," Mac said to himself. Maybe he will take the smallest drawing pad and blend in with all the reporters. He sat over the waste basket, pushing the sharp one-sided razor through the soon faceted wood of his veri-black graphite pencil, then lightly shaved a sharper point. Another pencil, and another, until he filled the breast pocket of his white dress shirt. Tips up. These he would hide beneath his suitcoat. The inside suitcoat breast pocket held his press credentials from *Life*.

It was too early to call Irene. Maybe after breakfast and before the kids were awake. He pulled the rubber eraser apart, squished it together and pulled it apart to clean it from yesterday's erasure. As dawn lightened the sky through the narrow blinds, Mac slipped on his suit, tightened his knit tie and walked downstairs for a continental breakfast of coffee, toast and orange marmalade. The phone booths were in the hall by the bathrooms. Mac closed the door behind himself and a light turned on. He fed coins into the slots and dialed his home number.

"Good morning, Irene. It is a bit sticky here." Mac summed up his impressions of suspicious citizens of Mississippi over the lobby telephone. Irene was too distracted by eight-year-old Frank, who had just spilled his cereal bowl, to interpret what that meant. The twins, Pat and Elizabeth, climbed up, then jumped down the two living room steps. Andrew slid in his stocking feet down the concrete ramp into the kitchen, climbed onto the chair rungs and stared straight into her face. By the windows, Mary was quietly weaving nylon loops on a small red frame. Probably making a potholder. Nearby, Hugh, a toddler, took cautious steps from the coffee table to the couch, then to the Cyprus window frame. He slipped down and began to cry, looking at the splinter in his finger. Most had eaten breakfast already.

"You're up bright and early! What time does the trial begin?" Irene asked, grateful she knew where all her children were at a glance.

"I'm headed over to size up the place and see if I can get a start on drawing the courtroom." Mac heard the baby sob through the earpiece. The phone line crackled.

"Keep in touch," Irene said as the milk flowed off the edge of the table and across the concrete floor. She had already made their school lunches. Irene had barely finished sanding the Cyprus beams of their newly built home when Mac had landed in Sumner County, Mississippi, to draw the September Emmett Till Trial.

These Southerners are still peeved about last year's *Brown vs. the Board of Education* decision, Mac thought as he stepped out into the dusty dawn. He stayed a few blocks from the red-brick county courthouse, with a clock tower that sounded 6:30 a.m. A few police officers chatted by the front door. They were not letting reporters in until seven. Across the street, Mac drew from a coffee shop the arched windows and doors of the courthouse on a small sketch pad that fit in his inner suitcoat pocket. As soon as the doors opened, he flashed his credentials and found a seat in the middle of the empty "White" press section. With his sharpest pencil, he drew the jurors' seats, the witness stand, the door to the chambers and judge's seat surrounded by the United States and Mississippi flags. He was drawing the stage for what became five days of court theatrics and 67 minutes for the jury's decision.

Mac was jostled as the press section began to fill and the spectators shuffled into the courtroom and gallery seats. From a lone crow, to a sparrow amongst a flock of birds, he mused and erased a stray line caused by a reporter who bumped his elbow.

"Eh, Mac, sorry," the reporter said with a distinctly Chicago accent. The less said, the better with us sounding like that. Mac redrew his line, then glanced around to see several reporter friends settled into seats.

Okay, relax, Mac thought. Let it flow, stay alert. Where's the story? Nah, the segregation in the courtroom or the press section is not news. His pencil captured the body language of stylish and elegantly dressed Mrs. Bryant. The heavy heat in the crowded room evaporated while he focused. Fourteen non-sympathetic and arrogant white male jurors set the tone. He captured their likeness and lackadaisical body language as they slumped in wooden chairs. Leave out the juror's beer, it's judgmental, he decided. Mac didn't feel the heat, though he'd already soaked his T-shirt and dress shirt as the hopeless fans noisily churned above.

The story unfolded about Emmett Till, a black fourteen-year-old visitor from Chicago in the last days of August of 1955. Emmett had been taught to whistle to calm his stuttering. After he struggled through b-b-b-b- to ask Mrs. Bryant for bubble gum, he let out a bit of a whistle to calm down. Accused of flirting with a young, white female grocer, Emmett was abducted from Mose Wright, his uncle's home, and cousin's bed, on August 28th. The trial was held just a few weeks later. Sighs were breathed by the black community, dressed in their Sunday best. The audience of neighbors, friends, family and fellow parishioners sat in the upper balcony seats. Their chairs scraped the wooden floors. Emmett was beaten in Leslie Milam's shed, shot and mutilated, then found in the Tallahatchie River. Pencils slowed in the "Negro" press section. Fabric rustled from the gallery in a nearly squirming silence. Not a breath was drawn from those in the rear seats.

"Can you identify the men who came to your door?" the defense asked. Graphite scratching the textured paper interrupted the vacuum of breathing as Emmett's uncle, Mose Wright, stood up. With a shaking arm, he pointed to the white men, Roy Bryant and J. W. Milam. "There's he."

"There, it happened!" Mac nearly said out loud. Mac's pencil flew to capture the tension in the air. He shucked 300 years of United States history! he thought and drew. Mac's graphite lines captured the electricity in the room in the form of the shaky, outstretched and elongated arm, the force of gesture in his stance, the quaking suspenders on the pants. Then, a loud lurching *thud* was heard. Mose Wright sat. That *thud* told what strength it had taken for him to stand, point his finger and state two words, "There's he."

The judge's gavel echoed in the thick air as he called a recess. After coming out of his drawing, Mac folded up his pad and tucked his pencils in his breast pocket. He and another reporter silently walked across the street for a cup of coffee. At the coffee shop door, they were surrounded, closely, by a few white male citizens.

"You Northerners go back home and leave us Sumner folks alone." Shirking off the comment, Mac had his coffee at his hotel instead. He redrew the sketches on larger sheets of Arches paper. *Got to get the quiver in his spine*, he thought. His hand shook from fatigue. *Life* had a tight, and strict, Saturday night deadline. To finish the art on time took long nights and early mornings, then days to mail. Mac mailed the notebooks and drawings from the hotel desk, in a brown, flat package, directly to a New York City home address. From the corner of his eye, he saw *The New York Times* headline, "The First Time in Mississippi History a Negro Testified Against a Sumner County Citizen."

Ahh, they beat me to it, Mac thought. The cab picked him up for the airport at the motel door with only his aviator's bag in hand, not knowing if his drawings would be published.

Part I: Early Years

Chapter 1: Airdrie, 1960s

Socks. They seemed to be the main reason for varying levels of raucous arguments. Stockings, garters, lace anklets, Sunday shoes and muffs were searched for in a flurry of thunderous scrambling upstairs. We were too young to watch over those younger than us. "Where did you put it?", "Those are mine!" and "Oh no, one stocking has a run! Can I borrow one?" churned from bedrooms. Dad was already up. He'd wake early every morning, very early, and finally got out of bed at 5:00 a.m. If the cat meAAAAWWWEdd! at 3 a.m., he was up for the night, after having tossed the cat over the bedroom balcony. That's when he became quieter. *Why take it out on the cat?* That Sunday morning, he was at the kitchen room table, reading the *New Yorker*, sipping black coffee and crunching wheat toast with orange marmalade. That's the way it was.

"Is the cat okay?" I asked Dad.

His eyebrows seemed to say, *That cat woke me up!* "Cats legs are made to spring if they fall out of trees, she'll be okay," Dad said. He went out to warm up the van in the courtyard for Mass. Thunderous footsteps cascaded down the grand front stairs. Orange juice and milk were consumed on the fly as we tumbled out the portico door from the kitchen. "Off we go, into the wild blue yonder, flying high into the sky…" we all sang sleepy and slow as the van passed through the front gates.

Under certain circumstances, there is no other day more desirable than Sunday. The Lord's Day, a day of rest and fasting, of Communion and dinner with family. On this particularly splendid spring morning, a red-tailed hawk soared with the Lake Michigan breezes below and *altocumulus* clouds over the shoreline, up the steep cliff to cast widespread winged shadows over a stately home with its back to the lake. Leaded, slightly open windows reflected the flight. In the center of a first floor bay of windows is a double door overlooking a long wide carpet of a stretching wide lawn. This bay offered a morning sun to warm our grandmother where she sat during her weekly visit. The hawk flapped its wings beside the chimneys to land on a branch of a grand old oak over the courtyard as the Volkswagen van wound its way through the maple and oak forest onto Mayflower Road.

This house is named Airdrie and we were its second family. Capped with arched terra-cotta tiles, the stucco walls stood facing an acre of trees secluding it from Mayflower Road. The shape of our home was welcoming with outspread wings inviting visitors into a high-walled courtyard. Though lined with windows facing east, Airdrie gestures westward to a winding drive through a forest that bowed, in the breeze, to the grand old oak in its courtyard. The hawk ruffled its lightly colored down breast and settled onto an oak branch. The springtime fragrance of tulips and forsythia, summer lake breezes and fall burning leaves created airs of expectation for Gramma Mac's large brown Packard to park under this oak on Sundays. Our Volkswagen van entered the narrow gate barely containing a boisterous family of eleven returning home from St. Mary's Mass.

"Why are you arguing? Be glad you have each other," Dad said.

Called "Mac" by family and friends, our father quietly exited the driver's door with two newspapers under his arm. He was intent on an agenda he'd laid out during the quiet moments of Mass. The world knows him as William Franklin McMahon, nationally-awarded artist-reporter. Broad-shouldered, six-foot-three-inches tall with dark hair thinning from a rounded crown, he strode purposefully to the front door with a serious expression on his clean shaven face. The van's side door slid open and four boys in penny loafers, blue uniform slacks, white shirts and loosened clip-ties leapt from the van. The third of four girls, I was lucky number seven; I jumped out with black patent leather shoes and lacy white bobby socks into the thick pea gravel to make two divots. Three girls followed. The oldest lifted the youngest to the ground. Their shouts exploded upon their escape from the crowded van and eternally long Mass. Turtle candies, tiny green army men with parachutes, balsa wood planes, rolls of black and white film and a paper kite purchased at Walgreens drugstore were clutched in our hands.

"Grandma will be coming soon!" said our mother. She was wearing a fashionable paisley dress with matching high heels. Her community knew her as generous, caring and insightful. "Change into play clothes, supper will be served at three. Roast-a-Beef-a at three!"

Inside Airdrie's eclectic Spanish-style courtyard sat the dark-paneled home, both grand and comfortable. Tall ceilings over hand-plastered walls and dark-stained oak paneling were graced with art pieces collected from world travels of both the current and previous owners. A leaded glass star fixture hung in the bay door that led to the expansive back lawn. Two stuffed tea chairs and a table filled the sunny bay. A *New Yorker* magazine was set on the table, awaiting our Grandmother's visit. I joined my little brother and sister, in pedal pushers, and we sat around the strewn newspaper sections and couch pillows, on a very long couch that faced an oak fireplace, embers figuring out what to play. We jumped on the couch springs like it was a trampoline. Then pillows were arranged into cells, separate forts facing the fireplace. We looked into the fireplace flames and rattled on from our imaginary world.

Dad stepped into the foyer where two sons competed to fly their balsa wood planes further. "Pilots, set?" "Set!" they called. One rose and crashed. The other glided into the living room. Dad quietly stopped to bend up the tips of the wings and adjust the metal crimp on the front of fuselage. Winds and the lift of heavy things was in our vocabulary. Through the bay doors and across and the expansive lawn, children ran with a twisting, twirling kite that nose-dived into the uncut grass. Dad stepped out of the door onto the brick patio. A plastic parachute hovered and a tiny green army man drifted towards him from the balcony.

"Hey Dad, please throw him back up!" Hugh called. Dad twisted the parachute around the tiny soldier and tossed the toy up to a catching set of hands. It took two tries.

Dad, at the end of the lawn, held the nearly broken paper kite. "Get a thin cotton rag from the laundry room." He slid the tethering bowed string to a one-third position on the harnessing string. A thin strip of old sheet was ripped and tied on the bottom for a tail. The kite still dipped in the strong wind off the lake. Two more strips were tied to the pointed tail end. Patrick held the kite while Elizabeth ran into the wind. The kite flew! By pumping the string, the kite rose and dropped until it caught an updraft from the steep cliff and shot into space. Cheers erupted until the steadily dancing kite was barely visible in the clouds.

"Dad! Gram's here!" I called from the bay door. Sheba was barking.

Dad hurried up the acre of lawn. The hawk rose from the branch and flew over the lawn shadowing Dad as it glided out to the lake. He entered the bay door. His three youngest children were sitting crossed-legged in side-by-side cells built of slumping couch pillows. Dad loved a hearth fire and always had one burning in his grand fireplace. He looked away with a *we-were-only-playing* look as we carried on in our imaginary world. Dad circled the tea table with *The New Yorker* tucked under his arm and greeted Gram with a reassuring hug in the dark foyer. The dog barked incessantly.

Mom was picking up the balsa wood plane shards that lay splintered on the Iranian rug. "Please put the pillows back, your grandmother is here," she said while untying her apron. The barking did not stop. Mom rang the dinner bell. Stomping clamored down the front hall as our family gathered from bedrooms, forests and lawns. Dad and Gram sat at the afternoon dinner table with twelve blue-eyed McMahons and recited "Bless us, O Lord, and these, thy gifts, which we are about to receive from your bounty through Christ, Our Lord…" over interlocked fingers. The table was a length of laminated wood cut from the Lake Forest Bowling Alley that closed the previous year. The long length still showed the dings and divots from dropped bowling balls. Singer sewing machine cast iron stands with a peddle at the bottom levitated the alley length at the right height for most of us. A collection of press-backed chairs with cane-woven seats circled the table. The five-door black and white oven had a series of recently used and nearly empty pots on its eight-burner gas range. "Amen," we all ended with a clatter of forks.

I don't remember mirrors in my childhood home. I'd had no image of myself beyond the back of my hand and my reflection in ten family members circling the kitchen table. What I knew was: silver-haired Mom, Irene, sat at the refrigerator end with curly-haired John in a high chair to her left side. By the stove, ebony-haired Jean, Elizabeth, Hugh. Chestnut-haired Dad and Frank on the other end. Then, on the side, Andrew, me, Mary and auburn-tipped Patrick sat. All had blue eyes. Half, but not all boys, were left-handed and the youngest was ambidextrous. Our birth years stretched three decades. Less than half saved the tip of their pie slice for last to make a wish. It seemed family dinners would continue like this forever, yet, change was inevitable.

I yearned to be seven again. We were under the same roof in 1963. We flowed together like a flock of birds. We still had a promising future led by the first Irish Catholic president. Our mother guided us loosely according to patterns set before I was born. When my unknown grandfather died,

Gramma Mac abruptly moved to California, which ended her Sunday visits. My two oldest brothers went to boarding school that fall, which started the peeling off of a sister or brother every year for college.

"Please pass the mashed potatoes," Gram said over the long kitchen table. The morning rain from Chicago had followed her thirty-five miles north to patter against the darkened windows.

"Why do that to a potato?" Dad joked, spooning the steaming mound onto his plate. "JFK plans to launch Ranger 7 this summer. I just heard from the *Tribune*. I'll go to Cape Canaveral and cover its take-off."

"Oh Franklin, that's very exciting!" Gram said. "You'll paint a remarkable work."

"When is the launch?" Mom asked.

"July. So I need to book flights now," Dad said.

"What will Ranger do in space?" a brother asked.

"This mission is to take television photographs of the moon's surface," Dad said. "NASA is interested in finding out about the dark shadows of the moon. To see what they are."

"Bess, do you want some apple pie?" Mom asked as she carried a plate to Gram and hoped to change the subject. She stayed grounded while Dad painted the excitement of the space race. "Would you like more ice cream?"

"Can I be excused?" Patrick asked, making a wish as he finished his pie tip.

"Yes, you can," Mom replied.

"Me too?" said Elizabeth, Mary, and Frank.

They got Dad's nod.

"How will you draw the spaceship taking off?" a brother asked. "Won't it go too fast?"

"I plan to get there a day or two in advance and draw the scene," Dad said. "Then, on the launch day, I fill in the people and the action." Over the clatter of forks, half of the family made a silent wish with their last piece of pie. The revolving door spun in for a full house at summer, and out for echoing halls seasonally. They never really came home again. I adjusted to the unraveling of us, as they moved into different lives.

A single warbling thrush repeated its song as the day began to glow. When I was five, I woke up early in the quiet of morning, looking through my eight-framed, second-story window at a red sunrise over the lake, through a three-story cherry tree canopy. Chirruping, trilling, then a quavering chorus of birds cheeping and twittering filled the warming air. The rising red, then orange ball made a pointillist reflective path that skimmed over the water straight to me. Each frame of the window offered a new composition of stark, purpled-brown branches against a blue or grey sky with the backlighting of a new day's early spring sun. If I shifted slightly I could change the arrangement of wintery branches within the glass pane. For hours, I composed this tree. The spaces between the branches took the shapes of dragons and unicorns that moved as the clouds blew past. As the window panes warmed with encroaching spring, buds emerged and burst into fragile pink blossoms that consumed the dark branches. The blossoms clung to the branch in clusters of five. Saw-tooth-edged and shiny, pointed green leaves made a dappled shade to cool the warming air. The breeze flipped up a downy underside. The sun burned white-hot, making liquid silver paths on the lake, then dots and dashes of watery reflections as Mary stirred in the next bed. Over the weeks, one petal at a time dropped as light green spring leaves unfurled to new arrangements. Each year, these leaves turned pink, then orange, then cherry-red before dropping out of the frames of my window. As I composed a falling red leaf before a clear blue sky, my mother's high heels could be heard on the long wooden hallway, "*Arriba! Arriba!*", she called and the house started to grumble for Mass, "Sunday Mass in a half-hour." A long hall of snores became a rumble.

"Sky's the limit!" Our mother cheered us on over a quick cereal breakfast. Dad and Mom kissed goodbye as he drove to the train. She put on a coat to drive me to my first day of kindergarten. If everything you need in life is learned in kindergarten, mine was an adventure. Mom and I talked as she drove along Sheridan Road. I clicked my new brown Hush Puppies saddle shoes that stuck straight out from the back seat. She and I entered Gorton's east door, past the auditorium to a cozy kindergarten. My first day of kindergarten began with my little hand in Mom's graceful one.

"You'll be with your classmates for a while. I'll pick you up for lunch." Our hands dropped their hold. I gaped wide-eyed at children crying and comforted by strangers.

"Why are they all crying?" I turned to my mother. She was gone. I sobbed. A stranger helped me hang my coat under a square that told the day in the week with felt symbols for weather underneath. She asked me what the day was like. "Sunny," I responded. I was shown how to peel off the round yellow felt sun with spiky edges and place it on *Monday* in rainbow colors above a row of cubbies. Painting with too-thick brushes on a papered easel, I set out to compose the cherry tree in my framed bedroom window. Blossoms scattered along black cherry branches, against a blue sky. Then I remembered the sunrise and dipped a new brush in red. The brush was raised to dab…

"What a lovely painting!" a teacher said too loud. My brush pushed into the paper and the red paint dripped.

"Oh my!" she exclaimed, flustered and upset. Why was she scurrying about? I stared at my ruined image, the dripping brush. She pointed to the piddle between my new saddle-shoes. I had no idea where that came from. Did something spill? Was I too focused?

"I don't know where it came from." I said.

"I'll send your painting home when it dries," she said to my back as I was whisked to the office. Thick padded undies and a plastic bag were handed to me. I changed into the novel padded pair and went home in Mom's car full of silence. Why was she quiet? I never returned to Gorton.

I started kindergarten again at my sister's Catholic school. I would have picked a cloudy felt image and put it on Tuesday's square at my first school. After buttoning a Peter Pan collared white blouse, and safety pinning on a too-big plaid skirt, after fourteen shoes laces were tied, eleven sets of teeth and seven heads brushed, faces washed, nine bowls of cereal were eaten—two with coffee. Seven sandwiches with apple and chips were in brown paper bags when Mom cheered, "Don't take any wooden nickels!" My four brothers in blue pants and white shirts and two skirted sisters led me to the bus stop a long block from home. The bus opened the door in the girls' playground near the marble of St. Mary's.

My too-tight pigtails pulled as I was introduced to my teacher who looked Muslim in a long black draping habit with a tight white headband and veil below-her-shoulders like women in Spain, until we recited, "Hail Mary, full of grace the Lord is with thee, Blessed art Thou amongst women…" We were led behind her flowing habit in a line down a dark hallway when a loud buzzer sounded. We sat along the wall hugging our knees that slipped out of plaid skirts and showed our navy knee socks while nuns locked the windows tight to keep out nuclear air if a missile reached Chicago from Cuba. Back in the classroom, a boy sat facing the corner wearing a pointed red hat that had large letters, DUNCE, while we filed out to play. Mom looked hard at me when I told her about it at dinner. Silence followed. I didn't return to the Catholic school either.

Rain trickled down the window to my third kindergarten at Sheridan School. I would have placed a felt rain under a grey cloud symbol under the Wednesday square two kindergartens ago. Two large-windowed kindergarten rooms had an art studio with four walls of windows between them. I rushed through my schoolwork so I could roll snakes and punch my tiny fingers into soft clay. Thursday and Friday would have been sunshine symbols as I hurried through my schoolwork to work with clay. Was this school chosen for me to I discover I was an artist? I'll never know.

On Saturday, Dad lifted me up onto the window seat in the end bay window of his studio. I had padded into his studio with my pink bunny slippers. He was painting with encaustics, a mixture of pigment in hot wax.

"Please take those off," he said. I put the slippers on the seat next to me after being careful not to roll off the soft ledge. Dad's hand, with his wrist at a vertical right angle, held a long paintbrush up above a pot of hot wax. Turpentine and Damar Varnish fumes drifted into the two-story room. Above him was lit a large suspended white globe fixture.

"Will you paint my bunny slippers too?" I asked, disappointed in his silence. I sat very still hoping the slippers might be painted into the seat. He squeezed paint onto a palette, dripped on some oil, mixed it with a wrist holding a paintbrush horizontally. It was a pointy paintbrush and the titanium white blob now had a bit of cadmium red in it on one side, some thalo blue on another side. Would they make pink? I waited even longer while trying not to fall asleep. I didn't want to fall from up high. I concentrated on how he might make the softness, the light pink color, the little ears with white centers.

"So, how's the bunny slippers going?" I quietly asked.

"I am not going to paint in those bunny slippers." He was agitated now. I slumped, forlorn, wondering what else would he paint. He was trying hard to get something right. I watched him struggle to make it just so. Maybe he was happy when he said it was enough for the day. I wandered out but he kept painting.

Another day, I sat again. I didn't bring the slippers. I could tell he was relieved. His tall easel was set so I couldn't see what he was working on. He went back and forth with a brush or two in his mouth and a couple of them in his hands. He wiped something off with an old T-shirt rag. Oil paint filled my nose and a sneeze exploded. We didn't talk. With only eyes moving, I looked around the studio with its tall ceiling and giant glass doors. I looked through them at the magnolia tree and the lake. A giant fireplace was on my left side in an alcove. The double doors to my left looked out to Mom's impatiens garden shaded by the oak tree. The heel of my socks caught in the metal screens covering the radiator. My arms flew up to keep me on my perch. Dad reached out. I gained my balance. Stiff-necked, I looked forward.

I didn't want to be older, just seven my whole life. I'd cross paths with my Dad at the bottom of Airdrie's front steps, he'd lift me onto his toes and we'd dance the tango on the Iranian rug in the front foyer. Passing in the hall he'd show a few boxing steps and teach a fake undercut to the chin. That's when my grandmother still lived in Chicago. That was before my brothers left for boarding school. Everything once was whole and intact. We were busy every day and what was experienced by one of us was felt by all of us. We all strove to be together and fiercely struggled for our parents' attention, a chair in the TV room and second servings. The organism that was *us* moved like a swirling flock of swallows in unison as we shifted with needs, hurts and wants. Dad raised us with a few well-chosen words and a silent observer's eye. Mom created peace by flat-lining favoritism, never arguing with Dad and making a steady structure based on age. Boys had outdoor chores and girls indoors. Everyone did their laundry and the dishes in pecking order. Beds were made with military corners and teeth brushed before breakfast and bedtime. The straggler was given more one-on-one time at the kitchen table drilling math or spelling. The ever-present canopy of Mom's watchful eye allowed us to reach for the sky in her shadow.

"That's my chair!" was called out from behind as we watched the black and white skinny panther who solved the mystery for a missing diamond. Rows of wicker chairs diagonally filled the linen closet room. Cupboards lined the walls with shelves and drawers of sheets and pillows, towels and plastic baskets. The chair before me blocked half the small screen, the chair behind scratched the wooden floor while Jacques Clouseau inspected a door handle.

"No one was here when I came."

"I called 'Saved'!" Two windows reverberated the shouts in the small room. Nine seats barely fit. Jacques Clouseau's mystery was solved and the diamond was replaced in the museum. Mr. Maggoo and his suitcase scuttled into the small TV screen. I walked out down the wide creaky front stairs and opened the heavy front door. The door closed.

Rustling leaves, bird songs and darting colors filled the air. Forsythia and tulips lined the stucco walls with early smells of spring. A bright orange bird flickered down from the oak, darted into the woods. I ran after it. It disappeared in the bright green canopy. Beneath the branches were yellow trumpets and white pointed flowers carpeting beneath the brush. Layers of plants and colors. Darting birds, mosquitos and spiders were everywhere. A web glistened with dew. A spider scurried. I walked further down the middle path and saw green cones bent over with lined vertically striped leaves. Surrounded by flashes of color on all sides, I called "Saved." No one argued in the front woods.

I started first grade. "Good Morning Sister Mary Michaelina!" In plaid uniforms, we stood and chanted before our morning *Hail Mary* prayer with palms pressed together and fingers pointed up. After living in three homes, two countries and having gone to three kindergartens, I settled in for eight years at St. Mary's in a brand-new uniform skirt and sweater. We recited the *Pledge of Allegiance of the United States* with our right hands pressed over our hearts. "…One nation under God, for liberty and justice for all". In class, we recited "We the people, in order to form a more perfect union…" At home, we chanted "We shall overcome." While my parents planned an around-the-world trip, Sister Mary Michaelina led us single file to the art room to make resin angel sculptures for Christmas.

When Mom and Dad were on the other side of the world, school principal, Sister Davide, announced through sobs on the P.A. system that we were all being sent home by bus early. President Kennedy had just been shot. The nuns' responses were frightening. They cried. They turned red-faced. They yelled. They rushed us out of school to a bus through the bleak, steady, torrential November rain to our sitter, Mrs. Christianson, who was sobbing in front of the television. At dinner, she took a sip from a JFK coffee cup and choked uncontrollably. We were all sent to our rooms. Apologetically, she called us down for Oreos and milk. The rain did not stop. We were sent back to our rooms gently.

I ached for Mom's patterns. She didn't cry. She didn't send us to our rooms. Outdoors, yes, but not to our rooms. Suddenly, I became aware of Mom's patterns. While we were a cohesive Roman Catholic family practicing a weekly structure, each of us whorled and wove our individual definitions. Thank God she came home early from her world tour. Mom gathered us around to unpack boxed Japanese dolls with six interchangeable hair pieces and wooden shoes. The boys were given printed blue fish kites made of cotton cloth tubes on poles. Dolls from Amsterdam, France, Germany and Italy were unwrapped and placed on living room shelves next to the bay window. Dad returned home later with a Japanese brush stroke movement to ink his drawings, his fingers pointing straight down to a brush, from a bent wrist. The ink, pulled by gravity to the brush tip, swirled by his wrist to express direct confident lines. We were not told his father had died and he returned early to bury him.

Gramma Mac took us three girls to the Barnum & Bailey circus. It seemed a rite of passage and important to her that we have this experience. Tigers jumping through hoops of fire, clowns peddling unicycles with striped clothes, elephants parading from largest to smallest and a myriad of costumed chimpanzees that made us laugh. She took two of us to the fireworks on the 4th of July before we didn't see her for months. She called Dad to say she was visiting a friend in California. She called again to say she had bought a car. She called again to say she was married again.

"Jack O'Connor," Dad told Mom. "Mother married her high school boyfriend."

"Mom, what's Dad's favorite color?" I asked as dusk settled. The yellow kitchen glowed with the smells of stuffed peppers and lima beans. Mom was tearing iceberg lettuce into a salad. Chives speckled sliced tomatoes.

"Why don't you ask him? It's time for dinner, please let your Dad know." Passing the portico door into the mudroom, I paused where the TV was flickering *Hogan's Heroes* on my brother's and sister's faces in the waning light. A sister, at the long picnic table, was making a light drawing, plugging colored pegs into a light box, a Lite Brite. Her face was side-lit by the TV, but around her nose reflected many colors from the pegs.

A series of cupboards on the left had art kits and toys gifted by Santa Claus at the annual Artist Guild Small Fry Show. I passed the dark dining room opposite the front staircase, through the front foyer and living room into a narrow hall. Dad's darkly paneled dim office with a fireplace and desk by a courtyard window opened to a two-story high white stucco room with the effect of being outside at sunset. I silently stepped down two broad stairs with bare feet through a spacious lofty room filled with artwork. Dad was hovering over a painting over a single burner, melting brush marks into a layer of wax.

"I like the trees," I said.

"Thank you. What do you like about them?"

"The branches are like lots of spider webs. What is your favorite color?"

"Oh I don't know. I like all colors," he said.

"Which one do you like most?" I watched him add oil paint to the wax pool.

"The color to finish my painting."

"How is it that every kid in my class knows their favorite color and you don't have a favorite color?" I said.

After dinner, dishes washed, music practiced, homework completed, Mary and I took turns filling the bath when Dad appeared to say goodnight. A centipede crawled in the porcelain sink.

"Dad, it's gigantic!" I cried out with wide eyes.

Shaking out his pocket kerchief he carefully scooped it. "Let's give it a chance to live." He lifted the squirming bug outside to the window ledge, set it down and cranked the window closed. He then said, "I changed my mind, my favorite color is the color of your eyes."

Though Mom's dream of raising nine children was more than two full time jobs, she had already traversed the country by propeller plane, been a community organizer, had a degree to teach art, and was certified in Montessori. She had grown up in the Our Lady of Sorrows parish where she envied large families. She missed her racially and religiously diverse childhood neighborhood with heaps of kids in the neighborhood. When John, her ninth child, started first grade, Mom volunteered at a Catholic church in Bronzeville. On Tuesdays, she and her grassroots friends commuted to the Southside to teach reading and math with Montessori methods. Head Start or social programs were not yet extant. They drove along the Dan Ryan Expressway knowing the Black Stone Rangers ruled, knowing the kids they'd teach witnessed violence. They entered the Church back door and stepped down to the basement.

"Did you hear what happened last night?" a student from Ida B. Wells asked when they entered. The volunteers let them talk about the shooting, who was killed, what teen was pregnant, and what the Black Stone Rangers did after dark. They showed bruises on their arms from an uncle who got too close. These women listened and parented, until one student would say, "Our parents want us to learn, we want to learn, let's forget what happened for a while. These women have come to help us." Still in winter coats and with gloves on, they wrote their names in script, solved math problems and turned pages of a book in an unheated church.

Dad's latest brown paper packages slumped, with worn edges and torn corners, behind his pressed back chair. After our stories of getting detention for bangs in our eyes or a dislocated shoulder at volleyball, Dad's images of historic moments on heavy paper, captured by a veri-black pencil and watercolor paint, brought home the gestures and likenesses of Eisenhower and Goldwater, JFK's funeral, MLK 's freedom speech, LBJ's mutual contempt with Bobby Kennedy. He explained the speeches while showing paintings from "a guy like Babbit, or Dukakis, or Mondale or McGovern who didn't make it." Before dessert, Dad would lift one drawing from the package. What came out, one at a time, was a world's fair of contemporary images of injustice not seen yet in *our* nation's heartland: religion, race, economy, segregation, women's rights, health, environment, housing and education. We saw paintings of barefoot boys playing soccer in Egypt or the Ayres Rock in Australia, a bamboo scaffold used to build skyscrapers in China and Japanese letters in neon lights in Tokyo. He would show us about the Bishops Synod of Vatican II in Rome, Robert Kennedy's ambition, Martin Luther King or a Continental Bank in London. We learned compound words: *Embrace ecumenical; We shall overcome; Ave Maria*. He showed us the poverty and wonders of the world through pencil on paper and told us stories of what it was like to be there. He gave us an international understanding that inspired world peace and a wonder about other religions and customs.

History and solutions came to life as Dad described the Korean War, the Bay of Pigs and the Civil Rights Movement. President Johnson's War on Poverty with Head Start, Legal Aid, VISTA and then the Peace Corps were explained with his infectious excitement. I was in school the day he covered the Marquette Park riots, but knew the event from our dinner conversations. I experienced it through Dad's art and heard the stories that became confusing when I jumped rope at St. Mary's girls playground. Daisy, give me your answer true. It won't be a stylish marriage, but you'd look sweet upon the seat of a bicycle built for two. We talked about crushes with boys while I struggled internally about recent protests. If it was his experience, told with imagery, was it my experience too?

"Sticks and Stones may break my bones, but names will never hurt me," we sang as we jumped rope. Growing up in Catholic schools during Vatican II was watching adults undergoing profound personal change of beliefs as if our noses were pressed against glass, frosted by the hurried breath of change. While I was learning to read and add, St. Mary's Sisters of Mercy wore full habits and were decreed by Pope Paul VI to meet each other. Nuns resisted, stating they had made vows of being cloistered. The girls in my class toured the convent to see sparse tiny cells, a tidy twin bed with one dresser and a closet. Pope Paul VI demanded nuns meet at a conference. Mercy in heaven! Once they met no one could stop them! One nun may have stopped wearing her veil or looping a rosary through her belt. As the years progressed nuns shed their habits, one bit at a time, for blouses, pumps and a hair style in a flip. The world had not yet met a country of women who only took care of children six hours a day. They led civil rights marches and their pledge to Jesus included housing and medicating the poor while feeding the hungry. The old guard dug in their worn heels in the convent. We saw and felt the discourse in the classroom. Dad painted the Irish Catholic Kennedys and walked on water at school. Nuns treated me with respect owed to him and glorified him beyond a mere father. Teachers asked me for his autograph. He walked by silently. When I bumped into Dad in the front hall, rather than dancing the Tango like three years ago, I could barely say hello.

Mom and Dad went to report on the peaceful Selma to Montgomery march and the John F. Kennedy Space Center Gemini Program launch. With a press pass, Dad joined his Catholic clergy friends to drop into Selma to draw this moment of history. Mom's empathy gave her the courage to let him go, then decided to join him. March 7, 1965, the television penetrated

into our home showing the Edmund Pettus Bridge police massacre of peaceful southern protestors who wanted to vote. Police on horseback chased unarmed, elderly women and children, beating them with bully clubs. They were there to terrify, but the clubs cracked skulls. We watched the protestors herded into a black enclave of three brick churches and a row of public housing. Dad heard that protestors escaped into a church only to have firecrackers thrown through the windows by police. An older woman who fell in the melee had a lighted cigarette burnt against her buttock. Children were left home alone while adults were hospitalized or jailed.

Monday night, a young Unitarian divinity student who was active in enabling black voter registration was cornered and beaten to death. Father Jack Egan made it clear that no clergy was to step outside alone and without their collar or habit intact. Within the circle of the Catholic clergy, Dad created a safe, protected corner to draw the Civil Rights Movement while Mom wrote her impressions. By Wednesday night, he was in a church jam-packed with civil rights characters and locals. They held hands in the cross-breasted custom with laborers who had broken hands and sling'd arms to sing "We Shall Overcome." At Holy Communion, Dad was moved by the protected white cleric with smooth and scholarly palms, connecting to the brave working man who wore bib overalls and denim. Thursday, Friday, and Saturday, the days blurred.

Dr. King did not come until Monday or Tuesday, but everyone else was there, staying in houses and apartments, being fed by traumatized young teenagers whose parents and grandparents were hospitalized or jailed. There were many meetings for careful planning of the next march. Dad was fascinated with the intense basement planning meetings with crucifixes glinting at the end of rosaries. Archbishop Iakovos appeared on the altar-platform of the church for one of the rallies of song and inspirational witness. The crossed arms were tricky for him, as he propped his Archiepiscopal Cross in a bobbling arrangement between his elbow while swaying back and forth. Dad told me he was grinning, as if no liturgy he had ever known was as wild and as much fun as this one. A beautiful sight in his tall crown and veil, and a worthy successor to the Apostles. Sunday, Dad watched small groups that went out to attend services in local churches, but were blocked from entering. They knelt on the pavement outside for prayers. Dr. King came and inspired the clergy, Northern protestors, Southerners hoping for voting rights, children, grandparents, angels and archangels and all the company of Heaven. Dad joined the masses that gathered and sang "Holy, Holy, Holy is the Lord of Hosts. The whole earth is filled with His glory!" He was careful to draw from a corner to not be noticed.

At dinner, Dad told us about being on a bus full of singing and shouting demonstrators in Montgomery. Outside, a group of Southern white men, carrying flames, started to rock the bus. Dad stood up, raised his hands and calmly reasoned with the Northern protestors to stop singing. They quieted. The rocking of the bus subsided. The perpetrators moved on and the driver hurried away. *Forgive us our trespasses as we forgive those that trespass against us.* Mom and Dad published an article about the Gemini Program space launch that was testing two astronauts, Gus Grissom and John Young, as they orbited the earth three times, tweaking their direction by firing thrusters and presenting the question if we could do that on Earth with the Voting Rights Act. My family was held tightly together by that strife that loomed outside our Airdrie's walls.

Winter

Holidays began with Halloween. Autumn's splendor and glory brazenly warded off insect and disease invaders with orange, red and yellow leaves as angled sun beams pierced our blue eyes. We burnt wine corks with matches to smudge our faces with hobo moustaches or witch's eyebrows, sewed patches on blazers or dressed all in black. With pillow cases in hand we set off to knock on mansion doors, deep in old oak woods at the end of long winding driveways. Knocking on very tall doors with dark windows was scary enough. One neighbor required we perform a trick, like a cartwheel or somersault, for a treat. "One hand only," another neighbor grinned, who offered a bowl of nickels. Mrs. French invited us in to walk around her dining room table of homemade brownies, popcorn balls, hot apple cider and cookies while her dozen cats circled our costumed feet.

We headed north on Mayflower, east on Deerpath, to Lake Street that ended at Lake Forest cemetery. Offshore wind in old oaks, creaked branches. An owl's hoot sent us running all the way home with our half-filled pillow cases knocking our backs and knees. In the linen room, we sorted our candy and traded until we slept deeply before waking with a traditional runny nose and cough. Five-foot-tall, white-haired Gram Leahy arrived in Airdrie's courtyard in her red Dodge Dart with a carload of Betty Crocker Cookbook treats: sandies; rice pudding; and shortbread. Gifts of knitted hats, crocheted slippers and tea pot cozies were unwrapped. Her charm bracelet jingled a comforting tune. Each etched round charm had one of her nineteen grandchildren's name and birthdate.

On Thanksgiving weekend, brothers and sisters returned from college. We squeezed around the mudroom table to halve potatoes and carve stars, trees, mangers, sleighs, in reverse for printing Christmas cards. The wet, freshly carved surface of the potato was tamped on a towel and pressed onto a stamp pad and folded card stock. Around Thanksgiving, a large box of tubed Container Corporation wrapping paper arrived from Walter Paepke. Mom and Aunt Mary Marg alternated holidays of hosting our potluck dinners with cousins.

"Let's do the razzle-dazzle play!" Dad always said in the huddle. Dads quarterbacked the kids for Turkey Bowl, then Santa Bowl and Bunny Bowl—touch-football with Uncle Harry and the Leahys opposing Dad and the McMahons. Razzle Dazzle had a lot of zig-zagging diagonally while the toss was mostly to the youngest player for first down. "Dinner!" called us in while the buffet was still steaming hot. The grandmothers fussed with a chocolate cake. Two sliced roasted turkeys, cranberries both jellied and sauced, herb stuffing, mashed potatoes with gravy, green beans, always Jello with embedded canned fruit in a ring mold shape. "Jello is good for the nails and bones," Gram Leahy said, wanting all of us to be together. Gramma Mac handed all the cousins Kennedy half-dollar coins.

On Christmas Eve, our eleven socks hung together from the mantle with care, clementines and walnuts stretching them into bulbous distortions. An evergreen, glittering with colored lights and metallic red, green and baked dough ornaments, stood in the bay window beneath the star light. We read Christmas poems and fables to each other, lit by a roaring fire before Midnight Mass. Every Christmas, Dad gifted Mom one-hundred single dollar bills in unique wrapping like glued pages of a hard-covered book that opened to a cut-out hollow filled with a stack of bills. The cousins came at three o'clock for Christmas dinner every other year. Spouses and great-grandchildren challenged even our ample homes for hosting until we cousins disbanded into two dinners.

Dad's stories and paintings evolved into films. A movie crew filmed his studio, panning across the cityscapes, crowds and events in his drawings to show how it felt to "be there". The active lines captured the energy of the room and the cadence of the music. Mom taped people's reflections to voice over impressions. In *American City at Christmas Time* Mom's captured sound and Dad's art tell of a dichotomous cathedral mass blessing. Reverend Jesse Jackson chanted with prisoners in a jail, "I am somebody. I may be poor, I may be unemployed, but I am somebody! I am God's child." on Christmas day. One Sunday evening after dinner, we all walked along the wooded path to the Harkin's home to watch Dad's film on a color television. We crowded around the giant color screen with built-in console speakers to watch Dad's first movie on WTTW that earned him a Peabody Award. *Real Violins* captured the Chicago Symphony Orchestra becoming World Class by a tour through Europe then Japan, conducted by Sir George Solti. Dad transformed a room off the kitchen for *Rocinante Sight and Sound*, his film business. We watched his Emmy award accepted on our black and white television not knowing where they had gone that night. Hooting and hollering exploded when his name was called as he rose to thank his wife and collaborators.

Spring

Annually, boxes of honey locust saplings arrived to signal spring. The rain softened the clay cliff so we could poke holes with broom poles to insert sprigs with a tapering root and kick-sealed hundreds of sprouts. Boxes emptied over the weeks of us traversing the slippery clay cliff under two to ten-year-old trees whose roots grew fast to hold the eroding bluff. At dusk we descended a winding path of railroad ties held against pipes driven into the clay cliff for steps. Left above was the structure of school, clubs, sports, music lessons and patterns of meals with place settings and centerpieces. Down the cliff, time passed at the moon's pace of lapping waves and the changing tides as if the world ticked to the moon's pull. "Smelting is a Chicago tradition!" Dad made us part of Chicago's spring ritual as a driftwood bonfire crackled. After beaming flashlights into submerged nets stretched into a square, squirming smelt were raised dripping at the end of a taught rope. Squiggly silver fish sprayed sweatshirts and pants, letting the cold night seep in.

"Bite the head off first!" a brother challenged. My stomach flipped. No one bit the head off, yet this chilly ritual call endured. Frying smelt sizzled in a cast iron pan on the sandy beach. The tide swelled towards the flames. Wet shoes were soaked by surf. Like the reflective moon dancing a path across the water, Mom presided with hot cider made in a large red kettle. Satisfied with our outdoor dinner, Dad directed us to the blinking constellations. Lazy bulbous clouds revealed strips of sky. He pointed out

Orion's Belt, Cassiopeia, Taurus, twin fish of Pisces after spotting the Big Dipper and North Star in case we needed to find our way home. Weary, we climbed the cliff.

When Dad's loud whistle sounded, we'd alley-oop to line up like ducks into the Volkswagen van. My mother's pattern corralled us with *you don't ever want to miss a moment*. Once a year they'd take us to Arlington Park Race Track to make $2 bets. A philosophy of life was taught, to let go of a loss, to make a better guess for the next horse. Optimism was trained.

On a Saturday, pre-dawn, we all sleepily piled in the van for a tour of murals in Pilsen and Bronzeville. A mural was spotted, we woke up, saw walls covered with faces and names of admired neighbors and slept again. Pilsen's murals were colorful. We walked around Maxwell Street, one of the remaining industrial tool exchanges from Chicago past. I treasured my second-hand wood carving tools wrapped in cotton cloth. Dad showed us Henry Moore's *Nuclear Energy* dedicated above the Manhattan projects lab at the University of Chicago.

We drove around the Picasso sculpture at Daley Plaza at its unveiling.

"It will rust superficially, sealing the surfaces of steel for hundreds of years." Dad said. We jumped out and ran up, slid down the inclined front while he circled the block. "Don't look in the warehouses," Dad said as we trekked around the stockyards of packing houses on 47th street. My curiosity led me to look in to see cows' rear hooves tied and hooked on a track, their necks bleeding black liquid into sandy dirt. A packing house worker looked concerned and closed the door. My stomach lurched. I tasted the smell of blood mixed with acrid smelling steel mill fumes from nearby and became vegetarian that day. We loaded in the van for *Man of La Mancha* who rode his horse Rocinante with a lance to conquer windmills for his beloved Dulcinea. The visual echoes of reality, images in mirrors of an idealistic man facing his own exuberance echoed in our belief to dream impossible dreams.

Careening through semis and slushy snow, ten families migrated south with the spring to a spit of sand called Santa Rosa Island off Florida's panhandle for spring break. Vans bulging with tents, books and beach gear squeezed through narrow gaps of tall trucks. The snow turned to rain as we raced to our overnight campground. Were we in Kentucky or Tennessee for gas fill up? "If we lose sight of you, we'll meet up in Florida," was said. The second day we opened our windows to the hot and humid smells of salt, palms and sand. Friends of my parents, with teenaged children, camped in a circle at the end of a Fort Pickens State Park. Over many years, we blistered our skin, suffered heat stroke, had an appendix removed, menstrual cycles began and ended, oysters and paella were served for a beach dinner, stories were told and songs sung.

Dad told about "North with the Spring" while driving north to distract me from the carsickness from the raw oysters. He turned off the highway, meandering on small roads of Alabama. We stopped at otherworldly gas stations with tanks of baby alligators, peacock bedspreads and foreboding Confederate flags. Redbuds and dogwoods flourished in the woods. The dirt was red.

After returning home, I searched at Lake Forest Library through the card files for "North with the Spring" and came across *Silent Spring*. Discovering Rachel Carson burst my world open. What mankind can do? Through rhythmic poetic writing she taught me hard science. The bald eagle, great blue herons and whooping cranes were nearly extinct. If shells aren't strong enough for birds to hatch, what are chemicals doing to us? *Silent Spring* led to reading Jane Goodall and her writings of our commonality with chimpanzees. These two women emerged as my heroes. They beautifully wrote of what I yearned to learn. Of how nature connected and was changed by us. How we could change our selves for the better. Jane Goodall's *My Life with Chimpanzees* landed on Mom's pillow for her night's read. She responded with a ticket to a Jane Goodall lecture at the Auditorium theater. Our definition of being a superior intelligence is based on making tools. Jane photographed a chimpanzee making a tool. Humankind was redefined.

Easter Sunday was all about bonnets and starchy dresses, black patent leather shoes, stockings and muffs for church. Leaving the car on Illinois near Greenbay Road, Dad walked on the street side of the sidewalk, "In case a car splashed," he said. We entered the church door from the rear nearly on time. Our pew, twelve from the back, was waiting for us. It's not that it was ever assigned, the parish knew we filled the same two pews every Sunday. Most Sundays doilies or handkerchiefs were quickly bobby-pinned on the way into church. The entrance procession began with a hymn. On Easter, bonnets flounced throughout the church. Women had veils over their faces and white gloves on their hands.

"So and so is still in mourning!" Aunt Mary Marg said seeing a woman in black with a droopy wide-brimmed hat. "Look who has a new baby!" Mom might tell Mrs. Harkins. We'd return home to an Easter hunt for eggs, chicks, jelly beans and bunnies. They represented what? Rejuvenation, rebirth, Jesus leaving the tomb, resurrection? Dying by crucifixion to resurrect to heaven? The meaning of Easter was a tough holiday to grasp.

Summer

June through late August, days were spent on our beach. Thousands of dried, curled alewives littered the beach. Their crisped fins sliced our feet. They floated on choppy waves and piled in the thousands above the gravel. Hot sun rotted the piles of stinking flesh. House flies followed. We avoided them underwater. In July, fatty Coho salmon lazily floated in the calm clear water, some as long as I was tall. I imagined reaching in to grab one for dinner. They were introduced to eat the alewives and stored the lake's DDT and mercury. Our soles toughened to leather running over the pebbles and sandy shore. Great flat stones captured light as they were spun to bounce in arcs on an inland sea. August brought high waves for riding into shore and migrating birds of prey.

Mom carried down a breakfast of toast and juice, eggs scrambled on a campfire and peppered with kicked sand as the sun glistened off the morning lake. She settled into her book when I first swam by stretching out my legs, walking my fingers along the sand and kicking. Silvery schools of minnows darted around my arms. The gentle waves lifted me to a float and lowered me for my fingers to touch sand. Kicking and paddling until I no longer touched down.

"Look, she's swimming!" was shouted from the Three Posts, the end of a washed-away dock. My dog paddle merged to a breaststroke with a whip kick that propelled me into the waves. My rite of passage to swim that far came with rewards of jumping. Ladder-like branches were tied for steps. Repeatedly, a wooden diving board was nailed on top of the rotting end of the dock posts. The gap with the older kids closed a bit. Practicing flips and front and back dives with our own Olympic competition scoring consumed weeks. Tying driftwood logs together with rope into rafts took hours or days. We pushed the raft, with a long green sapling, from one beach to another and dreamed of crossing Lake Michigan. Though too young, the older ones took care of the younger ones who looked after the even younger ones. Too much bossiness, too many rules invented to contain and herd what was out of control. I often felt squelchy by being reigned on by parental messages delivered from children.

Our hand impressions were pressed in recessed wet squares of sand. We added compositions of driftwood-sticks, shells and feathers weighed down with rocks. Mom mixed Plaster of Paris with lake water, and poured it into the square. She placed a metal wire in the setting plaster to hang on the stucco wall of the dining porch. Another day we might make sandcastles ringed with seaweed for gardens.

"Everyone out of the water!" Dad called down from the top the cliff, "there are seiche warnings!" We scrambled up the cliff carrying bags of towels, sand castings and water. Later, waves broke up our raft scattering the driftwood again, ripped off our Three Posts platform, and shortened our beach into our eroding cliff. The railroad tie steps collapsed into a vertical cliff and a climbing rope was installed. We pulled our way up the steep clay steps.

The summer of 1966, curled up in pedal pushers and a T-shirt on the couch reading, my hair still dripping wet from a solitary morning swim in the lake, I sat beside the bay window. The living room was floor to ceiling books in darkly stained shelves. A fifty-gallon aquarium bubbled behind me, the huge fireplace in front not even noticed. I devoured Laura Ingalls Wilder's *Silver Lake,* horrified that Mary had become blind due to a fever and wondering how she could possibly adapt to…

"Time to go!" Mom called from the bottom of the steps. I hadn't heard her high heels and jumped up, taking my book with me. My fingers reached out the passenger window to slice down the parkway trees. No trees fell. At the highway, I cranked up the window, the no-vent windows were pulled open. An aroma of tree-lined streets and summer prairie flowers rushed in. We rode for the time it took me to finish my book. Mary did go blind and Laura described in detail everything she couldn't see. When my stomach got queasy, I pushed a fingernail through my wind-dried hair along the midline of my head and started to braid it into two tight pigtails with a rubber band at the bottom. Already the summer sun had lightened my brunette hair to blonde.

Mom explained the Head Start program as she cruised along the four lanes laden with traffic of the Dan Ryan. Smells of steel mills and packing houses increased my queasiness. I closed the no-vent window, glanced about for a horizon line to steady my stomach. She told me about the Southside children she taught early-childhood math and reading skills. One of her students ,Vanessa, would stay with us for a couple of weeks. My sister was away at camp and Vanessa was my age. She would stay in my room. The highway was dug under the sidestreets with houses with high concrete walls filled with spurting patches of yellow and blue flowering weeds. I concentrated to keep my car-sick stomach behaving. A few whimpering coffee trees and broken-windowed brick buildings rose above the crawling car.

"This is the Dan Ryan Expressway. It's named after the Chairman of the Cook County Board," Mom said. Her tone told me he was like the conversations I'd heard about Cardinal Cody, but didn't understand. It was something about racially divisive actions in neighborhoods that she didn't like and that she was doing something about. We pulled off onto the side streets the wooden buildings slumped onto brick buildings. Some front gardens were seeded with flowers but not weeded. Sheets and cardboard filled in cracked and missing windows.

Young children played on front steps. Empty lots were filled with crabgrass and high with ragweed. Listless men clutching paper bags, slumped silently in front of diamond-shaped gates of closed stores. Radios blasted percussion that vibrated the windows and horns that rose to another rhythm. Liquor and Hostess snack signs were displayed in all the windows. Mom sneezed into her always-present tissue and pulled in front of several light brick tower apartments with a low-rise Head Start center. Stench of the stained streets caused my weak stomach to somersault. Earnest, coifed black mothers walked hand-in-hand with tiny daughters dressed in pink birthday party dresses above pinchy, patent-leather shoes. "For some, the dresses are all they have," Mom said.

Mom and her friends taught Vanessa, a girl my age. Quiet Vanessa, in tightly twisted pig tails with rubber bands at the tops and tips, arrived in her Sunday best with a brown suitcase. She sat primly in the back seat of our station wagon. My worn red Keds and her black shiny dress shoes dangled diagonally from the back seat, toes pointed in. Her tightly braided stiff pigtails touched my arm. The crisp ends poked. In the hourlong car ride home Vanessa was very quiet. She must have been one of my mother's favorite students. I showed her my Laura Ingalls Wilder book and told her all about Laura's Pa who worked the horses to plow the field and milked a cow. In the evening, Pa enjoyed playing the fiddle, or a violin. Her eyes moved left to see, but her head was straight. Mildly interested in two names for one instrument, I told her more about his folk songs and toe tapping.

"Laura wrote about her own life in the woods and by a lake in many books," I said. Silently, she looked out the window as we sped along Edens highway. There were more and more trees as we approached the northern suburbs. A stream of tears flowed down her cheek. Mom glanced in the rear-view mirror. Two quiet girls sat side by side. My shy place in a large family had become an awkward strain of entertaining a reluctant new friend. The feeling was worse than my queasiness. By the time we drove through our front woods on a winding driveway, Vanessa appeared to be terrified. Sheba ran out of the woods barking at the car tires. Even Mom's voice couldn't calm her. Inside the courtyard, Vanessa didn't want to leave the car, so Mom left the door open and brought her suitcase inside. Later, she took her hand and cajoled her to come inside. Vanessa had not spoken a word.

Our home had seven bedrooms, three staircases, eight baths, a five-room apartment and a three-bedroom coach house wrapped around the courtyard, a garden of azaleas and a tall, old oak presiding over the entrance. Mom made sure that each of us had an art studio. Our oldest brother's darkroom was at the top of the attic steps. Hugh made his own bedroom there too, painted in black and white checkerboard to strum his guitar. A sister's loom and brother's drum set filled entire bedrooms. My wood and stone carving studio was on the back screened-porch overlooking the lake. There was music all the time. Flute scales were stacattoed behind my closed double bedroom doors. The piano room was just off the living room. Guitar, drums, harmonica, and flute scales, rocked songs with blips and mistakes up and down the hall.

Early morning hullabaloo quieted after the oldest brothers and sisters skittered down the front stairs for summer jobs. Around the corner, a closet off the mudroom with a wall of hooks for sweaters, coats, scarves above pairs of shoes where we picked a sweater or coat right for the day. I planned on wearing a pair of Redwing boots for the muddy day ahead and hoped they were still there, though they were too big. The few kids on our block of three-acre estates, and Highland Park cousins, came to our house because something was always going on.

Vanessa sat on the bottom of the grand staircase and cried. I sat to console her. Sheba whimpered and barked. Sylvia meowed. My heart ripped for Vanessa. I was hopeless at calming her so frustration set in. Vanessa watched teary-eyed from inside the bay window. In the east woods by the lake, we decided to dig a hole to China. It had to start off pretty big. Enough for four shovels to fling dirt on top of ripe "stink bombs", white fungi balls that grew as big as volley balls. "Those smell so bad!!" "Hey, let's use them for nuclear bombs!" We tossed, as high as two of us could, to explode their stinking white and black powder all over the freshly mowed lawn. The whole yard and woods stunk.

We went back to digging. Over time, our hole got pretty deep. Deep enough to let us know we were not going to get to China that summer. Thin plywood was laid over our hole and branches and leaves laid on top. We slipped into the hole and slid the mossy cover shut so nuclear bombs couldn't get us. We planned to store dried milk, more water, chocolate and beef jerky for that ominous imagined day. Dad's old Army mess kit with metal spoons and fork was set on a board, then we ran to the basement to make pottery vessels.

Once Dad made us wooden rubberband guns in his basement wood shop. Carefully and slowly he carved in jointed wood, with minute detail, a replica pine .45 pistol with a wooden clothespin screwed on top. The rubber band on the barrel head was stretched to the closed-pin mouth. "Only aim at fences or trees," he said. The older boys had aimed and shot at each other before they were up the back basement steps. Immediately, all the pistols were confiscated by Dad. "And don't chew a gun from your peanut butter sandwich either," we heard at the table. Midway through the first week, Vanessa and I felt more comfortable together. We'd grown accustomed to our awkwardness with each other, though I was compelled to join the *we* of my family that often left her alone.

For long days, weeks, maybe years, we played Kick-the-Can. A circle was drawn with a toe into the pea gravel in the courtyard and an empty large tin can carefully placed in the measured center. Teams from ten to twenty kids were selected and a coin tossed to decide which team held the camp, or hid in the woods. Vanessa did not want to be picked first or last. She, in her pink party dress sat in a cast-iron chair, once a tractor seat, on a tri-pod of legs and watched from the portico. A name was called out while the caller's foot was on the can to capture the enemy who waited in the circle. Teammates could run through the circle and kick-the-can to release all the prisoners. The game started again. Chin to knees, I hid in the courtyard yews and swatted a hovering bee's hum. The first sting and flail of my arms angered the hive. Half a dozen red welts erupted on my face and I let out an explosive holler. I ran past Vanessa's slight smile, swatting a circling of bees to the kitchen.

"We will only live for four years if all the bees die," Mom consoled me while pressing copper pennies on the red blebs. Vanessa came in to silently help Mom pat my swollen and red face with a cool, wet towel. Vanessa wiped my stream of tears.

Capture-the-Flag consumed other days. The front woods were positioned around a central path to the tennis court, neatly dividing the dense underbrush in half. It seemed I waited forever to be picked for a team. Each team was given a red or blue bandana to hide on their side. Each team strategized to find and capture the other's flag. Cousins made up opposite teams: Stim covered Frank, Pike hovered over Andrew, Bow guarded Mary, Pat restrained Elizabeth, Peewee blocked Hugh, Noreen impeded Patrick. Underestimated little ones were tools of the schemers. I ducked down low and hid from the trunk to the trunk careful not to step on trillium. Mosquitos buzzed, webs tangled with fleeing spiders, brambles caught my T-shirt in the underbrush. Chases went on. I spotted the flag. No one noticed. Once captured, I hid it in my shirt. Skirmishes continued. The flag had to be rushed to the safe side of the woods before the capturer was tagged. I sauntered and made it to our home base. No one believed me when I called out, "Captured!" though I was standing there holding the flag.

Vanessa sat in the staircase landing window, looking out through the courtyard gate as a dozen of us friends ran through the woods. I looked up to see her watching us with intent. We were called in for dinner with a large hand-rung bell from the kitchen's screened porch. Vanessa sat next to me at the table where my sister, who was at camp, usually sat. She slept in my sister's bed. We bonded from being next to each other each day, girls the same age. After back porch dinners, we had enough for two softball teams. Vanessa watched from the back brick patio framed by two screen porches as sixteen-inch softballs were caught without a mitt. Batting order was usually by age. Pitching was always by the oldest boy on each team. When dusk settled to darkness, flashlight tag, ghost in the graveyard, or capturing lightning bugs filled our summer nights. We filled the bathtub to soak off the day's dirt. I read while Vanessa splashed in the tub. Her pigtails stayed tightly braided most of the week. My pigtails were braided at least every day. Vanessa and I dozed off to sleep watching a jar of blinking lightning bugs sitting on leaves.

Mornings, we woke up together and talked quietly. Our room was at the end of the hall, more quiet as we heard feet hit the floor, water flush and shoes hit the stairs. Slowly we changed, brushed our teeth, treasuring our quiet time before the day began. She told me about her brother and sister. How they shared a room and liked to play pick-up-sticks. I told her about how Mary and I played spelling games. "Am I spelling or saying O-R-E-O?" Rainy days found us in the large attic room playing darts or with an electric train sent by our Gram Leahy; we built a tunnel and two tracks intersecting at blinking lights that captured everyone's attention. We tried to be fair about who ran each of the two engines. Younger kids, like me, usually watched a train disappear into a tunnel, then almost collide with the other train until something broke.

Vanessa liked the attic with its six dormer windows and slanting roof. She liked the four-square game with a rubber red ball that could be bounced so high it ricocheted off the pointed ceiling. Numbered tiny pots of paint-matched outlined numbers on a board. Instructions were included to fill in all the #7s spaces with red and #2s with yellow until an image appeared. She laughed. I relaxed. We sat in bean bag chairs and braided each other's hair.

Vanessa seemed isolated, lonely. She cried at the bottom of the steps. My cousin arrived by car to play with Vanessa. We decided we'd make some money to buy candy at the Little Store, the farthest we were allowed to walk. Rice Krispies bars were made by melting marshmallows in butter and mixing in Rice Krispies cereal, then spreading those in a buttered pan. Once it cooled, it was cut into bars and placed in a wax paper lined shoe box. Frozen lemonade concentrate was mixed, ice added. Napkins, towels and Dixie cups were packed in a brown box. Our toy cash register was found and filled with coins and single dollars. The wagon was wheeled from the shed and wiped down of spider webs. Vanessa was petrified of spiderwebs. With a towel on the bottom of the wagon, we carefully pulled the box of bars, Oreo cookies, and lemonade down the long driveway and to our bus stop corner on Maplewood. A car pulled up asking for Rice Krispy bars and a cup of lemonade. I turned for change from the cash register, but the money was gone! I looked at Noreen, then we looked at Vanessa. She looked away.

"Keep the change," the driver smiled.

We decided to traverse the steep eroding cliff to swim in the wonderland of the lake. Vanessa slipped on the muddy stairs. I tried to hold her hand like my sisters had held mine, but she pulled away, slipped and scrambled up. We tried drawing, television, piano. I was in pain for her and exasperated tears would begin again. Some days, nothing would subside her stream of flowing tears. Sheba barked at her tears. I barked "Quiet!" at Sheba who barked at Vanessa. The cat was nowhere to be seen.

"Vanessa, your mother is on the phone," Mom said. Vanessa talked through her sobs. She took Mom's hand and closed the swinging butler's pantry door to talk with her mother. Mom and I silently sat in the kitchen.

"Mamma, I can't climb those stairs one more time!" Vanessa said. "I am worn out from climbing upstairs and downstairs. When I get halfway there's a window looking into dark woods that wolves run out. I can't climb one more set of stairs Mamma! Please come get me."

Mom and I drove Vanessa back to her highrise home. She stepped out of the car, all full of bravado.

"Oh, hi, Mamma" she said nonchalantly. She gave her mother a hug and walked past her. Her mother raised a brow and followed her. I wondered if Vanessa would introduce all kinds of new games to her family and friends. She chatted nonstop to her friends in the lobby.

Mom turned to me. "Would you like to stay with Vanessa's family?" This was our mothers' plan, to exchange homes and see how each other lived. Since that question, I have wondered what it would have been like to live in Bronzeville. Just as I was not part of the conversation to have Vanessa stay with us, I was not privy to why I didn't get to stay with her.

Vanessa's absence was bigger than her presence. Not an ordinary absence, it was a wondering-what-her-life-was-like absence. Was she happy at home? I wondered. Was she playing "Kick the Can"? Did she open a lemonade stand? Did she win at pick-up-sticks?

In the empty feeling after, I tried out my brother's idle Sailfish and spent the rest of the summer learning to sail. A strong sailing wind enticed a walk along the beach to launch our sailfish at the public beach to capture the breeze. My tacking ability was honed by following the path of more experienced day sailors. I sailed as far south as Fort Sheridan's airstrip when the wind whipped off the land and as far north as Lake Bluff. Chinook salmon and rainbow trout swam in the July's clear water. Only a few alewives shriveled on the beaches. After being caught in a thunderstorm, I learned to watch for the storm-building patterns of *cirrus* to *stratus* to *altocumulus* clouds. In high school, I taught kids to sail with the Sunfish. As we got older, it led to more friends and other beaches. It had been an idyllic, sun-burning, callous-forming, constant and ever-changing paradise until it inverted.

Someone on the beach asked, "What are those gulls hovering around? It smells like a dead Coho." A bloated, long-since drowned person's fingers poked out of the sand. A flurry of calling the police and watching the papers defined the last weeks of summer. The mystery was intriguing but the true effect was our lakefront paradise now had an element of horror. Our fearless abandon in a world that we conquered each season now had caution and trepidation.

Chapter 2: The Times They Are A'Changin'

A few weeks earlier at another lively dinner table conversation, Dad quietly said, "Let's have a moment of peace, Ommmmmmmm." We all surprisingly hummed, then laughed. He'd just come from Allen Ginsberg's peaceful protest in Lincoln Park with about a hundred people. It ended quietly with police shouting through bullhorns as the park closed at 11 pm, August 24th. The Viet Cong of North Vietnam had launched the Tet Offensive, a coordinated attack on three dozen South Vietnamese cities and a direct challenge to American troops. For the U.S. Forces, the price was maybe becoming too high to continue the war. The first protest on Friday included a black and white pig named "Pigasus the Immortal" advanced as a presidential candidate at the Civic Center. Jerry Rubin was arrested. Each night was progressively more violent. Protestors chanted "The streets belong to the people" and "Revolt" after police bludgeoned teens to the asphalt, clubbed photographers. Overworked police were fatigued, hungry and thirsty. Monday, August 25th, the first day of the Democratic Convention, Chicago was prepped for battle.

Wednesday, our family jumped in our Volkswagen for the Democratic Convention. I jammed in the third seat fretting about my 6th grade homework. We couldn't get near the barricaded Convention at the International Amphitheatre, so Dad painted candidates as they spoke in the Conrad Hilton Hotel lobby. Mom taped interviews with people in the audience and hovered with the younger kids. The rest of us scattered. I saw a chimpanzee wearing a McCarthy straw hat, a tall man holding the chimp's hand. The toe of my worn Keds tripped on a watch. I leaned to pick up the heavy silver band with a large ticking clock face. The chimp had already been escorted out. While I was walking down a long hall looking for lost and found, my brother came running, "Come on! We got to go now!" with unquestionable panic. I ran out into a crazy, mixed-up street and jumped in the van side-door with tear gas in the air.

"Close the windows!" Dad maneuvered the van through the shouting, disordered scrambling crowd, turning west on Balboa. The '68 Battle of Michigan Avenue broke wide open. Mom hugged my brother on her lap. There was a chaotic buzzing with shouts, horses rearing on hind legs, thumping and stomping. We listened to the muddled radio broadcast on the way home. Distressed commentators started to tell a confused story. Something else happened. As events rapidly unfolded, they told the next compelling story. Safe at home, we watched the hectic and unruly violence on TV. Police chased down teenagers, bashed them. Some fought back. The police kept clubbing the teens. The Chicago Seven defendants were arrested.

Rearranging snapdragons or reading poetic rhythms calmed me before the nightly dinner discussions. Unraveling *Canterbury Tales* gave me something to digest while six older teens, Frank, Andrew, Mary, Elizabeth, Patrick and Hugh, sorted their lives. Dinner table conversations revolved repeatedly around who got one of the two cars, menacing draft registrations, or conscientious objection to the war. I slipped snapdragons, after squeezing a blossom into a roar, into a vase expecting a long-lost cousin who was coming for dinner.

The doorbell rang. A golden sunset through September leaves streamed into the dark oak foyer. Kathleen had reddish wavy hair, deep dimples of a familiar Roger's smile accompanying her charming entrance. We were introduced in the living room as Mom set down a tray of purply grapes, candied pecans, cheeses, and Triscuits. After lemonade, mixed with a silver spoon, and cocktails in the living room, we walked through the dining room to the dimly lit screened porch. Hand-print sand castings hung on the stucco wall around a triple, eight-pane window. Bees bounced against the north screen, drunk with cherry juice from the north woods. The lake, on the east, reflected the orange-red sky at dusk.

Tart, spiced chicken was served with crispy, hashed potatoes and a heaping salad bowl filled with carrots, iceberg lettuce, celery and tomatoes, oil and vinegar, salt and pepper. Ice cream bowls waited on the sideboard buffet. Iced water, frothing milk and white wine surrounded the snapdragon arrangement, of mauve to purple tones, on the lazy susan. Dad's wise and witty remarks were not part of this conversation yet. Quietly, patiently, he waited for the subject to catch his fancy.

"Tell us about your work as a flight attendant, Kathleen?" Mom said.

"I've been part of the commercial MAC Operation since '67. I've flown thousands of Vietnam-bound military men around the Pacific," Kathleen said. "My father didn't want me to fly military to the Pacific, so I didn't tell him. The Marines were a cross-section of America that all had the same haircuts. My older brothers served in the Pacific during WWII, this was my chance. At times, you could hear a pin drop in the aisle. Or, pillow fights erupted on the flight. Part of the Marine code was that everyone was a winner! They drilled that into our heads during the flights."

Mom stopped eating, passing plates and serving. Memories of flying with United Airlines in 1944 overwhelmed her. "When I was flying I felt on the edge of my life," she said for the first time ever. "The closest I'd ever felt to being me while facing the fear of the unknown. I could feel the blood moving in my skin, my fingernails growing. My hair and face were full of electricity! I glowed silver. When I was flying, I was in control of myself. I knew who I was."

"I was twenty when I first started flying," Kathleen said. "My first Vietnam assignment was MAC, leaving Vietnam with a plane of tired, weary men who had just a few months before been boys. Within a month, my spirit was as old as water. They saw our round, not Asian, eyes and didn't say a word. That told us, the flight attendants, how it was with them. We didn't expect them to talk. We were proud of them. We were happy to welcome them home to Honolulu or El Toro or Travis or some other base. We knew returning home would be tough for them. Nobody, besides us, really understood."

"The waiting was worse than the flights," Dad suddenly said. He had been stationed in Molesworth, England in 1945 between bombing missions over Germany. "Imagination could be our undoing, so we kept ourselves occupied in London, with theatre, movies and dinner. It lightened our load of worry, the echoes of memory. It lightened the load of what officers shouldered that others couldn't. I carried the soil from training in Texas and Arkansas, Glenview and Pennsylvania. The soil of England was still in the seams of my clothes when I parachuted from a burning plane into Germany. London dust was caked in the cuffs of my pants." We paused in silence with these revelations knowing not to ask more.

Kathleen broke the silence, "My airlines scheduled a Christmas Eve flight with the Marine Corp from El Toro, in California to Da Nang base in Vietnam—that had not happened before. We said our goodbyes to the Marines in Honolulu and thought they'd gone on." Cicadas hummed a beat, blue jays cawed in the rising dusk. Forks and knives scraped the plates. She looked out the screens as if it was happening beyond the porch. "There were the Marines, the next day," she said. "They were waiting to go to Okinawa with us. Like old friends, we sang Christmas carols and actually made gifts for each other—mostly poems." She paused. "The twelve-hour flight was filled with stories of 'The Best Christmas was (or will be) with...?' We landed in Okinawa after all flights were cancelled. Who knew why cancellations were made? We'd be leaving for Da Nang the next day with the same passengers at 11:00 pm, Christmas Eve."

The telephone rang several times. "You have reached the McMahons, Please leave a message. CLICK, Hummm" No one got up to answer it. Four brothers were bracing for the impending draft, scrambling to find a way out.

Patrick said quietly, "Is my college application essay going to be about learning or war? Learning seems another lifetime, another person. I'll be told to kill someone or be killed for my country, by our legal system, by my loyalty. My choice is to follow this order or give up my girlfriend, my home, my family, and go to Canada." What will my basketball team say? Am I a coward, a traitor? No one could order me to shoot another person. I could die. Could I become Canadian? Patrick looked like his innards dropped, or his stomach ached? "Maybe my birth date will be a high number?"

"The flight from Okinawa to Danang is not that long," Kathleen said. "But we made the best of every minute. We were so young and far from home. But, Good God, we were brave and we did have Christmas. The crew had made this landing many times before. Everyone knew where they were going. We all saw red flares dotting the sky. Blasts of hot, humid air swallowed the coolness in the cabin. We all quieted on the final approach. A voice from the middle of the aircraft started to sing Silent Night. Softly, we all joined in until the plane landed and they opened the door. Maybe our flight would not make 'The Best Christmas was...?' list, but it's one that I will never forget."

We looked at the crumbs on our plates as the cicadas' hum rose and fell with the crickets. Darkness descended. The glow from dim lights cast shadows. The snapdragons smiled a darkening blue menacing from their vase.

"They'd get me first. I couldn't pull the trigger. My skin pulls tight," Mark said. "Leave my country forever? Stay and be killed? What about allergies, hernias? Get a physical and find something wrong. This cannot happen," he said. The screen porch spun around. The windows vibrated like a breathing membrane. The separation from home began. The separation from trust of government, belief in school, religion, education, and sports dissolved. The only reality was to accept this luckless fate or run like heck. Mom ached. Dad went stone-faced. I tried to understand.

Across the table and above the alert snapdragons, Frank squirmed in his seat scared of his thoughts, "What is this War that I oppose?" he said. Shame. Such shame. Hot stupid shame! "As long as I am in college I'll express my conscientious objection to war."

Dad, who never talked about his service, recalled landing his fifteenth mission in England. "The release from tension on returning to home base," he said. "The intense pleasure of aliveness as the B52 landed back in Molesworth. We'd defied the angel of death again. Triumph in life! Exaltation of nearness to death brought everything more to life! The smell of grass mixed with burnt fuel, soil and singed rubber, asphalt and holly. You want to be all of the goodness and decency after that evil. To be for justice and courtesy. To be a good man. What is valuable became crystal clear. The sunset became worthy of study and capturing each and every streak and pink-lined grey cloud. You want to be what is best in the world." Dad said he was in a place he didn't belong that had become his reality. My parents were missing the war and flying?

Dad said he couldn't tell his World War II story. It was beyond telling. There was no moral to attach. There was no advice that comes from any episode. The thrill of life and death meeting couldn't be explained. The sensation of those flights was like trying to tell someone how chocolate tastes. No way to explain. The adrenaline from pushing beyond what is humanly possible was not fatherly advice. The same draft as 1942 was being reinstated next year and four of his boys were of age.

Mom had barely breathed since the beginning of Kathleen's story. "The adrenaline rush of taking off became a necessity. Then, an unwanted craving. The intense glow fueled an energy. I could have flown without the airplane." Mom told us of her propeller plane transports. "It is the stitching together of tragedy and loss that remain and become part of us. The trauma barely happened, but it is the object in the room that entered our lives and wouldn't leave. None of us died but a part of each of us did." Mom told of her intense migraines, and the long-lost look in the returning military mens' eyes. She poured chocolate sauce over vanilla ice cream for peanut-sprinkled sundaes, a maraschino cherry topped each before being spun around on the lazy susan. The snapdragons glared a deeper purple above the disappearing bowls.

Over the snapdragons, I could see my glum sister was missing her friends. She had another week of being grounded for wearing pants to school and she knew all her friends were together. "I can't see them because of wearing pants to school," Mary said. "We can't call on the phone. There are people dying of hunger in Africa while we are punished, suspended, grounded for what we wear!"

Hugh skidded his chair back and said, "Can I be excused? I've got wrestling practice." He stood up stiffly and walked away. A melancholy transitional air draped the conversation. This table of yearning yippies transpiring through time to their own unique beginning. No one else noticed the increasingly louder crickets dominating the porch or the snapdragons going limp.

Kathleen had everyone's attention. "I recall a Texan becoming fast friends with a New Yorker," she said. "You couldn't get a word in between their stories. Neither listened. They both just talked. When the guys left the plane I often stayed behind to sign paperwork for our cargo or fallen soldiers. I helped a Latino family walk from that chain link fence at Travis. At the aircraft, they received their son's coffin. I held the grandmother's fragile hand as the flag was placed on the coffin right before us. She was such a little woman. She wore a black mantilla. The massive red sunrise was orange and purple and seemed to hold us all in its brilliance. I looked straight into it as I placed my hand on the flag. We heaved great sobs. On my own, in a bus to San Francisco, I watched the sunrise disappear in clouds."

The scraping of plates softened as the night enveloped the tenderly lit faces reflecting each other. A human soul is a slight thing. Is it our duty to care for our body so the soul can progress? Are we stewards of the soul we carry so that it remains whole and healthy to life's end? Is our soul the same since the beginning of humankind? It is a vague slight notion of who we are and become in a lifetime. It is the only thing we are measured by in God's eyes.

Chapter 3: They're All Sunday Drivers

The summer after my eighth-grade graduation, I flew to Europe with my parents and younger sister and brother for a car tour. Dad was commissioned by Continental Bank to draw banks in Milan, Paris, Brussels, Munich, Frankfort, Zurich, Lichtenstein and London. He packed Herman Wouk's *Winds of War*. We traveled as a professor's family with Youth Hostel cards and slept where we landed each night, sometimes using camping gear, with no reservations anywhere. Dad and Mom wanted to show us Europe. Their older kids had the Spain experience.

"We're going to crash!" I woke up shaking Jean. "The plane has stopped!" Northern Lights danced on the tips of our wings convincing me that the plane had frozen in mid-flight. My sister calmed me with hushed whispers. Sleepy, disturbed passengers barely looked out the windows. Did I somehow remember my infant flight with the failed engine? We landed in Milan and shopped at the Galleria before visiting Dad, who perched on his wobbly camp chair on the sidewalk, hunkered over a drawing with throngs of onlookers who watched each line become a representational, then cubistic interpretation of the city scene before us. "I draw what happens over time," Dad said to the spectators, "and what is around the corner. It is a timeline of one day." When Dad wasn't drawing, or driving our tiny Fiat, he was reading Wouk's reminiscence of WWII. We revisited his war experience from Wouk's perspective. Dad didn't like to camp at home, but we camped in Europe. Already six feet tall, gangly three of us shared the Fiat back seat, squished while rounding the switchbacks in the French and Swiss alps.

In Switzerland, I awoke at dawn to hike a cow path up to a tiny, icy, and clear turquoise mountain lake for a morning skinny-dip in melted snow.

A few birds offered melody to clanking cow bells that gave rhythm to the red glow of a dawning day. As the sun warmed above the mountain peaks, I retraced the path down, greeted by a stream of hikers speaking dozens of languages: "Good Morning." Suisser-duetch *Buongiorno.* I'd repeat *"Boungiorno"* to the next person who would reply in Spanish "Buenos Dias." I greeted the next German hiker with the Spanish version, then German to an Italian and so on for tens of languages and hikers. At thirteen, I was horrified to think of how many would have seen me swimming if I hadn't dressed even moments later.

"Switzerland was a neutral country during the war," Dad said. Fresh water flowed for our tooth brushing. The bathrooms were clean and free of charge. Near Munich, Dad stopped the Fiat at a fork in the road. Mom and he talked in hushed tones for a long time. They kept glancing at the sign on the post—*Dachau.* They were deciding whether to show us a concentration camp or not, then took the right fork instead. In Munich, Dad ordered my first beer, a Bavarian wheat beer, in the Hofbrauhaus. Mom looked sideways at him through raised eyebrows. It was the tall, ceramic stein with HB and a thumb lever on the handle to lift a ceramic lid. After I had had a few sips and felt the effect, Dad explained that this was the place Adolph Hitler started his Nazi party on the third floor in Festsaal.

"Here, the twenty-five-point National Socialist Program was introduced to 2,000 people in 1920," Dad said. It was a year before Mom and Dad were born. "You don't need to drink all of that." he said. "With beer, Hitler was able create a nation of followers. It was in this beer hall that Adolph Hitler created the Nazi regime that spread throughout beer halls." The stein was feeling heavier and I sleepier. "That's enough," Dad said taking away the half-full stein. In Nuremberg, the bombed blocks of homes and buildings were prodigious. I stared in disbelief at block after block of ruins. Dad rolled the window down to ask a crutched man missing a leg and an arm for directions to the Youth Hostel. They talked in a cluster of German-English phrases intermixed with laughter. As I gazed at the surrounding blocks of bombed-out buildings, they shared their own mixture of bonded camaraderie. I was amazed that a German and American could speak in their own code. It could have been Dad's B-17 that took this man's limbs! He could have shot Dad out of the sky! When I asked my mother how could they talk so freely without anger she said, "We should have shown you Dachau." Maybe they had both been drawn into a battle that made no sense to either and wanted desperately to go home. That night we walked past destitute people who sat along purpling walls exposing gruesome burnt leg and arm injuries.

"Sometimes people purposefully maim themselves," Dad said. Our Youth Hostel beds were lined in two rows of twenty-five, side-by-side, in a grand old building's galleria-type rooms. Men slept in one wing and women in the other. At breakfast, Dad divulged that he woke in the middle of the night and remembered sleeping in this building when he was marched as a prisoner to a nearby camp.

"Don't use the water to brush your teeth!" Mom said. On our way to Belgium, we stopped in traffic. One European driver got out of his car to talk in German to a driver, then French to another in the next car, then Spanish to a third. When he got to our car he lifted his hands and enunciated in clear American English, "They're all Sunday Drivers." I realized how isolated the Midwest is from the rest of the world and, even more so, Lake Forest from the Midwest. When we visited the Calais beaches Dad read from Wouk's book while a horse cantered along the surf at sunset. Churchill had to decide to allow a camp of Allied forces to be bombed for a large number of England's army to have the chance to cross the channel to England. Private boats picked up the soldiers from the beach to transport them to England as military ships were bombed. Dad wanted to camp here, Mom wasn't sure it was safe. We found a hotel room. I was still vegetarian at the time and grasped enough language to request pasta *parmesan solemente* or *sans boeuf.* French waitresses were very concerned. "You must eat meat!" they said.

We stopped at each little French town for a loaf of fresh bread or *pomme frittes* that held me over. We drove into Paris late at night with no hotel reservations during Bastille Day weekend. Every hotel was full. Very late, we all got out of the car to knock on a door in a sketchy block of Paris.

An elder woman with half her head black and the other white opened the top half of the door, "*Bonswaana!*" she greeted us. Haunted I thought, but nodded when Dad asked me for an okay. The pull cord loo was on a landing shared by two floors. When I opened the French doors to our railed porch in the morn, a naked man stood across the street singing from his balcony. I quickly shut doors to keep my younger brother and sister from seeing.

"Remember, don't use tap water to brush your teeth," Mom said. I walked along a bank of the Seine and into a pet shop that had squirrel monkeys and parrots, squirrels and minks. Dad and I visited his favorite art stores in Paris, Berlin and London where he replenished his preferred 100 pound Arches paper and veri-black pencils. One day in Paris, my mother and I searched until we found Auguste Rodin's Museum where I felt the spirit of individual men through their sculpted bronze faces. I saw Rodin's bronze-cast eyes expose the souls of men who lived a hundred years ago. I felt the vitality and mentioned to my mother that I would like to try that at home. We drove out of Paris and passed elaborately dressed women sitting or walking in windows with red lights.

One month in historic Europe made me aware of the gift of fresh water and a desire to sculpt. At fourteen I started finding people's faces in clay. Sylvia Shaw Judson, who sculpted *The Bird Girl*, came to dinner and politely viewed my first attempts. She invited me to work with her on Saturdays in her Ragdale studio. Sylvia sculpted small and quiet things made powerful in form. She taught me that the visible form expresses the spirit within. She taught me how to testify to the enormous importance of life forms while showing me how to build an armature for clay, make a mold, and cast it in bronze. Sylvia showed me a woman could be a sculptor as well as a mother. With my driver's license, Mom arranged for me to take Tuesday mornings off school to sculpt with the internationally-known artist Abbott Pattison who taught me carving, constructing, and modeling techniques. Sculpture burst open with new skills to make representational and abstract art.

Over three summers, Pat and I, with friends, canoed in Quetico. With

Duluth packs on our backs and canoes on our shoulders, we portaged from rock to rock, poured salt on the leeches and started our life-long birdwatching. We dragged a fish line for cooking our dinners, charted courses to stashes of jellies and slept in canoes and witnessed one of the most remarkable Northern Lights displays of our lifetime. Multicolored dancing lights filled the sky on a night without mosquitos. I learned later the light shows were caused by explosions on the sun. We slept in the open, exhausted from a full day of traversing lakes and portages.

"Bless us oh Lord and these thy gifts that we are about to receive…" The churning repetitive hum of summer cicadas raised our decibel level. We were sitting on the back porch at dinner, each of us before the folded napkin on the left then the fork, a plate and knives and spoon on the right with a glass above those. Freshly cut zinnias were in a low vase in the center. The sand castings blended into the stucco wall. I positioned myself to overlook the lake. The complexity played itself out in a discussion of who got the car that night. Sheba leapt at a morsel of dropped food. The phone rang.

Pat called, "Do you want a horse?" She was given two to care for by her neighbor.

"*Yes!*" I answered, not believing the moment. We had talked about getting horses for years, shared our birthday week through grade school, bird watched and canoed together. Mom noticed my excitement. Pat and I would ride horses together. I couldn't believe it was true! Pat's friend had gone to college and the family wanted to keep the horses in the barn and field. And so my high school years included taming a wild Duchess to not run at full speed into the barn, to jump low fences in the pasture and race and race through corn fields. Pat, with Nugget, and I, with Duchess, trotted through West Lake Forest's fields and woods.

Along the western edge of Lake Forest, we rode our horses to McCormick's Pond, slipped off the saddles and swam on horses bareback. They shot off their last foot hold to dog paddle at a trot speed. We strapped sleeping bags on back of the saddle with saddle bags filled with food and grain and camped overnight. One Thanksgiving, my cousin and I rode ten miles to Lake Michigan, then back after dinner. For Halloween, we buttoned raincoats over our heads, carried Jack O'Lanterns and rode around the streets surprising trick-or-treaters as the Headless Horseman. In the winter, we'd harness one horse and she'd ski behind, while I rode bareback. West Lake Forest's prairies were a completely new environment from the lakefront forests. I worked Saturdays at Lake Forest Bookstore, babysitting and as a lifeguard to earn money for vets, oats and hay.

Robin, a biology classmate, explained *virgin prairies* had *native plants:* crown vetch, spurge, burdock, fleabane and spiderwort in biology class. Some plants still sounded like weeds. With a heightened awareness cinquefoil, shooting star, turks cap, lupine, Jo Pie and butter and eggs emerged as we appreciated the root and seed producing systems of prairie plants. Red-Winged Blackbirds and bluebirds flitted their colors in the glistening dew of the turkey foot grasses. Great Blue Herons and Whooping Cranes were endangered. Robin controlled burning the prairies to reduce invasive species and release seeds by heat. From the priory in Lake Bluff, he and I walked the creek path behind Ragdale and into their prairie. We discovered the artesian well in the middle. He was excited that Ragdale's prairie was possibly a virgin prairie that had never been farmed. Robin, with a naturalist, came to see me at the Lake Forest Bookstore. They wanted an introduction to Sylvia Shaw Judson. After that meeting, she and her daughter Alice Hayes gave the back fifty acres of virgin prairie on Greenbay Road to the Nature Conservancy—now cared for by Open Lands. The mother and daughter decided to open an artist retreat with the front four acres, Ragdale house and red barn.

That summer my mother asked, "Would you like to live with Gram in a Lake Forest apartment during your senior year?" Her hardwood carved furniture, depression glass and china were moved from California to an apartment above Deerpath Theater. Gramma Mac and I ate bacon, liver and caramelized onions for breakfast, lunch and dinner. I spent our time asking questions about her family and Dad's childhood while she envisioned deceased Jack passing by her furniture and through the apartment. I never met any of my great aunts or uncles, but she was from a large family.

"Margot, just look forward." Gram would say. Or a thought-provoking phrase, "my parents were bedridden. Eva and I were busy working to feed the children who were on their own. I hope you will never know the difficulties in the life I have known." How could I not keep asking questions?

"There is a place near Ausable Forks," she began. "It's near Lake George. Lake George is grand! I was married near Ausable Forks in a church. I wanted my savings for furniture not a big wedding," she trailed off into memory. She'd point to an ad in a magazine, "See how beautiful her neckline is…I always wanted to be an artist."

My cousin Noreen and I couldn't find Gramma Mac in her apartment after school one day. I called Dad. He searched by car. Noreen and I scoured the town. Gram was found getting off the Chicago Northwestern train after "visiting friends in the city." That evening she had a massive stroke. I moved back home to Airdrie and visited Gram in the hospital. One late afternoon, while the shadows were long and just before the darting swifts were replaced by swooping bats, Gram passed away. At her wake, I met a lifetime of family, friends, work associates outside of Gram's Sunday visits. I knew nothing of her work life or siblings.

"She was a remarkable woman," a gentleman paused to tell me. "Always looked out for others and felt her way clearly through life. Very classy." I wanted to know more. I drove fast on Westleigh Road to West Campus classes with the car still bouncing a bit from going over the bridge. I hit a low point of missing her, my independence of us watching out for each other, and loss of living in an apartment in town. Frustrated with my questions she deflected masterfully, "It was all grand!" My grief settled in and I pulled over. I felt her say out loud, "I have no hunger, no thirst, no want or need. I don't have pain or sorrow. Don't be sad for me because I'm myself now without burdens. If you are sad it is for yourself, not for me." I didn't feel sorrow for her passing again.

With Dad ensuring we were educated before college, I heard Buckminster Fuller explain comprehensive design science of artifacts like the geodesic dome for sustainable living, John Cage's music from everyday staccatos of sounds and silence. Both influenced my audio taping of springtime cardinal robin and chickadee songs to arrange into Hayden's *Spring Sonata Allegra* patterns for a music composition assignment. I had the sand of Lake Michigan and the soil of the prairies still in my shoe laces. My Fry boots were worn by ravines in search of birds and along beaches collecting driftwood. My skin was darkened, hair lightened from the reflection of the sun from sailing Lake Michigan waves. My back was challenged by bareback horse rides through the forests, lakes, and prairies. I wasn't the same as the previous six brothers and sisters. I didn't transplant well. I won't grow straight with trimmed, transplanted roots. I tried, but had too much broad rooted, webbed inter-connection here. Friends flourished in various circles, connected by sports, ecology, literature or art. I learned to sculpt here. To reach my full height, as an artist, I needed to draw strength from my tap root. I will come home again. I packed my bags for college.

Chapter 4: Fragile Flower of Lake Forest

7am: Garrison Keillor radio show; 8am: Renaissance Art History; 10 am: Biology; 1pm: Drawing I on Monday, Wednesday and Friday. 9am: American Renaissance Literature; 11am: French; 1-4pm: Sculpture on Tuesdays and Thursdays; 4pm: violin Thursday; 12pm: bagpipes 12pm Friday. Homework until midnight. I'd landed at Hamline University with a full line-up of classes in a consortium.

Thumbprints mashed into wet clay delineated differences. I sculpted one head with a raw honesty of my search for a likeness. Knives cutting the surface, scraping the form for my imagined image until the head was proportionately unique. Twice a week, for hours and months I pushed and sliced clay, then threw wet plaster at it to harden, making a thick shell mold in two parts. Both mold halves were broken away with prying metal rods. Burning hot wax was poured into the fragile interior of that shell with fine fins from etched lines, rolled around, poured out, then repeated. That wax image was seared with a white soldering wire to attach vertical tubular sprues that were fused to a cup. Hot metal pins poked through the thin skin to hold placement in the mold. Months of clay sculpting was placed in a metal cylinder. Vermiculite, sand and plaster were poured inside and around the wax shell and left to set until rock hard. When inverted into a kiln, a gas flame burned overnight to harden the mold and leave a lost wax space. I tended the burning kiln and lifted the mold's hotness with foundry gloves into a sand pit that steadied the pouring of sputtering splashes of molten bronze into the empty space. Surprisingly, transforming pliable clay into solid metal was seeing my sculpture for the first time. With a liver sulfate and iron oxide patina, I gave my first bronze portrait to Mom and Dad for Christmas.

What caused Dad and I to argue over a mere chickadee at the kitchen window feeder, I'll never know. We were sitting at Airdrie, having toast and marmalade at the kitchen table. He had a cup of coffee. I silently drank a vitamin concoction blended with beets that gave me three hours of energy to finish my extended class-work. Mom quietly hovered, used to the transitions from college, apartments, and visits with spouses. "You never come home again," he quoted some great author from *The New Yorker* on the table. We were at odds for many reasons and he wanted to remind me I hadn't been tested by life yet. In response to my new confidence from my sculpture and studies, Dad read a cartoon: "Pointy heads that can't park a bicycle straight." Though my pre-med track was woefully compromised, I'd come home after being hospitalized with hepatitis in college. They were concerned.

"Don't forget to do the dishes." Dad saw the confidence I'd come home from college with and wanted to remind me of a woman's role in life. I chafed at his demeaning ancient ways. How does that advice match his liberal point of view? "Wear stockings and a dress to your interviews," he told me. Not anymore, I would only take a job where pants were allowed— blue jeans preferable. Mom rolled her eyes at the opportunities I was snubbing. "If you can type you can get a job anywhere," Mom said.

"Would you look at that chickadee!" Dad pointed to the black, hooded, gray bird upside down at the birdfeeder.

"That's not a chickadee!" I surprised myself with how the words exploded with confidence.

"That is a chickadee," he said and stepped out of the room.

...or nuthatch, I thought. The silences of our arguments were louder than a bomb. We'd been negotiating my preparations for a summertime mountain-climbing trip with new college friends. Three days a week I'd jogged through St. Paul's snowy sidewalks to get in shape with friends. We rock climbed on Saturdays at Taylor's Falls and ice climbed once or twice at the Mushroom Caves while I swam one hundred laps a week. My parents considered climbing a waste of time. My belay lines, carabiners, crampons and ice pick were purchased from my summer landscaping job. My parents didn't engage in more conversation, sure climbing would blow over, pretty sure their "fragile little flower" as my father called me, would come to her senses. I was too tired to care. Obsessive, wearisome waiting to hear about grades ground me down. During the end of two tedious months in bed, my Uncle Harry visited. He had never been in my room before.

"Hey, I'm sorry you're under the weather. I've been there," he showed a compassion I hadn't seen before.

"I don't have energy for anything. I can't even read novels."

"Something good came from my bout with hepatitis. In recovery, I watched oil ships pass by New Guinea and thought it might be a pretty good career to pursue," he told me.

"Why were you in New Guinea?"

"It was hotter than Hell," Uncle Harry said. He had served in the 33rd Quartermaster Division of MacArthur's Pacific theatre. "In Hawaii on July of '43," he said, "our army training was in an ocean of tiny islands I hadn't learned about in geography class. We trained hard in jungle warfare to calm our fears while guarding installations." It was May of '44 when he arrived in New Guinea. To hear his story in such detail made me feel chosen.

"We trained again on this dash of an island with dysentery, malaria and stuff I couldn't name." My image of a jungle, from *Tarzan*, merged with my uncle lying in a hammock, like on *Gilligan's Island*. Vaguely, I didn't know where New Guinea was, vaguely imagining Hawaii on inserts on maps. Later, I found in an encyclopedia, the place where General Yamamoto had been killed the year before my uncle's troops arrived. The Japanese had not lost a battle in eighteen months before that year. The Yanks took out the mastermind of the Pacific theater. Their honor was bruised, and they fanatically expressed their outrage on the army in September on Maffin Bay. U.S. LST ships released their back ends to spill army soldiers into a barrage of machine-gun bullets that blasted down the beaches from caves. Missiles volleyed from entrenched enemy fire. "I tried to wait for a pause in the spray of bullets," he said. "Adrenaline revved through my fatigue. By the grace of God, I was spared. For a bit, ship canons had protected troops, until the Americans' front line was on the beach. Even the Allied planes stopped firing. Patrolling the perimeters of the Wakde Airdrome and the Toem-Sarmi sector, the troops found the fighters to be non-stop and fierce. Those Japs would not fall back!" He looked at me. Did he really say "Japs"? "The island of New Guinea was a fierce foe. You couldn't even joke about stealing a swine to barbecue with the way the natives honored pigs." In December, he was transported to the west coast of Morotai, where he contracted hepatitis.

"How did you get it?" I asked. "My hepatitis probably had come from dissecting sharks in bio class." But I had been dreaming in my childhood bed while my uncle had been alone in a tent with bugs everywhere.

"Who knows? If it wasn't one thing it was another," he said. "Before Christmas, though, nothing felt like a holiday, we controlled the island perimeters. Patrols in the dark jungles at night encountered scattered resistance that popped up out of nowhere. The Japanese were fearless, ruthless—not afraid to die. Our nerves were always on edge." Natives tattooed with crocodile patterns, covered in mud, honored salt-water crocodiles occupying ocean beaches and the freshwater Sepik River. "The crocs, with eight-foot-long jaws, could pluck a man off the beach and swallow him whole. Defending ourselves from crocs meant encountering another angry native. We were steaming in our fatigues and couldn't go near ocean or rivers. Couldn't touch tree bark, it might be poisonous. The loudest birds you'd ever heard woke us night and day. Swarms of bugs carrying disease hummed in our ears, low pitched in the day and high pitched at night. Giant cicadas sounded different on cool nights. We could never let down our guard." He paused as a deep sadness from deep within him. "Life was a crapshoot. It had little value." I wondered why was he finally telling his story? *I should be writing this down. What if I forgot!*

"About February," he said, "we landed in Lingayen Gulf in Luzon. Some guys opened valentines. They must have paid someone to send them, the way those guys looked and smelled," he said. "We drove into the Caraballo Mountains in the most brutal scene of humanity. What happened can't be told. Ah, the things humans can do. We can overcome any obstacle if presented the chance. We can be horrendous. It troubled our minds." What a gift he was giving a tired, bored college student. I was aching for some kind of adventure but couldn't move.

"The 33rd Division's objective was to capture Baguio, the Philippines' summer capital and General Yamashita's headquarters," he said. "A line of Japanese fighters, neighbors, classmates and friends would run straight into the Americans' firing to build an embankment for their second line to hide behind. Their relentless sacrifice was beyond human comprehension." Limestone caves were dug at beaches' ends to protect machine gun gunners from airstrikes. Marine and Army troops invaded along those beaches. Every man was wounded. The Japanese entrenched themselves in caves and pillboxes (concrete poured guard posts) in the hill so air backup couldn't protect the Americans' safe passage. They dug miles of caves. The Americans shot flame-throwers into caves to flush out the enemy. No one took prisoners. "The ferocious intensity of battle defied human instincts. Every inch of our path was covered in gruesome deaths as we took Aringay. Then we took Calugong and Mount Mirador around mid-April." I nearly held my breath so he would continue. "Baguio and Camp John Hay fell the next day. We had not a moment's rest. Don't let your guard down and watch each other's back! Pockets of furious resistance erupted and were squashed. We kept going. The San Nicholas-Tebbo-Itagon route was captured a couple weeks later, and it was all over. The Australians exploded in celebration. It must have been the beginning of May in Hell's hole with my liver kicking up a storm. 'Heaven is Java, hell is Burma; but no one returns alive from New Guinea' was a popular Japanese saying. I laid in the infirmary. Guys around me had bleeding gums and bones from dengue so painful they felt broken. Gambia parasites from monkeys gave shivering chills. Malaria was everywhere. We started to get vaccinated. Some of us felt a bit better. We finally got a rest, but were racked with guilt. Every day we wondered, why me? Why had I survived? By the Grace of God, a lot of luck and prayers maybe? We were commanded to rest, to rehabilitate. Wished I could have enjoyed the beer, but my liver was shot. I could feel my swollen liver under my right rib throb. I took a chug now and then. Paid for it. That's when I saw the oil tankards pass. Now that's a living, I decided. In September, we occupied Honshu Island in Japan, fill our hollow bones until the ships brought us home."

He stopped talking, looking at me quizzically. He seemed embarrassed to have told me so much. How had he remembered so many details, when he could barely keep track of his work load?

Awkwardly, he started to leave. "Sorry I dumped that on you. I hope you slept through most of it?" Patterns set long ago meant I wouldn't hug my uncle. He wouldn't hug me either. I was close to him and loved him, but mostly he joked and I stayed polite. His story was the kindest gift. I waved, thanked him. I knew I needed to get some fresh air, move. I needed to get out of bed. I had to get going! I had to get out of this malaise.

A few days later, the cold January sun came out. Inspired by my uncle's story, I attempted climbing down the backyard cliff I'd easily traversed since preschool. I could barely balance, and squatted with vertigo. I reversed down the steep incline on all fours. The walk along the beach didn't last long. I climbed up clinging with my fingertips and toes. *Tomorrow I will try again.* A week of walks and eating regularly helped. I packed my clothes for school, and would recover.

Well enough to return to college in February, I studied the course lists. Asian Literature and Micronesia Art History jumped off the page. The repetitions of schedule set in: Garrison Keillor, Art History, Comparative Biology II, Drawing II, Literature, Sculpture II, Fencing. Homework until midnight. In spring, I joined the tennis team to get back in shape. We practiced with down jackets on outdoor courts with dirty, drifted snow along a cyclone fence. Clumps of snow clung to the diamond patterns and fell to explode into crystals if jolted by a wayward slow bouncing ball. Matches were played in Duluth, Mankato and Rochester. My partner and I laughed so hard at mistakes we'd fall on the court.

In literature, I'd read about folk characters, a monkey spirit traveling between earth and heaven with wisdom and mischievous antics. India's Hindu deity Ganesh, with multiple arms. The five-thousand-year old Sepik River culture honored crocodiles that grew to twenty-five feet long, with jaws as long as a person. I learned the Hooli lived in the mountains and prized the family's pig. The boys grew eighteen inches of hair, had it ceremoniously cut and woven into a wig. Paint was carefully applied to the wigmen in spirit houses. The Fresh Sepik River was the largest body of fresh water in Micronesia. Eight hundred and thirty-two New Guinea languages, including sign, kept clan secrets and made New Guinea the most linguistically diverse place on earth. I learned the locations of New Guinea, the Philippines, their proximity to Japan, China and India. For my final report, I carved a Sepik River fertility symbol in mahogany while imagining myself being a Hooli artisan. In sculpture class, I made in clay and cast in bronze a full figure. Our drawing model actually had six toes!

Chapter 5: Among Fields of Ice

O nly take calculated risks," Mom said. Turned out, she and Jean came to convince me not to climb mountains. Mom drove to my Wisconsin camp where I taught sailing for the summer and hoped to take me home.

"I've worked hard for this all year," I said. "I bought all the equipment." It was 1976 and I wanted adventure.

"Why don't you let it go?" my mother said.

"Because I can," I said. "I want to do this, Mom." My family didn't drive through to view mountains. They experienced, witnessed and documented travels. I promised to journal, to photograph and draw. After all, my mother had climbed into sputtering propeller airplanes at my age. She may have quarreled similarly with her mother.

"That was for a greater purpose," my Mom argued. Mom reluctantly agreed to let me go. "As long as your sister joins you," she said. Why did I feel the need to climb mountains?

A week later, my sister Jean, a friend, Mike, his friends and I packed our equipment to climb the Bugaboos of the Purnell range in British Columbia and Athabasca by the Columbia Icefield in Jasper Park, Alberta, Canada. Caravanning in a Beetle we named *Athabasca*, we push-started across the country. The car's starter quit in the Dakotas. I grew nervous about my sister's safety. How could I have endangered her? My sister's frustration with my company in a caravan of young men driving to the mountains to bike and climb was valid. We stayed in Golden overnight and provisioned with rosehip tea, dried beef, eggs and rye bread. I was shut down with a barrage of emotions knowing I was responsible for Jean. What had I gotten us into? The expansive, snow-capped grandeur of the

Canadian Rockies was awe-inspiring! After wrapping our car tires with chicken wire to ward off porcupines, we ascended rocky traversing paths with fragile, brightly colored flowers emerging from the fresh snow, finally reaching the tree-lined beginnings of glaciers in the Purnell range. "There's my fragile flower," was how my father had often greeted me.

We trudged with heavy packs upward and raised tents in a great snow that fell day and night. Waiting for the weather to clear, we played cards for three days. Low, distant rumbles alerted us to poke our heads through the unzipped tent to watch the collapsing avalanches explode down valley chutes of the enormous, sheering, calving glaciers. Here in the tent was fine by me. A rainy day below our tree-line was a blizzard above on Crescent Glacier. After days of reading, playing Hearts and visiting the domed huts at Boulder camp, we set out. Our glacier goggles shielded our eyes from clear skies and blinding snow. Crampons were essential. Ice picks were also, as we were about to find out.

We traversed the Bugaboo Mountain glacial field, roped together because of snow-covered crevasses. On top of Bugaboo, we crossed an open field of ice. Suddenly, our leader, Mike, slipped into a crevasse that curved under so fast he seemed to disappear in front of us. *Act now! Minimize danger! Stay calm. Decide on a solution.* The more he struggled the deeper he slipped under.

"Just stop!" I called. "Don't struggle against the ice. Stay still!" Mike dug in his pick and hung on. Panic set in with the climbers. Mike was our leader. I had to act fast. Second in line, I pulled my line taut to hold him, clung to a grounded pick while lying prone, crampon toes dug deep in the snow. After a moment's pause, a plan emerged. We chocked, or fit a trapezoid with a loop, into a rock for the next climber of the chain to belay, with my line taut. The loop held fast on a chock in the fissure that allowed a carabiner clipped to it and if the belayer's waist harness to stabilize the climber to the rock. The belay line end was held tight across the climber's pelvis. The rope was released or shortened by holding both ends around the belayer's hip.

The fourth climber came around to pull Mike out, while the third belayed the rescuer. All four climbers remained linked by lines. Slithering forward, I tightened Mike's line, replanting my pick, as he was pulled out, thankfully with no sprains or breaks. I worried whether Mike's limbs were intact, and if he could continue climbing. What would Voytek Kurtik, pioneer of alpine climbing, do? Our adrenaline was spent, but we managed to restore Mike's energy with oatmeal snacks and resumed ascending one of the twin peaks. My sheer exaltation of having extracted Mike from the curved fissure was inspiring. The views from the summit were beyond belief gorgeous. On the summit, we celebrated by adding stones to the cairn, empowering us with climbers before and after our ascent. The things humans could do!

Climbing Mount Athabasca was trickier. We started before dawn, consistently roped together alpine style, we each carried backpacks of crampons, chocks, carabiners, picks, helmets, water and snacks enough for a one-day climb. The traverse under the rise was a wonderland of ice bridges and drifted snow canyons. Of the five of us who began the deep glistening snow hike to the face, only Mike and I continued past the first ice bridge to the base of Athabasca. There was no way I was coming this far and not cross that bridge! Thank God we accepted their food and water! I guess we were headed for a light day of alpine climbing, Voytek Kurtik style. Voytek and his friend could climb Polish mountains like no one else! Obsessive, meticulous, precision made him the best. *Time to channel Voytek.*

Our metal teeth of the crampons strapped onto hiking boot soles bit into the crystal-clear twenty-foot long ice bridge. I roped around a rock and belayed Mike as he crossed with pick in hand. The arching bridge didn't break! I was belayed from the other side. With disbelief, I cautiously stepped on crampon tips over a two-foot-wide blue ice bridge that was likely thirty feet above fluffy white snow. If I can cross that, I can do anything. Knee-deep in fluffy snow, we arrived at the Athabasca's face. Snow shoes would have been helpful. The sheer cliff rose to the left of the active and moving Columbia Icefield.

Two, eight, twenty rope lengths, we repeatedly belayed one climber from above, while the other ascended by tenaciously ice pick pulling up the sheer face. My crampon tips kicked into slick, white ice, like ladder climbing, as I chopped the pick tip above and into ice to pull myself up. I reached Mike's belay spot, then climbed a rope's length above him. I set a belay and he climbed the length up to, then beyond me. Often a chock was wedged too firmly in the crack and left behind. The deceptive mountain face had a sloping, rounded, vertical wall. Each of our rope lengths looked like the last belay one to the summit. Methodically, Mike and I ascended, but how would we get down? This climb is too sheer to back down.

"Should we keep going or head back?" We discussed at each passing of the belay line.

"There is no way I'm going down that sheer face! How much farther?" Mike said.

"It should only be a few more rope lengths to the top?" I said. "Let's go!" My energy increased with the adrenaline, the beauty. I recognized myself on this sheer rock face. *I'm supposed to be here.* The thick white snow was far below us as we ascended the icy, bowed rock face. At first it didn't seem very far to the top. I was fooled over and over again by the bowed perspective. At the far end of the valley, we pointed and waved as tour buses stopped for viewers to add a quarter to the binoculars and watch our ascent. Tourists could see how far we had to go. Every twenty rope lengths, I nibbled on a power bar, gaining energy from the magnificent snowy peak under a summer sun. Beauty was a communication with a higher world. The views made our strenuous effort worth it. Already we rationed water. Eight, ten rope-lengths higher. The summit lured us, teased us. No other climbers were on this face. We had a guide book and our will.

Voytek had invented a word, "CREA". It was mental oxygen, friendship. CREA was about creativity being more important than creation. As long as CREA functioned within us, we were alive. On that climb, I felt what CREA was. CREA was energy from the surrounding beauty and dependence on another. We were constantly just two rope-lengths from the top ridge all afternoon. It was like a bad dream when you can't reach where you are going. Fear-fueled adrenaline kept us going. Hours of endurance wore us out. Why was I here?

At sunset, we reached the razor-edged crest with wind whisking up from a several-mile-deep back side. I feel made to climb mountains—who knew? Any cairn of rocks, piled to recognize the peak of Athabasca, was buried in drifted snow. Bright white snow blew powerfully from both sides of the thin ridge into red reflections of a waning sun. We dared not take a break. Hiking just below the wind's edge at dusk, we traversed drifted snow to the scree-sloped side of the face, not daring to descend what we had just ascended. Twelve hours of climbing, with mere nibbles and sips of water from day packs, and now we couldn't keep the icy wind from whipping through our clothing. I added snow to replenish my water bottle. I am at home on this wind-blown ridge. From the flat Midwest, how is this familiar? Ahead, the Columbia Icefield was a slow river of frozen ice. The expanse of miles of fresh white snow stretched to the horizons with a setting golden sun and rose dusk. CREA; I climb for the connection to nature and the beauty.

"We're not going to find Tom Crean here!" Mike joked in a shout. "Wouldn't a herd of long horn antelope look nice along that expanse of ice." Tom Crean was a Kerryman who joined Captain Scott to be one of the first to reach the South Pole. His remarkable personality, calmness, courage and endurance saved many adventurers' lives during years of traversing the Antarctic.

"Good idea to channel Tom Crean now. Voytek got us up the mountain, Crean's courage will get us down," I said. "It has got to be easier to crisscross a glacier." A nearly full moon reflected off the snow with a bright glow. Our humor kept me calm. "Let's keep descending by moonlight," Mike said. They must be wondering about us at camp? We ARE going to make it back safely! It's like I've lived this before.

A food and water break caused hunger. Exhaustion and delirium set in under a full moon reflecting off drifting snow. Mike and I descending a scree-path just as darkness set in. The wind calmed. Fatigue ruled. Though our adrenaline was high, we chose to chock to a crack in the cliff above a leveled scree-ledge to rest until dawn. We ate most of our chocolate with dried fruit and rye crackers. Rationed food would fuel our tomorrow. This tethering to the side of a mountain is also familiar. I had learned from sculpting that safety came first. Tools and protection allow more to be done preserving effort. That training was easy to adapt to climbing. Because of the cold, we took turns, sleeping and waking the other every twenty minutes to jog in place and warm the extremities. Water from snow was not an issue. It melted inside our coats. Stomp your feet. Wiggle your toes! Thawing my fingers took time. My toes no longer warmed up. While rummaging Mike's pack for food, I pulled out two fist-grips with alligator jaws.

"What are these for?" I said.

"You slip this side of the juniper onto your rope and when you pull down the grip tightens." Mike said. I tried the juniper. Haphazardly, one juniper was put into my pack. Most of our conversation was planning how to get through a narrow chute with only one chock left. We needed two. Even with this broken few hours of sleep, we greeted dawn rested, concerned, and ready. The expansive warming sun shone over the colossal glacier. Its rise encouraged our descent along its edge. Scree gave way to a steep cliff. Slowly and carefully we wound our way across the glacier of snow and crevasses sometimes backtracking if the cracks were impenetrably webbed. When no rocks were available, one of us would go forward and lie prone with crampons and ice pick dug in for the other to advance. Progress was slow and tedious. I could no longer feel the cold in my legs and arms. I was hours beyond hunger. Only careful, cautious forward motion mattered. I have the endurance and drive to be a good climber. Horizontal and treacherous crossing of the deceptive glacier tested their nerves.

"What would Tom Crean do?" I asked.

"Probably go unleashed—forget it," Mike said.

In the lead, I came to a light, fluffy area in the snow along the scree bank. Not so different from other fissures in the glacier surface but we had reached a dead end in the maze between crevasses. I signaled back that the snow looked airy, then poked at the spot with my pick. I hammered the spot harder. Mike dug in with his pick. I sat down and kicked it with two heels, then signaled back. Cautiously, carefully, I stomped on the light snow. I signaled back that I was going ahead and Mike nodded. I took another step. Silence.

No sun, no wind. Kaleidoscopic, effervescent rainbows of every shade of purple, red, yellow and orange vibrated in midair and unfathomably deep into blueish tones, blurring vapor and reflections in solid ice. I was mesmerized with wonder. Perplexing dancing pigment floated below, above, and around me. The air was vibrating with bright white falling flurries. Deep in the ice colors sparkled, green, gold, then red, dancing in swirls. *Alice in Wonderland.* This was beyond what I had ever imagined. Vibrancy and prisms, endless depths of dancing color. Overwhelmed by an intense beauty my mind transcended tangible thought. An unrecognizable world swirled around me.

"Margot!" Mike called. Where was he? Above? I looked up through two slick, widening, clear, blue-ice walls. My ice pick dangled several feet above my reach. A broken hole above that and sunlight streamed down spotlighting floating snowflakes. My crampon tips were stuck with a tip-toe hold on either side of a steep vertical chasm that narrowed hundreds of feet below me. Rainbows of bright rose, glistening gold, animated blue and energetic green. I was surrounded by pure beauty, the walls vibrated with hues. Disoriented, I heard "Margot!" being called from above the hole that was up twenty-feet from where I had fallen through. *This is a crevasse.*

"I've tied your line around a rock," Mike said. "Come straight up the hole you entered. I'll belay you up. Take it easy!" Mike's even calmer than usual voice caused me to be concerned. This hole of ice was like a beautiful dream that I didn't want to leave, but I need to get out. Reality sank in. "I'm in a crevasse! A person lives fifteen minutes before hypothermia sets in." I started to think fast. The juniper! I fished the hand grip out of the top of my back pack. Without losing the toe-hold of my metal points in ice, I slipped it on the taut line and pulled myself up to my ice pick. With two crampon-tip holds, the ice pick and sliding the juniper up the rope, the climb out was possible. As the rope slackened, Mike set up a belay to keep my line taut. A sloping shelf gave me a place to dig crampons into a surface. I started to climb across an ice bulge into a bright spot in the snow and broke through the snow above with my pick. I climbed out a freshly opened hole and sheepishly said. "I know, I'm not supposed to exit another hole, but I'm out."

"Not to worry, grab onto a rock." Mike was even more composed. I was concerned.

"Untie your line, I'll pull it through the holes. I'm still chocked to the rock," he called out. I clipped my carabiner to a chock in a wall crevice, dropped my line through the hole. Mike coiled the line and tossed it to me above the openings. When I was clipped on belay I began to move from the rock. I wondered if he'd gotten hurt while stopping my fall? He was awfully quiet. He must have been dragged as he slowed my fall a rope length.

"Thanks for slowing my fall so I could gracefully land a toe hold," I said.

"I got scraped up while being dragged." Mike said, "But, I'm good enough to go."

Miles below, we waved to what looked like Jean and their friends along the moraines at the bottom. They must be a mile away. Jean and the other dots paused and pointed up, and started to run to the base of the glacier. Busses emptied tourists at the "pay to look" binoculars again. The joy of seeing Jean! Stay calm. Relief. Keep your wits about you! They waved back.

A tough decision lay ahead. We could go around a rock wall which would take a few more hours or slip through a narrow gap between to two rock outcroppings and be down in an hour. There was a stretch just below the passageway where one of us couldn't be chocked on for the second belay, because we had only one more chock and needed it on top and below this gap. If Mike could take out the top chock, we'd have it for the lower levels. I would descend on belay through the gap, brace against a rock and belay him to where he can move the chock. With our fatigue and exhausted food, we chose the shorter route.

"If we make this, I'm going to nominate you for an American Alpine Climbing Award?"

"After we make this I'm going to give my crampons to…?" I said. Humor helped us to swallow the fear, kept our muscles from twitching.

Mike could stop quicker if he slipped, so I went first. Our guidebook said to head to a wall on the left of the narrow chute to a fissure for a chock. I was learning the power of will and what humans could endure. I learned I could transcend my fear for a greater gain. I learned the importance of belief. Believe you can do this and it will happen.

"Be careful," Mike said using our last chock to belay my advance through the narrow gap to as far as our line would extend to the left. The snow was deep. Tensions escalated. I needed to make each step a careful one as I crossed the chute of deep snow. Total concentration mattered. This was the real deal. Knowing my sister was headed to the base of the mountain pinpointed my concentration. Act carefully. I advanced to the outcrop on the left with trepidation. In me is the answer to why I climb. I am good at this.

"I found a chock another climber left!" I locked my carabiner on a chock and called back.

Safely, Mike was belayed through the gap and down a length of deep snow. He used the last chock again on a rock to belay me down two lengths. Within several line-lengths we were off the face and on level ground. We could unleash and run down the cascaded snow. Jean and a few friends ran to greet us at the bottom of the deep snow chute. We scarfed down peanut butter sandwiches and chugged Gatorade. Hugs of relief calmed the anxiety they hadn't allowed to surface. Stories in babbles of moments without a coherent story line flowed. It was mid-day over the Columbia Icefield.

The next morning, we cut the chicken wire off the VW Beetle's tires and headed east to Minneapolis, push-starting at every stop. Mike and I assembled a slideshow with a script, drawings and photographs. Jean, Mom and Dad, and Mike, and his parents gathered at Airdrie's dark living room to see our narrated show. Mom had not grasped the harrowing moments until the story was projected. Maybe it was better Mom didn't know? With my parents' unified love of cutting-edge flight and travel, a part of them understood. A part of them would have done the same thing. That was the way it was.

Chapter 6: Ireland, Manhattan and a First Job

Sophomore year, I entered the William Kugler Musical Instrument Museum for advice as to why my clay flute lost its tone after being bisque fired. For the rest of my college years I popped into this museum to help with the school tours. From tall walls of instruments on wheels, we handed ostrich egg sitars and black sea comenches to small children to strum. One wall were examples of the centuries-old progression of string instruments that lead up to making violins, starting with the Black Sea comenche. It was his nickelodeon collection the Smithsonian was intrigued with. Those lined the walls covered in tarps.

January term of 1977, my cousin Sheila and I traveled to Ireland to visit relatives on her mother's side. We earned independent study credits for Irish music from an Anthropology of Words for her and Art History of

Musical Instruments for my course. Her Aunt Letitia Gorby in Bray was our base camp. We traveled by train from Dublin along the North Sea during a fierce storm. We repeated: 1 Martello Terrace, Strand Road, Bray. The Bray station was across Strand Road and a park to Aunt Letitia's home. 1 Martello Terrace, Strand Road. With our backpacks on, Sheila and I linked arms and stepped into the ferocious wind across Strand Road. One foot forward and two blown back we inched across the park in what seemed like an hour. Unrelenting wind and driving horizontal rain forcefully pushed us from our next gliding step: 1 Martello Terrace. If we raised a foot we'd lose our balance. Is 1 Martello Terrace the left side or right side of the row at the end of the green? Our eyes watered, our mouths zipped from the cold rain, our soaked heads down. The diagonal traverse ended at the last door right on the sea.

"You look like drowned field mice," was Aunt Letitia's greeting. "I've been watching you since you started across that blimey park. What a sight the two of you are. I wasn't sure you'd make it until tomorrow." We sat after changing our drenched clothes for a pot of black tea and biscuits. Her stories started when we entered with nary a pause as she fluidly covered family, Irish life, her connection with Aunt Mary Margaret and gratitude to Uncle Harry with amazing details that I'd wish I'd recorded in her lovely and lively brogue. The waves of the sea continued to pound in the side of her jolted three story house. I settled into the soft winged living room chair worn from the jet lag travel and weather. I thought I'd never rise again. She jumped up to fetch a book.

"You're an artist I've heard. Come here and sit in the dining room. Now look out that window." I glanced back over the park with rain plummeting diagonally in sheets on the soaked green. The wind roared.

"Here, read the first paragraph." The cover of the book was James Joyce's *Portrait of an Artist as a Young Man*. I read the first page.

"He wrote those words about sitting right here in this house looking out that window," she stated with the full impact of Irish literature history and storytelling. Sheila and I learned everything we could about Irish story telling. We heard the Gorby stories of relatives from Cavan to Dublin, Bray and Monkstown. She'd arranged for us to visit an Australian uilleann pipe maker in Monkstown as soon as we'd dried our things. A Gorby would host us there. As her quick and lively heavy brogue triggered story after story, our heads began to nod beyond what strong tea could revive. Quick as a rabbit she leapt up to the whistle of the tea pot on the peat burning stove to fill our red water bottles to heat the beds. We climbed her staircase to the second floor with the rain dripping from the clerestory. Buckets and rags helped.

Our huge double bed had four posts with curtains to contain our warmth. The rubber water bottles were tucked in for our toes. "No need to use the wash basins, the bathroom is down the hall," she cheerily guided. "Now find you pajamas and brush your teeth before bed. I'm delighted with your visit. Good night girls." Uncle Harry had provided for Aunt Letitia through the troubles in Ireland when she was widowed and struggling to make ends meet. Her daughter Astrid had hosted us in Wales where she lived in an abandoned chapel with a basement carved out of chalk and was married to a deer manager for an extensive estate. Every meal was venison: curried, stewed, ground for burgers. Her son Ambrose, a delivery man, would pick us up in several days to see the family's home in Cavan County. We were asleep before our heads hit the pillow.

I heard Aunt Letitia up before dawn. Sheila and I laugh at our toes reaching just over five feet of person next to six feet of person. We rose to help as the storm had been worse overnight with the waves hitting against the wall of the house and splashing in and down the three story staircase. She was mopping buckets of water. "Don't go near the sea, girls. It's rough today." Sheila and I visited Monkstown with lighter packs to learn about making elbow drone pipes. He directed us to Galway for uilleann piper's music. "Find Seamus Ennis." The ullieann pipers and Aunt Letitia's stories set our path to explore Galway. We boarded a 10 pm train expecting to sleep all night and arrive the next morning. Surprised we arrived in Galway two and a half hours later. Now to find a hotel at midnight in a foot of snow in a small city. It was the coldest winter in forty-five years with wanting heat. We stayed bundled in down coats and sleeping bags under blankets and still could see our breath through shivers. All for the sake of art.

Because we were American, we could sit in bars, being the only women. Dark wood, peat fire smoke in the air, new spills on old spills of Guinness. Whiskey was not served until afternoon. We had our notebooks out for armor and took notes of conversations and musician's haunts. "I'd give you my farm house if you like Ireland. All the heat is by a peat fire," an older man offered. "If you're lookin' for an uilleann piper you've got to hear Seamus Ennis at Kings Head. He'll play in any pub that he enters, so keep your ear to the ground. I've got his pipes if you see him. He went home without them last night."

Tig Coili might have Tommy Keane.

Eugene Lamb at the Crane Bar or look for Liam O'Flynn or Ronana Brown, they spend a lot of time in London.

Another good bet Skeff's for Willie Clancey.

O'Connors Pub is always a good bet: just see who's there. You can't go wrong.

We wrote in our notebooks and ordered another cup of coffee. Just then the man sitting next to us rose from his Guinness pint and in a clairvoyant voice sang a lilting limerick about a young lass in the green hills left behind in a young man's search for self. He confronted a series of impossible tasks to achieve the love of his life.

Was it an angel on our shoulder, or the luck o' the Irish, that we happened upon the legendary Seamus Ennis half way through a set? It was enough to catch the drones and trills that echoed a five thousand year old storytelling culture amidst vibrant green hills. That is how his music sounds, ancient with misty, bright green, mystical toe tapping. The "Morning Trush" composed by his father who awoke to a thrush singing every day. Seamus found the music and played it with the mist in the air and clarity of a rested lyrical repetition. We heard the magic of Eugene Lamb and Tommy Keane before flying through London to Minnesota.

Junior year, I was granted a January term scholarship to intern in Manhattan at *Scholastic Magazine*. My friend and I shared a room at the

Biltmore Hotel across the street from Grand Central Station and several blocks from our office. Writers said they couldn't afford to go out at night, but we skimped and never stopped exploring jazz clubs, museums and visiting artists in their studios. I discovered publishing and loved it! I researched the white seal cubs of Canada being clubbed for making soft and furry keychains, coin purses and muffs. The article about depleted populations causing near extinction was written at a third-grade reading level. I didn't join the others at lunch for a week to write and rewrite for deadline. If I could get the school kids to understand, they'd tell their parents to stop buying trinkets. I was driven to find the right words to save the seal pups. "Hundreds of letters from children came back about her Baby Seal article," my boss's letter reported to my college advisor, "letters are still arriving."

"Why are you racing through college?" my sculpting professor asked.

"Lucky-number-seven," I said. He required that I take one sculpture class to finish my major. I enrolled at the School of the Art Institute (SAIC) before May graduation. At SAIC, a few of students and I found an empty courtyard classroom with natural light and asked Professor Eldon Danhausen to teach us figure modeling. We met 9-4:00 Saturdays to learn how to sculpt the glisten in an eye and kissable lips in grey clay, splash-coat hydrocal with a surface slap, and mix and paint rubber molds. We cast in bronze in the school's foundry. Mom and Dad traveled extensively while I cared for Airdrie. I received a call for a second interview with World Book Encyclopedia where I had applied in February. By March I was drawing for the editorial department of the annual encyclopedia updates and fourteen page descriptions of new discoveries in science, art, ecology and politics.

Well connected environmentalist, Rafe Pomeranae published that the Jasons, an international scientist team, had just determined the earth was getting warmer. National researchers dove into analytics and developed the same conclusion. A cocktail of sulfur dioxide from coal power plants, nitrogen from car exhaust and ammonia from livestock waste and fertilizers mixed with water vapors across the Midwest to rain acid on the Adirondack forests. Already half the red spruces died from the calcium sapped from their foliage. Forty one percent of the lakes measured acidification resulting in fish having heart attacks from bursting red blood cells. Fish were eaten by humans. New research on oceans warming made larger hurricanes and tornados, denser, heavier rain and encroaching coastlines were exploding with importance. Carbon dioxide was warming the earth. We could turn it around, but we had to work fast. We had thirty years before life on Earth changed dramatically. Humankind was at fault and at risk. It was called global warming.

I researched, consulted with scientists, then drew how bigger hurricanes formed from higher ocean temperatures making more powerful storms to cool the equator by transferring heat by evaporated rain falling in temperate zones. Shortages of water was, even then, causing sink holes in Florida. Greenhouse effect visual descriptions were constructed and photographed with three dimensional felt to show how ozone holes allowed more sunlight into our atmosphere. Stop using aerosols and Freon for refrigerants. Chlorofluorocarbons (CFCs) in aerosol refrigerant propellants that burned holes in the ozone were banned in the U.S.

Locally, Hazel Johnson, Chicago's Mother of the Environmental Justice Movement, from CHA's Altgeld Gardens, became an environmental activist following the death, by lung cancer, of her husband in 1969. Her children suffered skin and respiratory ailments from Altgeld Garden's contaminated earth. Nationally, the Jasons revealed importance of the reflective white glaciers rebounding the sun's energy away from earth. The prediction was if concentrations of CO2 doubled in the atmosphere, global temperatures would rise by 2 to 3 degrees Celsius. The most devastating feature was the effect of rapid melting of the arctic ice sheets. The oceans would rise, beside a calamity of drought.

Genetically Modified Organisms (GMOs) were still experiments. DNA coding was made in painted clay and photographed to explain to readers. New breakthroughs in understanding how the plasticity of the brain could be rewired with new synapses around damaged areas were visualized for illustrators to make finished art. After a few articles, I became the go-to person for designing genetics and DNA coding explanations. GMOs were being developed and discussed for moral implications. While tomatoes were bred square for packaging, the best GMO use might be to grow rice in brackish water. The seas would rise in the Bangladesh rice fields first. We described the new science at a third-grade reading level and sent our update warnings to Bangladesh, the Arctic Poles and Iceland. Northeast trees and lakes were dying from acid rain.

Daily temperatures recorded for decades indicated global warming and scientists sounded an alarm. Gordon MacDonald advised Dwight Eisenhower on space exploration, Richard Nixon against coal, and started an Office of Carbon Dioxide. Roger Revelle advised every president since the Manhattan Project and helped the Weather Bureau establish continuous measure of atmospheric CO2 on Hawaii. He told LBJ humans have "altered the composition of the atmosphere on a global scale" through burning fossil fuel. "Future economic and political impacts would be beyond comprehension."

We wrote articles on solar and wind power, integrated and loved electric cars, wind turbines, synthetic fuels and solar panels for power. Despite Three Mile Island, nuclear was considered better than coal. Many aspects of water from acidity to unequal distribution poisoning food sources and production. Sink holes, evaporation, the motion of water cooling the earth with rain. The possible shortage of drinking water due to weather changes. Drier areas, flooding elsewhere, melting ice, rising seas make larger and more frequent storms. Still no one could fathom the first truly global question we'd ever had to face: how to slow the rapid heating of the earth with our dependency on fossil fuels. I biked to work. I grew a rooftop vegetable garden, purchased organic food. I was too consumed with studying for the MCATs with my roommate.

Earth is between two planets. One has too much CO2 and is too hot for life. The other is too cold. Our imbalance could go either direction, but most likely towards too hot with added CO2. In 1979 ecology was news and not political. Everyone was on board to save our quality of life on earth. World Book told the story of sink holes and large hurricanes worldwide. We warned India, Africa, Micronesia, New Orleans, California, Nevada,

Oregon, and Virginia. As World Book encyclopedia laid off 750 editorial creatives in one day, my thinking grew to express the importance of each decision being about life on earth, primarily humankind.

I remained to publish another set of updates while applying to Yale for graduate school. I chose an MFA in sculpture. At SAIC I had learned to focus my attention on the importance of an ear, or details in a hand, as a piece of the whole. Sculpture must look more like the subject than the subject itself—hyper-seeing while making rhythms in form. A few of us traveled to Italy to tour museums of Renaissance sculpture and painting in Rome, Venice and Florence. I sculpted a bronze *Reader* for the Winnetka Library, Northfield branch children's courtyard and that spring was accepted into Yale.

Chapter 7: Representations Amid the Conceptual

I matriculated to the 1982 Yale Master of Fine Arts class of eight sculptors, of which three were women, to sculpt nature: human, plant, and animal forms. As the first representational master's degree student in twelve years, I was terrified as I presented my first slide show to my fellow classmates. I was so nervous that I could barely speak. My fellow installation and conceptual students did not know what to say, but the look they gave me seemed to say: What rock did you crawl out from under? By this time, my sculpting heroes had expanded to include post-war European sculptors, Alberto Giacometti and Marino Marini.

"I will be hiring a sculpting assistant," Erwin Hauer, Yale Professor for Undergraduate Sculpture Studies, said at a welcome event in Yale Museum's courtyard. My ears perked up. I applied and was hired. As his assistant, I taught drawing and sculpting for undergrads on Tuesday and Thursday mornings in Hammond Hall. I studied drawing with William Bailey and Art & Architecture with Vincent Scully. I was off to a good start in an overwhelming place full of amazing people.

I worked with two other students, Tom and Julie, modeling for each other. One day it was Julie's turn to sculpt my portrait in clay. Julie was moving clay around to get the proportions of my mouth and forehead in relation to my eyes. She worked in silence. I watched, but could not see what she was sculpting. I could only see the back of the clay head. Julie wheeled the clay on a stand behind me to shape the angle of my neck in relation to my jawline.

"Take more charge of your critiques," Julie said. A visiting performance artist had thrown me off in my group crit by chiding me for sweeping up the floor of plaster chips and clay dust. "They are there to help you with your work. Ask questions to define the conversation for your needs," Julie said.

"If I sneezed, I'd be analyzed for my velocity or timidity," I said.

"I know what you mean," Julie said. "In my last painting crit, the professor told me I needed to open my eyes and look harder." My jaw dropped and I spun around. Julie's face was calm.

"The eternal optimist!" I cried out recognizing my grandmother's optimistic expression when I saw the clay portrait of me. "That is my grandmother! I didn't know I looked like her!" This was the first moment I recognized our likeness. Julie was taken aback. My surprised exclamation, out of place in this moment of quiet, raw creation, might have been confusing for her. "It looks like me and my Gramma Mac," I explained. This discovery triggered questions and longing. Was I like her? I didn't know anything about Gramma Mac. I didn't know anything about most women.

During my first semester, I was sculpting three full-scale women discussing art around a table when the department head, David Von Schlegel, asked if I would teach Erwin's undergraduate sculpting classes. He had taken ill and was in the hospital. "There is no one else on campus who can teach figurative sculpture." For half of my first semester I taught Erwin's classes and became friends with the undergraduates.

I'd tell myself to calm down on the way to classes. Julie and Tom were in my class. Up until now I'd sculpted with the students, helped Erwin with building armatures, keeping the water based clay workable, the classroom and casting room clean. Erwin told the undergraduates, "The power of the image comes from convex form pushing against the space around it. The horizon of the form softens at a full roundness and hardens at darker, sharper edges defined by crisscrossing of lines like fishnet stockings, or grids on television golf course terrains. Form extends beyond itself and into the space around it to transform the area," he'd explain in words and images. I stayed calm, arrived early, imagined where their sculpting was headed and offered ideas for a next step.

Remarkable teachers steered my figurative art in experimental directions. Erwin had studied with Marino Marini in Europe before coming to the United States. His work involved repetitive abstract architectural elements. During my first year, Garth Evans told me that talking with Alberto Giacometti was exactly like experiencing one of his sculptures. It was as if the fog of Paris were eating into the essence of an isolated man. He told me Alberto used few words, and was worn raw. Giacometti was a sparse man who survived the Great Wars. Natalie Charkov, who had taught me at Yale Norfolk, where I taught as well, had met Marino Marini in a cafe in Florence. They told me of how these sculptors' art was like being in the room with the artist; how knowing their art was like meeting them. Their stories helped me realize my charge as an art student was to find and express who seven o' nine is.

One week Alice Neel, a figurative painter, visited our class. We sat cross-legged together on the floor in the A&A common space with vertical boards filled with first-year paintings. Alice looked at each one and responded with stories or comments that might help.

My friend Gabrielle was sitting next to me. In the middle of the session she whispered, "I've got to go to the bathroom, I'll be right back. Tell me what she says." She was gone awhile. Long enough for Alice to get to talking about Gabrielle's painting.

"This artist is reaching into the past, covering the middle and making a contemporary statement. This is contemporary art. Who painted this?" Alice looked around.

"Gabrielle'll be right back," I said and, to keep the conversation going, "You have mentioned what I think she intends to paint. What critique would you have to share with her?"

Alice stared at me long and hard. "I have a reoccurring nightmare that I wake up as an art critic," she said fiercely. "I shake and sweat when I imagine myself criticizing artwork. Whatever did you think by asking me that question?"

Just then, Gabriel slipped into the spot beside me. "What just happened?"

"Here's Gabrielle, she painted that painting." I replied.

"You are a contemporary artist!" the visiting painter looked hard at

Gabrielle and moved onto the next painting.

Hammond Hall was on the opposite side of campus from the School of Art and Architecture and around a cemetery. It was surrounded by an empty lot and had an abandoned train track that had become a trash pit below it. I biked to the building and called the police for escort if I stayed beyond dusk. I was locking my bike to the indoor banister when I heard, "We're getting together in the back," a call that came up from the first floor of Hammond Hall. I grabbed a can of nuts from my counter, climbed down the steel steps across the two-story welding area and out the tall garage door. In a fifty-gallon rusted barrel, a fire had been started. Beer was buried under ice in the Igloo cooler. An arrangement of plastic and wooden chairs, logs and planks of wood on cinderblocks were loosely arranged surrounded the barrel. An abandoned train track dipped below us. A first-year was comfortably seated with a scarf around her neck sipping a beer. Another hurried in with a handled bag. A second-year came from around back. Another grabbed the beer cap with a set of pliers and pulled the cap off while someone else laid his cap over the edge of an I-beam and hit the top with the heel of his hand. A cloud burst from the open neck of the bottle, but he tipped it up before much of the beer poured out. I peeled off the cap of the nut can and set it on a log near the fire.

"So, what happened?" Ann asked about our lunch with Richard Serra, a New York artist who sculpted with nontraditional materials such as steel, rubber and fiberglass. He visited the sculpture studios annually. "What did he say?"

Ursula von Rydingsvaard, a sculptor (whose large-scale works are influenced by nature including cedar and other forms of timber) and I had joined the others at a circular table in S.O.M.'s red brick cafeteria. Second-year sculptors' trays were full of plates filled with fish, broccoli, salad and cardboard boxed drinks.

"Is that chocolate milk you are drinking?" Richard Serra irascibly gestured.

"Yeah, I like chocolate milk." Pete said.

"I've got to get back to my bourbon in New York," Richard smirked. "You guys drink chocolate milk here."

"So, Richard..." Ursula began a calculated art dialogue of NYC artists. It was a glimpse into their world for us.

Serra turned to her and replied authoritatively, domineering and demeaning. We peered into their dialogues and their references, with a history we were trying to enter. Ursula stood up and left. To this day I wish I had left with her. The air was ripe with antagonism.

"Never make a maquette," Serra said. He now had the floor. "Never raise your sculptures above the ground on a pedestal. Never sculpt an idea less than full scale that presses into the earth."

"Wait a minute." My Irish ire was up. "Rodin put the Burghers of Calais on the ground. It is not new to put sculptures on the ground; it has been done for decades. When Rodin wanted to raise a sculpture on a pedestal, he did."

"So, you know what you are talking about." Richard looked hard at me and the conversation traveled elsewhere. During my one-on-one crit with him he had called me a reactionary. I had responded that I wanted to start with the full range of life forms to develop my direction. That weekend, I went to New York City to explore galleries and saw a new exhibit of Richard Serra's. It was of steel maquettes on pedestals.

"What did he say to Ursula?" Ann asked. No one had a clear answer. "You've got to write him a note. Tell him you saw his work after your conversation and are glad he agrees."

"How would I get his address?" I asked.

"Send it to the Gallery. They'll see that he gets it," Ann said.

Anthropology of the Human Skeleton class was intimidating with students who were well trained majors. The history of how we know when indigenous people first rode horses was known by more broken bones during a period of time. We learned that suture lines told how the skull grew together to indicate age, that how teeth were worn determined diet— worn molars told of maize, broken front teeth indicated tearing meat. I took notes furiously, fascinated. We learned how a male skull had heavier brows, a female skeleton was more petite. Vertebrae showed strength or injury with ridges. If a hole had grown closed on a cranial plate it meant brain surgery happened and the patient survived. If the skull was spongy they died of syphilis. Every skull we studied had syphilis.

We divided into groups of five seated at large round lab tables. Boxes were on the table labeled Machu Picchu with numbers. "What is the gender, age, diet and occupation of the ancient skeleton before you? Here is a sheet of guidelines." We opened the boxes to see five foot plus long skeletons and removed the skull. We had one high cheek boned round faced female and a chiseled strong browed male. Both were eighteen years old and had been buried together. "Romeo and Juliet," we named them. "How did they die and what was their society?

Over the semester our group contributed a theory that Machu Picchu was a thriving community when the Spaniards invaded. The men left to fight them and were wiped out. Spanish soldiers found this village of women and brought syphilis, which decimated the remaining population. Equally convincing was the other groups' theories that this was a religious center of women who were killed by the disease or that this was a resort town or university. My 1984 thesis exhibition was of female friends on pedestals: Doreen, Julie, Gabriella, Lena and Laura. We completed a Yale education and tread a path for other Yale women.

Chapter 8: Machu Picchu

With my MFA art stored in boxes in New Haven, I met Barb and Dennis from Chicago and Edie and Dave from Seattle in Cusco, Peru's airport. We adjusted to Cusco's 11,000-foot altitude, preparing for an eight-day hike of the Machu Picchu trail. Our first Cusco day we walked an exhausted block or two to dinner. We were always in our hotel before dark for safety. By day three, I traversed the city's markets looking for propane. With backpacks, a stove, tents and lots of water, we climbed into the bed of a vegetable truck headed to Malnapalta. We saw a dozen children drinking cha chi while their mothers' ripped earlobes healed from pierced earrings being stolen. The truck carried gasoline tanks on the cab's roof. Our truck bed was filled with crated chickens, backpacks, full shopping baskets and mysterious bundled cloth bags. We lurched up the rutted dirt road with gasoline splashing back on us with each bump. The clutch didn't always catch at steep curves. We coasted back several feet. Everyone waited to hear the clutch to engage while children squirmed. The truck lurched upward.

"Not all of us are going to make it to Machu Picchu," Dave said. I was tired from finishing my thesis exhibit and packing from grad school. He kept me on my best guard. Malnapalta sat at the top of the next Peruvian peak, the hub of a spider webs of cow paths. Have you ever tried to follow braided cow paths that veer and loop and rise and fall like a loose weaving? It's hard to know if we'd followed the right one for days. With my forty-pound pack, I recalled and rehearsed Spanish words. Starting with numbers, then days of the week, fueled by the magnificent, blinding beauty of each turn in the path. Shining Path members were in the area and caused our vigilant alertness. We carried kerosene for daytime heating of water and camped far off the trail. We lit no fires after dark. Sleep after dusk, wake with dawn, stay aware. Spanish phrases emerged from my distant memory in the steady pattern of hiking. A few angels, in the shape of school children in sandals heading home for the weekend, showed us the way to their village. A sandaled boy grabbed my forty-pound pack and ran the right cow path with us hurrying behind. They knew to slow down for us to chaperone them past one farm that frightened them. After we passed that skulking farmer, the children dumped my pack, pointed out our path down the valley on the right and waved farewell. The temperature dropped. Edie started to get chilled, then started to go pale. Hypothermia was setting in. Dave set up their tent and bundled with her in their zipped-together sleeping bag. She slept deeply.

Exhausted, the rest of us fell asleep as soon as our heads hit the pillow. That night, a snowstorm buried our tents. We dug out from the drifts for an early start to cross the Salcatay pass before the afternoon rain or snow. A length of my tent pole and two stakes were left in the deep snow in our rush to get over the pass before the afternoon snow. Gaiters around our ankles and balalaikas around our necks enabled our steep, relentless hike in tennis shoes up through the snowy valley. We took turns flattening a path up to oxygen-deprived heights of 14,000 feet. If the cells of our bodies are replaced every seven years, does it include brain cells? Soon, the splitting headache increased the escalating pace to get over the pass and down to oxygen—fast! Matte tea brewed over propane cured the excruciating migraines. If only I had started my day with matte.

Five delightful and strenuous days of traversing the ancient paved Incan road lined with thousands of varieties of orchids at every turn inspired us. There were plenty of hikers at each campsite. Caves carved through the mountains, sidewalk size ledges, along vertical walls, carved above steep drops and bridges built over dips at a steady seventy-degree temperature. Huge square pavers leveled the dips and waterfalls replenished our thirst. The Inca Trail wove around mountain tops with stone surfaces so finished we could have walked barefoot. On rare occasions, the stone path dipped into a tropical rain forest, or rose to a walled and ruined village that required an extra sweater. There were many hikers at each designated campground from all over the world. *More people around is comforting, but watch out for your camera and propane.* After a sidewalk-width pack-snagging-on-steep-walls-traverse above a hundred-foot drop, we passed through the Sun Gate to Machu Picchu. Most of the traverse was visible from the guard's vantage. Guards with arrows may have watched for intruders along this face of the mountain. A yellow-headed snake reared its flaring head with red eyes as we entered Macchu Picchu valley. We froze, backed off and waited.

Edie, Dave and I camped overnight on a rock above the snakes that Hiram Bingham's map indicated was sacrificial. I found out later the Incas didn't sacrifice. After a deep restful sleep, dusk became dawn. June's summer solstice solar performance shot a streak of light onto the ruins as it rose through a crevice, spotlighting Hyna Picchu and the Sun Gate, the bookend guard stations of the valley. Sunlight cascaded over the homes of the elders, through their windows then to religious sites. Light flowed down the slope to wake the village. As the valley was lit by the morning sun, a shadowed arrow from the valley pointed to Macchu Picchu. I captured it on film.

Truck-sized rocks were cut accurately with stone age tools to interlock into walls that withstood earthquakes, time, history and tourism. We wandered with the llamas in awe of what humankind can do. There were stone pools carved to reflect the sun to keep solar studies from burning their eyes. Clean water was transported constantly along stone troughs. Pools were carved. Windows lined up with the sunrise. Terraces for growing food stepped down the mountain allowing variations in growing zones throughout the year. Stone storage buildings told us they grew an excess of quinoa, corn, wheat and barley. Barb and Dennis, Edie and Dave headed to the Amazon River while I took a train from Machu Picchu to Lima, saw the 150th Anniversary of bullfighting and flew to New York to move from New Haven to Chicago.

Chapter 9: Love in a Time of Purpose

Why did you move to Chicago?" I asked Daniel, my future husband, as he and I walked in a scruffy field of weeds edged by the south branch of the Chicago River and hum of I-290 rising behind us. The rounded towers of River City boxed the end of the field with Daniel's car parked on the east. Half-finished sculptures with bags of concrete covered in plastic were scattered in the field.

"Chicago has problems to solve," Daniel said. That was an understatement. Chicago had the most restrictive covenants of any U.S. city, confining African-Americans to specific blocks, causing excessive concentrations of poverty and blight. Public housing was built in an intentionally segregated manner, with the Dan Ryan Expressway dividing black from white. Wooden three flats leaned on other wooden three flats. When the apartments were quickly built after the Chicago fire, tenants didn't mend measly landlorded tenements. The Great Migration in the early 1900s exacerbated overcrowding and neglect of buildings and homes. A Bronzeville sculptor carved fallen, harvested porch boards. Just after WWII, government segregation worsened the confined, overcrowded neighborhoods of Chicago's Southside. The Black Arts Movement of writers, poets, painters, musicians emerged from this tautness of concentrated poverty. "Bronzeville" was written in a *Tribune* article and adopted in place of the previous name, "Black Belt." Funding for schools, parks and hospitals went elsewhere.

"What's a day in the life of Daniel Burke?" I asked a bit awkwardly.

"Oh, that's too boring, unless you want a pity party," he said. His brown eyes matched his brown hair, which was an emerging requirement for guys I liked. Daniel was soft spoken and made no apologies for the holes in the floor or the chugging start from a stop sign. "I commute from Humboldt Park to LAF's Uptown office to meet with other lawyers about tenant complaints of the day," he said. (The LAF was the Legal Assistance Foundation of Metropolitan Chicago.)

The legal aid lawyers discussed grassroots, political or legal pressure to solve housing issues that mostly lead to a phone call. Their last resort was to go to court. Court cases were heard by explaining to judges offenses like leaky windows, no hot water, elevators that didn't work and crumbling concrete. By the time the complaints got to LAF, they were pretty bad. Daniel summed up issues with compassion for intolerances and abuses. Awful circumstances explained intelligently with passionate solutions, with a clear distance from tenants' emotional turmoil. I liked that about him. The hot day got hotter. Carefully, I stepped around the hole to get out of the Datsun. Sculptors had left bags of cement and wood, covered with tarps, beside embryonic unfinished objects in a field of weeds. A bumble bee hummed, sparrows flittered. Solitary in the field, we invented what each artist might finish.

"The kids will have opened the hydrants today, and I'll have no water pressure for a shower," he moaned. The sun beat down; we ducked into the oven of a car.

"We could install water parks with on-off valves to let them cool off," I said, then invited him to swim in my parents' Lake Forest pool.

"How can I see your sculpture?" he asked.

"I have a one-person exhibit next Friday. It's opening night of the gallery season in River North."

Daniel called the following Thursday to say he was coming to the opening with an officemate. I was excited though I felt the complexity that I was also going with a friend. Friday night, my graphic design job delayed my leaving. My friend arrived late and was hungry. We heated up someone's leftover pizza from the office fridge. Traffic was heavy. I was caught in a bad dream that kept me from my sculpture reception. Parking was difficult and made me over an hour late for my own one-person exhibition. Daniel's friend had already left. Apologies covered my ire, jokes released tension.

"The show goes on!" Daniel said over the botched gallery reception. The bad dream dissipated.

Daniel called me for a second date, a Peruvian pan-pipe concert at Chicago Symphony Center. The wooden-pipe rhythms, strings and drumming resonated of Peruvian mountains. His thoughtfulness for another date that combined my world of having just hiked the Inca trail to Machu Picchu was impressive.

Daniel had volunteered for Mayor Harold Washington's mayoral campaign and as a precinct worker for Luis Gutierrez' city council campaign. Alderman Ed Burke was Mayor Harold Washington's nemesis since his election as the first African American mayor of Chicago. The fall we met, Daniel took a leave from the Legal Assistance Foundation to run an aldermanic campaign for Luis Gutierrez, who "needed a Burke too." Daniel pledged Luis to be chief of staff for one year. Each Saturday morning at 10:00, Luis set the agenda with a clear message for the following week. Running Luis' campaign began with a voter registration drive, targeting first-time African American voters. "We want every African American vote," Daniel explained. "Unregistered votes are the key swing for the votes in closely contested elections."

In 1983, the Federal District Court had found that Latinos had been unlawfully prevented from electing Latinos to public office. Luis had caught Mayor Washington's eye when he challenged Dan Rostenkowski for ward committeeman, and he gained credibility for an aldermanic campaign. Redistricting opened up a Latino majority ward. It would swing the City Council vote, so Mayor Washington cared. Luis and Manny Torres were in a dead-heat race for a less-than-one-year position. Mayor Washington was helping. At Friday night campaign rallies, Daniel and I twirled ballroom dance steps to salsa, then broke into college rock moves after rice and bean dinners. We sneaked in conversations at church tables covered in plastic over disposable plates and forks.

"Luis' theme is that the machine has never invested one dollar in Division Street, the Puerto Rican community's core business district. He wants to repair the vaulted sidewalks with community development funds,"

Daniel said. A path to make a difference on the west side was opened by this election. They were hopeful. This fierce campaign was about land use, resources and power. Some campaign workers hoped for jobs.

"Luis and Soraida's home was fire bombed when he was running for ward committeemen of the 32nd Ward," Daniel explained. "Omaira, their baby, was sleeping in the bedroom. They lived in hotels for months." Luis had lost badly to an Illinois Congressman named Dan Rostenkowski but was winning the war. Mayor Harold Washington supported Luis to run for alderman of the 26th ward. Gutierrez and Torres tied. The next battle was legal, with a recount of ballots. A debate was staged. Luis Gutierrez challenged Manny Torres to a televised debate on Spanish TV, knowing Torres did not speak Spanish fluently. Gutierrez trounced him. Some campaigners aligned with Luis's position on Puerto Rico's independence. I waited for Daniel to go back to LAF, but he persevered.

Daniel was the second staff person that Alderman Gutierrez hired after he won his first election for Alderman of the 26th Ward in 1986. Luis's goal was to become a congressman and to be a fighter for social justice and for those who had little power. His passion flowed from his core political belief that the island of Puerto Rico should have nationhood and not be a territory of the United States. As an "independista," the alderman fought for the rights of Puerto Ricans to be free from territorial status.

"Grande burrito." I ordered food at a six-point intersection Mexican restaurant on Milwaukee Ave. The lights were fluorescent bright and the burrito large enough to feed a mid-sized family. Not only did I order the grande, but Daniel was shocked at how I dove into the giant dish with a mountain of rice and beans. "Uh, sorry I haven't eaten since breakfast. I can't believe fire-bombing is still going on," I said. "How was your first week?"

"I was introduced to the Alderman's staff in his storefront office near Division, when Luis ran out the door." Daniel said. "He was punching a guy on the street." Someone had just thrown a brick through his car window. "The first punch I saw through the window," Daniel said. 'You broke my window!' Luis shouted at some guy. 'You said I'd be chief of staff,' hollered the assailant. They swatted at each other. Then Luis walked away straightening his shirt, running his hand through closely cropped hair. He regained his composure to return to the meeting."

That year, I taught drawing and sculpture at the Art Institute and shared a graphic design job at a university and was sculpting for the Botanical Gardens. Daniel worked early mornings to ensure Luis was on time for community conversations, long nights in Spanish-speaking campaign offices, and weekends to canvass the Western Avenue neighborhoods. They had an office, or more like a desk, in city hall and the campaign storefront was near Division Street. The job became basically city services and individual employment problems.

"Don't come to me about patronage," Luis told his campaigners. It wasn't that he didn't interfere with the Shakman decree from a lawsuit which abolished political patronage jobs or help get municipal employment. Mostly he obtained transfers for existing workers. The elections enabled Harold Washington to gain control over the city council with more independents elected. Policy changes from his office were written into ordinances and voted into action. Certain departments and bureaus could expedite requests from certain wards.

Once seated at city council, Luis worked to pass landmark legislation including a gay rights ordinance, sweeping ethics reform and a model landlord and tenant ordinance. Daniel was turning thirty and I hosted their birthdays at my family's Aerie Gallery, a River North gallery where I exhibited with friends. Luis and Soraida attended as did Josh Hoyt, our community organizer friend. Daniel's gift, from me, was a basketball and *La Boheme* opera tickets that provided Daniel a long, deep and pricey nap.

Daniel, a compassionate man, who called his mother Saturday mornings, had a fierce tenacity for justice. He cared enough to sink his teeth into complex social issues and wrestle with them until solutions were reached. His unassuming radar traversed any fundraiser to glean scraps of information that were processed into a plan by the time he circled back to the buffet table. Had he asked questions, overheard chatter, or picked up body language? His summaries were spot on. Twice a week he took

Spanish lessons to catch the *bochinche* in the office. "I need to know what they are saying about me," he said.

After a year of twelve-hour days, seven days a week, Daniel took me out to a lovely French dinner to announce, after a glass of wine, he'd been awarded *Puerto Rican Bachelor of the Year*. He also told the campaign office his year was up. "I let them know I wanted to spend more time with you," he explained. Alive and well, Daniel stepped from the lion's den of Chicago politics back to his legal services office. His friends wondered how long I would support his justice work. Daniel had amazing strategic skills and a lock-jaw memory. That he worked for justice with a solid background in American history balanced my optimistic, creative forward-thinking with a strong interest in environment and health. We admired our complementary differences of his being a realist and my being an optimist. We encountered challenges and solved them with creativity on a daily basis. Weekends were adventurous and travel was our priority.

Daniel's greystone apartment in Humbolt Park just north of North Ave offered basketball games and concerts at the Lagoon Boat House. My two-bedroom condo on LaSalle Street overlooked Bughouse Square kitty-corner from where the Dill Pickle had been. My parents were in Peru the week I moved in. They heard about Jane Byrne, the former mayor, staying at Cabrini Green, a few blocks away, while they walked through Machu Picchu. I walked two blocks to my Pallete & Chisel coach house studio. The River North Gallery district was several blocks south on Wells and Huron.

Fr. Jack and Peggy Roach were neighbors at Holy Name Cathedral. We met for a diner dinner on Chicago Avenue. "Why don't you sculpt the people in Chicago's neighborhoods?" Father John Egan queried. Just then, a plumber came up to our table to shake his hand with gratitude. Father Jack gestured after him. "Someone just like him—that is who makes up Chicago. Let's have a sculpture exhibition of Chicago's unknown heroes." I imagined a variety of occupations of men and women. One generation to show the variety of who wove the fabric of Chicago.

Spurred on by the racial turmoil at the School of the Art Institute I hired a few of my students to help with and learn how to create an exhibit.

We wanted to pay tribute the people who created the fabric of our city. With Fr. Jack, Peggy Roach and Ed Marciniak as advisors, we began our search of subjects. The Retirement Research Foundation funded the exhibit, The Chicago History Museum designed the exhibit, *Just Plain Hardworking: Ten Chicagoans who Have Made a Difference.*

I called neighborhood organizations for individuals selected by their communities to find five men and five women of various occupations. I then sculpted five more sixty-year-old women who wove the fabric of Chicago's history for a reception of Chicago History Museum's exhibit, *Just Plain Hardworking,* including gospel singer Delois Barrett Campbell; Cook County Hospital director Ruth Rothstein; restaurateur Florence Scala; artist Maria Enriquez de Allen; and homemaker Hildur Lindquist. As I sculpted women with the tools of their trade, the voices of professors and friends guided my thoughts in the studio. A black steelworker, a Chinese housing developer, a Mexican artist, an Irish priest (Egan) and a packing house union moderator described some people that made Chicago's complex fabric. *Just Plain Hardworking* opened with four collaborators to five thousand viewers at the 4th of July reception including Senator Paul Simon.

WTTW was taping the artists of *Just Plain Hardworking* art for the Chicago Historical Society exhibit. They taped Dad painting the Chinese arch in Chinatown and me sculpting Hilder Lindquist in clay then translating that to *Ciment Fondu.* Frank photographed the ten people and Jim Yisela Jr. wrote their essays. WTTW taped our meeting with the curator, Wendy, under the coach house magnolia tree. The National Portrait Gallery selected the statue of Delois Barrett Campbell, the Chatham neighborhood gospel singer, cast in bronze with a mosaic blouse for their collection. Fr. Jack's bronze portrait was collected by DePaul University. Fr. Jack officiated my June marriage to Daniel.

Chapter 10: Travel and a New Life

Sveti Stephan is the most romantic place in the whole world," Mom said. She recognized that Daniel's and my ceremony included one person from each of our thirteen families. With a ripple effect, she invited the families of in-laws to the weekend celebration.

"We're thinking of Sveti Stephan for our honeymoon," we told Mary Alice, Daniel's mother.

"That's the most romantic place in the whole world," Mary Alice echoed. At the rehearsal, I levelled questions at the annoyed pastor.

"Can the wedding party sit down?" I asked.

"No, everyone is kneeling while the homily is given," said Fr. Jack.

Daniel's and my aunts and uncles, brothers and sisters, in-laws and cousins met at the Lake Forest beach pavilion for a bar-b-que rehearsal dinner. What I didn't recognize was that this would be the last weekend we'd all gather. Meeting each other put a face to their names for years of stories.

The morning of our mid-day wedding was already ninety-degrees. My five brothers, Daniel, and his four brothers played five-on-five McMahons-Burkes basketball followed by a refreshing beer. I chatted and dressed with my bridesmaids: Elizabeth, Barb and Sheila. The forecast was over 100 degrees and we were the second wedding of the day in a two-hundred person *non*-air-conditioned church. Fr. Jack, who'd already had a few bypass surgeries, draped a stole over heavy liturgical robes. Barb, a bridesmaid, packed smelling salts. Fans twirled hot air into the church. By afternoon, changes were no longer possible. Fate would take its course.

Cool, calm and collected, I strode down the aisle with Dad. This walk had scared me for months. *At least it's a short aisle.* I calmed myself to sleep at night. I felt no heat, no fear, but delighted in the ring bearers and flower girls. I walked with a swagger next to my Dad. I knelt next to Daniel during the homily, the wedding party kneeling beside us. "Marriage is forever," Fr. Jack began, then for fifteen minutes we listened to him expand on definitions of *marriage* and *forever*. Fr. Jack found new ways to describe *forever*, then *marriage*. He caught his breath and revisited *marriage and forever*. I glanced at the bridesmaid—she hadn't fainted yet. Daniel seemed fine, but his blond brother next to him squirmed a bit. I was amazed I could kneel this long and feel no heat. I glanced at the priest; he was continuing. A loud, cracking *Thunk* echoed throughout the church. Daniel's oldest brother, the best man, fell backwards from a kneeler onto the marble floor. The video cameras spun up, then down. The fall itself could be his undoing. I froze a smile on my face. A blur of doctors from the pews circled our best man. Uncle George, who served in the Navy Pacific theater, Judy from Cook County Hospital and Mom, who nursed airsick WWII vets, recognized the fragility of life and ran to help.

"Mom, did Dad just die?" his son's voice was recorded. Barb's smelling salts were passed to the hovering doctors. I tried to keep positive, not knowing that Tom had been told by a doctor not to exercise for six weeks. This morning was his first exercise since a clot had formed in his leg from a baseball while playing catch with his son. The fragility of life from a mere basketball rivalry between brothers-in-law encroached this chapel of WWII vets and healing spouses.

"Don't worry, there are four more brothers, we'll get through this," Daniel's youngest brother said. Daniel's black-haired, second brother knelt on the kneeler. Fr. Jack summed up the homily and moved onto Communion.

"I've been to a lot of weddings," a sculptor friend mentioned. "This one, I'll remember."

The receiving line and reception were under a tent, "in the same back yard they met playing croquet," one of my now nine brothers toasted.

We honeymooned in Sveti Stephan, Yugoslavia, in a fishing village built on a rock island with a footpath off a deep, crescent beach and turquoise Adriatic Sea below steep mountains. The entrance to each room was on a different level of steps with cascading roses.

Dubrovnik and Split were a quick train ride away. Calamari and local wine, olive oil and the catch of the day was our daily diet. Ivan Mestrovic's chapel in Split rose from a Mediterranean bay like a white marble citrus press with angels carved. A circular room of hundreds of repetitive marble carved angels encased and energized the interior dome space. Rodin said of Mestrovic, "He's a better sculptor than I."

A week in Athens and Crete followed. In Crete, the minotaur's horns of the mountains were reflected in the placement of architect Daedalus's elaborate maze-like labyrinth. The winding pathways were commanded by King Minos for a minotaur, half bull and half man, to dwell in its mystical core. The best and the brightest young people were honored to battle the minotaur. Daedalus and his son Icarus strapped on wax wings to fly from Crete to escape.

"Do not fly too close to the sun, not too low to the waves," Daedalus instructed his son. With glee, Icarus soared through the clouds and heavens; his wings, melted by the sun, sent him crashing into waves. There's our mantra to guide both our marriage and work: "Do not fly too close to the sun." For our coffee table, I carved a Carrara white marble slab into a fallen winged man on hospital wheels to remind us to fly neither too high nor too low.

A terrorist attack of a Cycladic cruise ship from Aegina port included Saint Patrick's parishioners from Aurora, Illinois. Our travels escalated in awareness and long lines to board transportation. From Rhodes, we planned to ferry into Marmaris, Turkey and were told, "Maybe tomorrow." We hovered at the ferry waiting and could board another boat before nightfall. Our cruise along the Turquoise Coast was not arranged ahead of time. "Just walk the pier and talk with captains, you'll find a sailboat," Mom had said. With hand signals and brief wording a captain and ship were arranged. At the slip, we were offered a larger boat with another family.

Our four-day sailboat cruise, along the Turquoise Coast, was with a family from South Africa who traveled on their Dutch passports, and a

Captain whose only English words were "No problem." The blond mother was non-conversational. Her husband, a jazz musician and travel agent, chattily hoped for peaceful change in Capetown. Their son, whose older brother was in the military, wore a Rastafarian necklace, dreadlocks, remained silent and avoided his mother. In the quiet moments on the sailboat I mulled over Dad traveling with Fr. Jack and the Catholic priests in Johannesburg and Capetown to end apartheid. They gave advice learned in the '60s civil rights protests. The last day, the mother talked to me about her concerns raising her boys with looming turbulence ahead.

"We're headed north not south," I said to the Captain.

"No problem," he replied. Hours later, we anchored for dinner at a sponge diver's cove. Sponges were hanging from lines and fresh fish was being steamed in a pit. A small boat met us the next day to enter a river and see cave dwellings, the first inhabitants of the coast. We hiked into ruins of multiple civilizations along the river that used the same religious stones for a temple, then a church, shown by carved stars and crosses. The sail ended in Fethye where we caught a bus north to Ephesus on the side of the road. Twelve men changed our bus tire for two hours. We visited Virgin Mary's humble home and enjoyed a magnificently performed symphony with impressive acoustics in the ancient amphitheater. We flew home from Istanbul after five hours of security checks.

July in Chicago continued to be blistering hot while the city contentiously debated lights in Wrigley Field. Finally, August 8, 1988, the Cubs played the Phillies under lights. Daniel came home from the game with an opening night baseball cap and exciting news. "I've just been offered the chance of a lifetime. A new affordable housing business will renovate buildings in disrepair. It's going to be called Chicago Community Development Corporation (CCDC). They've asked if I'll leave LAF to work with them." With CCDC, a for-profit developer of high rise affordable housing, Daniel could actualize fixing up leaky windows, crumbling parking lots and broken elevators directly. Many aging apartment buildings could be lost to luxury lakefront housing or be renovated and kept affordable.

Their first building, 850 W. Eastwood, was in Uptown, a few blocks from the lake. A computer lab, playground, and daycare center were in the plans to allow mothers to train and work. As the elevator doors opened, cooking smells from India, Eritrea, Ethiopia, Puerto Rico, Mexico, Burma and Thailand wafted in from various floors. A mosaic of symbols from each country welcomed renters behind the security desk. "I feel like I died and went to heaven," a girl said as she moved back into her renovated bedroom. Her family had a new kitchen with new appliances, lights and windows that kept the rain out. Lake breezes kept the room cool in the summer. Daniel then applied to renovate more at-risk buildings along the lakefront in Bronzeville, Chinatown and Uptown. Each renovation included changing tile color patterns or adding glass walls for outdoor walkways. Punch lists were endless.

It was immediately apparent one Saturday morning as I stepped into our ash darkened backyard overlooking Bughouse Square that the world as I knew it was at an end. Our backyard was covered in large flakes of black and grey ash. The air was a black cloud that blocked the sun. Overnight, an entire block of galleries at the heart of River North's gallery district burned to the ground. With it large bodies of work and the dynamic and cohesive Chicago art world. The vitality of River North had changed; some galleries moved to West Loop. Daniel and I found a home in Oak Park where we hoped to slow our nonstop pace.

"We're not going to answer the phone at dinner." Daniel and I had agreed to turn over a new leaf in our new home in Oak Park. Two plates of steaming food at our first meal had just been set down…the phone rang. Furrow-browed looks were sent both ways across the table. Daniel went to answer the phone. "You have to take this," he said from the den.

"Good evening, this is Bill Kirby, President of the John D. and Catherine T. MacArthur Foundation, President of the John D. MacArthur Park Environmental Foundation, and board member of the Retirement Research Foundation. Do you have a moment to talk?"

I was asked to sculpt John D. MacArthur for a State Park in Singer Island, Florida. We set the price, the schedule and the unveiling date in that conversation. He told me, and I imagined, the image of John D. MacArthur at the moment he gave his fortune to the foundation. The image of Mr. MacArthur is as if talking on the phone while smoking a cigarette, without the cigarette or the cup, in the coffee shop of the Colonnades Hotel. Neither of them knew how much the estate was worth.

Mr. Kirby funded a WTTW documentary on the artists of *Just Plain Hardworking* that was broadcast a year later. A textured image of how Mr. MacArthur chatted with Bill Kirby at the Colonnades Hotel in water-based terracotta came to life in my studio. I captured a likeness from a video of Mr. MacArthur serving coffee, then returning to a calm conversation. His rounded shoulders, elasticity of his bowed, long arms and whimsical expression of his face were gleaned from the black and white. The feeling of his energy in the room was conjured from memories of my high school classmate, Jim MacArthur, his nephew. When one furrow on the sculpted brow was too deep for Mr. Kirby's liking, I flew to Singer Island to visit the Colonnades Hotel, as it was being demolished, and experience the state park that was being made into a manatee and bird refuge. At the unveiling with the board at John D. MacArthur State Park, I met the founding lawyers. The Mayor of Palm Beach toured me through the area in her red Miata with lunch and a stop to meet Mr. and Mrs. Jack Nicklaus at their fundraiser.

Daniel and I were able to attend my National Sculpture Society's award ceremony the last week I could travel before Mahon was born. I wore a long silky emerald gown and silver necklace. Then I had a one-person exhibit in River North for two months when Mahon was born. Mom was upset because she was ripe with poison ivy and couldn't hold my newborn. I panicked when I woke at seven o'clock—Mahon had slept through the night at 9.5 lbs!

Meanwhile, Daniel fluidly gained the trust of tenants, congressmen, senators, city attorneys and construction workers. His attention to detail meant late nights and early mornings. The seven-year cicadas humming was so loud we shouted over the buzz, concentrating on hearing our own thoughts while two interns and I sculpted a monumental father elevating a child on his bent knee. The rebar skeleton was set in a wet concrete foundation and the formation was modeled in concrete in a Homewood's Irwin Park by Dad's birthday.

Chapter 11: Family Life

A less than poetic rhythm of family and art making showed some strength and our own fragility of life forms during my era of making to-do lists. A diaper needed to be changed. I wanted to sculpt Tuesday, but the sitter's baby was sick. More detail in an interpretation made the object about someone else, less detail made a more universal symbol. The laundry, Thursdays playgroup, groceries and the space between the form and beyond it was as important as the object itself. My studio was then in a coach house on Woodlawn and 48th street. A foundry, metal shop with plasma cutter, wood shop with lathe and mold making room filled a five-room carriage garage and tack room. With the plasma cutter, I burned through steel plate, silhouettes of dancing figures, thinking about Degas' dancers. Figures extended and retracted their arms and legs as I walked around. The silhouettes were welded together at right angles and spun for the effect of dancing. I welded variations. These were enlarged in Corten steel and installed in Lake Bluff the same day as a monumental scale bronze mother and child were installed in Lake Forest. My sculpting rhythm was in thirds; commissions, non-for-profit exhibits and gallery and museum exhibitions.

One day at the grocery store, with Mahon in the cart, buried in groceries, and my daughter seat-belted by the push bar, I was focused on checking out. Mahon handed up groceries, Sophia held my purse. Just as I finished, I heard "Hello, Margot." A cousin had been standing in line behind me all that time. "How's it going?"

"Hi, Bill! How's Margaret and the girls?"

"They are fine. Looks like your kids are coming along fine!"

"Thanks." I had just hired a new sitter and wondered how work and kids would go. "If you ever find a house with a studio in the back yard, please let us know." Within the week they were back to us with a house that had been on the market for a year with a new two-story-high studio in the back. Not sure what to do with five bedrooms? Daniel and our two children and I moved onto the block of Humphrey with a new studio in the backyard and a hoop in the attic.

This was the year Daniel and I joined our book group. We'd been in a Thursday morning playgroup since Mahon was born. The book group met nine months of the year on Saturday nights for a potluck dinner. A neighbor invited me to join a book group of artists, doctors and lawyers that met on Sunday nights. Over many decades, there was only one or two times we read the same book. Both groups shared advice on raising children, travel tips, preschools and recipes. Both got involved with the education and the school boards. Oak Park had seven elementary schools feeding into two middle schools and one over 3,000-student high school. Each elementary had its own differentiated strengths amidst balancing the budget in an increasingly broke state. We hashed out ideas to avoid referendums. The most intense dynamic of the Saturday book group was that the two opposing little league boys teams were in 5-6th grade playoff for the championship. Two book group Dans coached each team in an alternating battle of wins and losses. "The Dans" became their name from that playoff on. Even college applications didn't reach the extremity of that week.

After a particularly cold winter, we'd tap our front yard silver maple for sap and boil it to syrup. Then I found out! This was the Catholic corner of Oak Park, along Austin and Washington. From Catholic Corner in the Adirondack Mountains, the Fox-Franklin-McKillips moved together to Catholic Corner in Oak Park. Sometimes the bucket was overflowing with sap in the afternoon. I wish for that many stories to have been passed along. My mother's maternal side of the family, the Rogers, lived across Washington Boulevard on the southeast sector of that corner. The Rogers' frame house was taken down for the Rectory of St. Catherine's Parish. The Rogers had moved there from the farm house on Waller and Lake Street where their milk cows grazed amidst the sweet clover in Columbus Park.

"Whoever can come is welcome at three o'clock for Christmas dinner." The *we* of my brothers and sisters with their children, gathered inside, under the reaching seventy-five-year-old Silver Maple branches in Oak Park at Christmas, by the hearth fire, for decades. Daniel and I hosted a Christmas turkey potluck dinner and shared Secret Santa gifts, one adult to another and one child to another for thirty years. When the kids were tiny, I boned the turkey so it would cook quicker giving me time for assembling toys. As the toys became more digital, I brined the turkey, then cooked it with lemon and garlic. I liked that my children's Legos and American Girl dolls, craft clothing, books and unwrapped digital devices were packed up and moved to their rooms for the house to fill with twenty-five to thirty cousins and friends at three tables. Santa Bowls, Turkey Bowls and Bunny Bowls of touch football were played before feasting. Easter was at Mom and Dad's, then the Beck-Marino's. Thanksgiving was at a brother's.

In September of 1996, Sophia started preschool and Mahon started kindergarten during the week Brie was due.

"I think after I die, people will remember me," Mahon said after his first day of kindergarten.

"I want to learn everything in the world," Sophia said as she came home from preschool.

"This is going to be interesting," Mom said as she picked them up at the maternity ward of Northwestern hospital, looked into the eyes of the midwife just before Brie was induced. The moment she was born she was whisked away for an Apgar test—passed with flying colors! They talked about her dimple and smile before I held her.

"Aubrie, A Most Unusual Girl..." the midwife sang the *Bread* song for us that night. Mom brought the kids to Oak Park for my recovery the first week to help. That's when I noticed Mom was not well. Daniel's brothers and Mary flew into town to celebrate and we baptized one-week-old Brie at St. Catherine-St. Lucy's Parish at the end of the block where Mom and Dad met in 1938.

That Christmas, my extended McMahon family gathered for 5:30 Mass while three-month-old Brie was a live, kicking and cooing Christ child for the Children's Christmas Pageant before 5:00 Mass in St. Catherine's, St. Lucy Church. Sophia was an angel and Mahon, a shepherd. "I would not have missed that for anything," Mom exclaimed.

Within two weeks Mom, Dad, Daniel, the kids and I were packing for frigid Washington weather for President Clinton's inauguration. We were invited by Mom's cousin Kathleen, who was high school friends with Hillary, for lunch at the White House. It was going to be below zero for the inaugural parade and ceremony. We stayed at my sister's in Maryland, and a lambskin bag was shared for keeping Aubrey warm. Mom and Dad had a hotel room along the inaugural parade route allowing Dad to paint from the window.

"We'll stay with the baby while you go to the White House luncheon," my parents said. "The cold makes it hard for us." More clues that Mom was aging. Daniel, Mahon, Mary Irene and I entered the back gate for social security clearance to the Arkansas Luncheon with the Clintons. My last name did not match up to theirs, so I was detained while they went ahead. By the time I caught up we were near the ladies room seeing portraits of First Ladies in the basement. Music started on the second floor. At the top of the steps, we turned left towards the music into a large reception room with windows to the gardens. Just then, President Bill Clinton stepped into a receiving line position. We stepped into line being within their first ten visitors. Daniel and I stepped up with the kids to greet Mr. Clinton.

"Mr. Clinton, I'd like to introduce my daughter," I said. He was delighted to say a few words to them. Daniel discussed an Affordable Housing issue; Mr. Clinton was fully aware of the nuance. At a certain point the President pointed his forefinger at Daniel and said, "Thank you!" The large sliding doors glided open and the line music continued as we were led into a larger room for lunch. We joined our friends from Illinois and had a good laugh about my being detained. Cousins Kathleen, Jimmy and Johnny Rogers were there as well as Betsy and Bonnie and the *Traveling Pantsuit* friends from Park Ridge. That night, Daniel and I attended the Inaugural Ball at the Air and Space Museum, seeing enough friends to have a great time. The actual inauguration the following day was as frigid as expected. We all left Mary and Tap's house in Potomac to park near Mom and Dad's hotel. Five-year-old Mahon ran into an elevator as it closed.

"What! He's gone!" I said.

"Did he know the floor number?" Daniel waited on the first floor and I went up to nine. There was Mahon knocking on their hotel room door.

The swearing-in was several blocks from the hotel and icy cold. "Your Mom and I will stay here. It's a bit cold today," Dad said. These are not the parents I knew. What's going on? When Mary and my family arrived at the crowd, we stood in a circle to keep warm as if around a campfire. Large screen televisions were everywhere. Thousands went quiet while the oath was taken. A cello played in the severe cold. I hoped the sound box wouldn't split. The inaugural parade was watched from grandstands in front of the White House.

The same week of my parents' July 27th anniversary, and our annual family gathering, their phone began to ring on Monday. By Wednesday, every brother and sister with their children was coming for the weekend. That never happened. Mom and I stared at each other. We were making lunch in her Keck and Keck kitchen.

"What is going on?" I said.

"I'll need help." Mom arranged an afternoon walk through Airdrie on Mayflower and the Greenbay Road Humrich house. I shopped at Costco and filled her fridge and freezer. We booked tickets for Shakespeare's *Tempest* at Barat College for thirty. With a day trip to the beach, everything seemed unusually full but fine. Mom was delighted with Saturday's walking through Airdrie's bedrooms and our playing wiffle ball in the backyard with her grandchildren. Some of us traversed the steep cliff to the beach. Photographs were taken everywhere. Mom was in a dream state of remembering this household and being surrounded with her family. We floated with her excitement. We brought a picnic to Barat College's front lawn for the *Tempest*, until the thunderstorm struck.

Hovering around Mom through the downpour while respecting her independence, something changed. *Why am I hovering?* We arrived at home drenching wet.

"Mom, you don't need to put the recycle out, there are eight adults in the house," I said in the hall.

"I just want to leave things in order tonight," she said and fussed in the kitchen. I decided I'd stay overnight with eleven-month-old Brie who took her first step that morning. The cousins slept in sleeping bags in the living room. After a restless night on Dad's studio floor, we woke to Mom already in the hospital. I finally got a turn to visit with her during the 6:00 news. Mother-to-mother, we shared our concerns about our children. We agreed that we would watch over each other's children. It didn't register that she might have made other agreements with her other children. It seemed like our conversation would continue. Mom was transferred to Northwestern Hospital for testing. As she was wheeled over the glass bridge, I asked the nurse to pause.

"Mom, if you look to the left you'll see the lake." Who knew this was her last view of her beloved Lake Michigan? Who knew that her stories and the library of her life story had not been told yet and that soon she would not be able to talk? I can hear her say, "You will never know."

A family meeting with the doctor informed us that that she probably would not make it. Denial set in. If we had listened, her death would not have been sudden. I had seen medical students poke away searching for veins. Younger and younger doctors attended her after that meeting. "Please keep me from being a guinea pig!" she said to Dad. Her care declined, her energy waned. Long dreading of what was impossible to expect. Denial worked. "What do doctors know anyway?" one of us said.

Dad and I drove to Northwestern to visit. They'd had no time together. I paced in the hall, got coffee, then more coffee again. It all happened this fast. I learned about the art of medicine as they tweaked doses. I came back from the coffee shop to a small party of visitors. We talked about another volatile rain storm the day before. Another visit, I was alone with Mom. The doctor stepped in. She was no longer able to speak. "She will need intervention." I looked at Mom, who nodded knowingly to me, of a conversation we'd had in 1983. "She doesn't want any extreme measures," I told him. Why me? Where was Dad or anyone of them? "No extreme measures," she had said. Always the caretaker, she had watched friends suffer beyond their most vital lives. Aunt Rita asked that I make sure she received the sacrament of last rights.

"Father Jack, would you come to bless Mom?" I asked when I phoned him. "Father McNulty is on vacation. She may not make it through the night," I thought I said. The hospital family room was filled with every brother and sister, Uncle Harry and cousins.

"What are you all doing here? She's going to be fine." He gave her a blessing for the sick. "You can all go home now, she'll be fine," Father Jack said. Could we have both been right? I spent the night with her in her hospital room. Mom wanted me to write down a story about the hairdresser in the hospital, but couldn't finish sentences through the oxygen mask. Several times, the oxygen mask needed shifting into place when she slept. Her children were flying in from Georgia, London and New York the next day. Mom, who could not speak, summoned her children and they surrounded her like Celtic stones connecting heaven and earth. One tear slid down her cheek. Her heart stopped. We were all in a circle around her. We hugged. Between late summer and early fall Mom suddenly passed away. With her went all her reading, writing and travels that I had not yet heard. I read at her St. Patrick's Memorial Mass eulogy, "Sunday paisley pumps sunk into fresh dirt, Mom taught me to plant impatiens and zinnias in the studio garden after Mass. She captured my interest as it piqued, sacrificing her good silk Sunday shoes in the process. We planted snapdragons in the sunny borders facing the lake." My solace was to build the kids a treehouse in our Silver Maple.

"Grandma is not afraid to die because she is so holy," Sophia called up to me. I bolted two twelve-foot-long 2 x 8's to the trunk and added slider brackets to the studio wall. The joists glided as the trunks blew in the wind. "How many rooms will there be?" Sophia said. I hadn't attached the floorboards yet. Four vertical 2 x 4's then a salt box shaped roofline over a one-room plywood windowed room was added for their drum set. Mom conjured the best from everyone and created community by selflessly giving in random acts of kindness. She may not continue to be a part my children's growing up, but she'd already made an impact on who they would become. *What would Mom do?* entered every decision relying on the patterns she set for moving homes, prayers before holiday dinners, Sunday Mass at 10:00, gathering for fresh food meals, exercising and birthdays. Distributing our books, crystal, silver and collectibles were by her patterns of equality for all and choice by age.

"Make sure he is eating," people told me regarding Dad's mourning. I brought meals on Sunday, others covered Tuesday and Thursday. Dad and I planted a flower garden at his driveway entrance. We dug deep, stretched fabric to stop weeds and planted daffodils and hostas. My mourning surfed on shifted tectonic plates, the map of the world had changed. Seas valley'd deep with tormented peaked waves. Dad painted in encaustic his toppled crab apple tree in full bloom.

"I'm too powerful, I need a break," Sophia said. "I'd like to take some time off until picture day. Just write to my teacher that my Grandmother died."

"Thank you Grandma for all the delicious chicken dishes," Mahon said at the wake.

"You know this is going to fall to you," Mary Philbin told me at the memorial service.

Father McNulty invited me to sculpt the under-construction new St. Patrick's Church, the oldest parish in Lake Forest. Daniel and I had been married in that parish, I read my mother's eulogy at her Memorial Mass there and our oldest children were baptized there. My sculptures were created over the next five years while Father McNulty guided me through *Anem Cara,* an Irish way to be Catholic with a profound spiritual connection to nature. Our intent was to sculpt Lake Forest's nature in the simplicity of stone, wood, earth and water to step out of marble-lined homes a retreat to granite, flowing water and St. Patrick's Breastplate: Jesus before me, Jesus behind me, Jesus within me… The granite bedrock of the Midwest was carved by fracturing with heat and cold water into a waterfall baptismal font with embryonic pools. An oak cross with Celtic knots unraveled at the intersections where Jesus died. While taking a stained glass class before designing the Ambry, I visited Bob and Bernice O'Brien's, stained glass windows in Hinsdale-inspired textured clear panes stirring a flow of water or bubbling brook with light entering. My stencil-painted family room of Saint Patrick's breastplate welcomed parishioners. Earth-like, twice-size Holy Family with Jesus as a teen stepping away from his parents in *Fondu ciment* fills a low arch. In an opposite arch, six-foot hands hold a rosewood Tabernacle.

"Those are my hands," John said about my five-foot-high *Fondu* sculpture for the tabernacle.

Part II: The Secret Lives of Parents

Chapter 12: Messages from Beyond

The August after Mom passed away, Dad joined Daniel, the kids and me for a Santa Fe vacation. Santa Fe was our discovery and haven. We loved the multi-faceted depth of history, variety of cultures, the music, Native American arts and dance, the cowboy and cowgirl rodeos, the ever-changing desert, and, the contemporary art world. Daniel and I first visited Santa Fe with three-month-old Mahon when I discovered the squash blossom silver and turquoise jewelry like my mother wore and the art galleries on Canyon Road. I feel so connected here. With the kids, we often rented casitas at Rancho Jacona on the San Ildefonso Reservation, halfway between Los Alamos and the opera house. Little and large casitas speckled a ranch with livestock, peacocks, rabbits and chickens. Roosters crowed all day. When they were young, the kids were mesmerized by water striders in the creek. They swam in a local river and the pool. As they got older, the family ventured to coyote legend-telling at the folk museum, balloon launches and friend's homes and ranches.

On this remarkably different vacation, we rented a casita for Daniel's mother, Mary Alice, for one week and Dad for the second. We picked Mary Alice up at St. Johns after her literature seminar. With Mary Alice, we were awed by Millicent Rogers' jewelry in Taos, Georgia's paintings in Abiquiu and Maria Martinez in San Ildefonso. Every night we attended the open-air opera. A sitter named Sunshine arrived to tuck the children in with contemporary Santa Fe stories. Mary Alice was an *officianato* of the opera and could tell in the first few minutes if the pace would be tolerable or not. "This opera is going to take until dawn," she whispered as she led Daniel and I out in the first ten minutes. The execution of nuns in the French revolution was sung with bravado, a pirate's tale musically told the next night. Mahon, Sophia and Brie joined Mary Alice for a magical lyrical forest tale chanted under the stars. Grandma recapped the opera before and after with the kids. They loved the late night and being included.

In the afternoon, we six were awestruck as we hiked Bandeleir ruins on a plateau and imagined the magnificent city once teeming with American Indian families. Suddenly, lightning struck, thunder roared. We dove into a tiny cave, curled under a low ceiling, cozy from the danger. Mahon discovered a small, tightly tied tiny cloth bag tucked into a little niche. He pocketed the bag as we stepped out to clear skies. The hand sewn bag was left forgotten on the dining room table in our casita.

On Saturday, Mary Alice was ready to fly home. My Dad arrived eager with a package of artwork the same afternoon. He showed Mary Alice his brown package of unfinished drawings. We were delighted to see his lyrical lines make scenes we had just visited. *Dad has been here many times, I wonder why?* At the airport I read a display of some of the earliest pilots performing stunts by diving into baseball fields and around county fairs in early 1900 wooden planes.

Their first night with Grandpa, the kids opened the tiny cloth bag from the cave to find several smaller cloth bags of silver amulets, a few precious stones, and a note to ancestors from a troubled soul in a difficult time. Their jaws dropped. *What have we done?* My father sat back with a *what-have-I-gotten-myself-into* look. "What are you going to do now, Margot?" he challenged me.

This happened for a reason, let's see what it means. I read the note out loud, "Ancestors, I am struggling to find meaning, I am low. These offerings are prayers to find a way forward. Please help me find my path forward. I am lost," the note began. We opened each and every bag, each note. Read them and closed the amulet sacks again. Reverently, I brushed the dust, gems and silver charms into the pouches and tied each in the largest bag. One object was added as an apology for the disturbance. Mahon and I went at ceremonious dawn, to replace the sacramental amulet bag in the same cave. I hoped it was enough.

On early mornings, Dad and I drove to Santa Fe square for him to finish, me to start paintings. The cathedral was one early morning destination. While there, a piece of paper blew against my leg with writing on it: I have given up my life and come to this city for a rebirth and transformation of life. I am a completely new person. My Dad said, "Does this happen to you all the time?" I laughed while I was reminded of a visit with my mother at the hospital. I asked my mother if she'd like to come to Santa Fe? "Next time!" Mom replied while putting on a brave smile. Santa Fe is still a spiritual place. Are these notes or signs from Mom? In all my visits to Santa Fe over decades and different seasons for art receptions and vacations, the notes came only when Dad and I were here together. Why am I so connected here?

I experienced my father's stealth at the Santo Domingo Indian reservation, where the whole family was invited by a pueblo guide to her tribe's Corn Dance and Ceremonial Day. We found the guide at home and asked for permission to draw the ceremony. The guide agreed, but no photography. My Dad and I found seats at the leg races, by the creek, to draw the ancient and annual competition. As I was looking up, my paper was swooped out from under my hand and ripped in two. A hot-tempered vigilante yelled indecipherably at me while tribe members lead him away. I glanced at Dad. He was gone! The irate man backed off, ripped my drawing to pieces. Worried, I scurried up my pens and watercolors to find Dad. He shielded his drawings, halfway to the car. He waved me away. "Don't lead them to me, I've got a start. I'll need the key." I tossed him the keys and turned back to the volatile scene to divert the chaos.

This is how he managed drawing at Marquette Park in the midst of riots, at Selma during the march to Montgomery and travels to South Africa in the mid-eighties to talk about a peaceful end to apartheid. With this stealth skill, Dad didn't fear bringing his family to the 1968 Democratic Convention when the Michigan Avenue riot broke out. He taught them survival and stealth. On the car ride, my father mentioned, "Irene lived in Las Vegas, New Mexico."

"Mom lived here!" I was surprised. That explains Mom's squash blossom jewelry. "Where is Las Vegas?"

We drove around the mystical Santa Cristo mountains, through spectacular Glorietta Pass, to Las Vegas. Uncle Harry had mentioned, the last night of my mother's life, in the hospital family room, that my Mom might have caught an undetected tuberculosis from their father. "Your mother was always taking care of Dad," he added. In a Las Vegas antique shop, I found a local history from the 1920s. Dad showed me places he visited with Mom. I took notes that I read back to my father at the airport as we returned to Chicago.

I learned Irene's Las Vegas preschool years were on 4th Street, a few blocks from the sanatorium and Catholic school for Harry, her older brother. They had moved to New Mexico from Chicago after a winter cold exacerbated their father's tuberculosis. At first, the household help was for him, as he took time from his Standard Oil of Pennsylvania job. They had moved from Garfield Park, when Rita was an infant, to the cool dry air of New Mexico. This explains Mom's courage to move her family, and an infant, to Spain. When pre-school Irene stepped off at the end of the line in Las Vegas she might as well have landed on the moon. Layers of ranch culture, various Indian customs, cowgirl drawls, Mexican language and food blended into huevos, tortilla and jalapenos for breakfast. This diversity must have been where Mom discovered the rich variety of cultures that inspired her to fight tirelessly for justice in Chicago's segregation.

Irene's mother, Agatha, was a tiny, feisty and energetic business woman who knew the importance of the spice of life. I imagine she strictly guided the cook to leave jalapeno peppers out of the green chile, "mild would be fine," and cook the corn with "a bit of honey not sugar." She would not change the cook's process of making a bean paste, though she found it too peppery. Her husband had a strict diet of fresh fruits and root vegetables. Her children liked simple, direct food. Sunday mornings, Agatha dressed her three to the T and marched the family to 8:00 Mass. They lit candles to pray for the health of their father, each other and for the extended family back in Chicago. Agatha finished an entire rosary of ten Hail Mary's for each Our Father before Mass began. Agatha, and her rosary, attended Mass every morning for her spiritual and personal time.

Irene treasured holding her father's hand as they walked from church. He stopped often to hold a handkerchief to cough a deep phlegm. She loved their life and shadowed her mother taking care of him, fetching slippers or bringing the paper. Irene brought him steaming tea or icy water as he rested. Irene was empowered by being able to help her father, unaware of his waning energy or increased coughing. Strictly held siestas briefly quieted Irene during the mid-day, dusty heat. She was encouraged to play with neighbors while he rested. As the sun dipped below the Santa Fe mountains, Irene's parents sat on the front wooden porch, rocking the baby while she and her brother played. She and Harry taught Gallisto, Mexican, Hopi, Navajo and Hispanic friends hopscotch and Red Rover. Their friends taught them foot racing and distance throwing games. Rita eagerly watched.

Agatha was relieved when Henry explored New Mexico with the kids. He and Harry drove through the gorgeous Santa Fe mountainscape. He and Irene browsed through town, chatting with shopkeepers and with her over lunch. The baby, Rita, was bounced on his knee. "Trot to Kerry, Trot to Lin, you'd better watch out or you might fall in!" he sang to Rita. Leahy family excursions included Montezuma Springs, where they slipped into the tribe's rotating schedule of soaking in healing minerals. If Henry was feeling well they drove a day to Ojo Caliente near Taos. Picnics of tacos or burritos along the Santa Fe Trail gave them a chance for optimism. The transcendent mountains energized Henry, but the altitude made it hard for him to breathe.

Treasured time together included jaunts in the Santa Fe Trail stagecoach to a baseball game held in the Albuquerque race-track infield. At the seventh inning, a Curtiss Model pusher airplane, made of wood, accomplished stunts over the infield. Irene was awestruck, as the smiling, vigorous Roy Francis swooped from heaven (or a cloud fifteen-hundred feet above) to the diamond, up-turning after a blown kiss and wave. The stunt flyer appeared like a messenger from God, connecting people with heaven in her four-year-old's imagination. Agatha kept a close watch on

Henry's energy and swooped the family home before weariness won. Their hopes peaked with adventures, followed by a week of Henry recovering. Perfilia tended scrapes and bruises of three children while their mother attended morning Mass daily before she visited Henry in the hospital several blocks away.

Agatha encouraged Irene's fascination with unfathomable flying and her son Harry's enchantment with cars by taking them to the Fair. At the Mexico Territorial Fair, automobile versus airplane races were held by Lincoln Beachly flying and Eddie Rickenbacker behind the driver's wheel. Irene cheered for Mr. Beachly. Harry was for Mr. Rickenbacker, and Rita clapped and squealed with delight from the roars of engines and crowd. Agatha hovered over Henry, who lay wrapped in a blanket, smiling with delight over his lively children. His spirit and charm overrode any ailment. His kids embraced the wonder of their life, unaware of TB's gravity. Excited conversations about spectacles during the race, Hopi dances, Mariachi music and cowboys roping cattle enthralled them most of the way back to Santa Fe. Like a pile of puppies, Irene and Harry leaned onto Henry's Bouncing over the rough Glorietta Pass lulled them into sleep. The wheels offered little give on the rutted roads.

Daniel's and my frequent trips to New Mexico gave me tidbits of recognition into Irene's love of diversity, social justice and precious life as her father weakened, was hospitalized, and passed away. Mom's spirituality was a blend of Native American, Celtic and Catholic. No wonder New Mexico felt familiar. Rita had been an infant when they boarded the recently extended tracks of the train, just as I had been carried on a propeller plane. Mom eagerly immersed me in Spanish culture before I could walk or talk. Spain might have rejuvenated her vibrant memories, her nostalgia for her intact Leahy family. Their affluent lifestyle of adventures and laughter was crushed with Henry's death.

Agatha financially crashed in 1929 with misguided real estate investments. Irene had cherished their summers on the beach at Chain of Lakes until they lost their property and her mother began working. Gram Leahy also died of a lung disease that the doctor diagnosed her scarred lungs were by knitting mohair? It must have been dormant TB? The layers of culture, from American Indian festivals, to opera, art and chamber music, to roping cattle was what Daniel and I adored about New Mexico. This was where Mom got her passion for flying and travel. This is where TB affected her lungs and caused an early death. I was bleary-eyed from reading about boom town Las Vegas, when it was the end of the tracks. Curiosity led to how my grandfather could have caught TB in New Jersey.

"Henry had moved west to cure his TB," I read. I visited Black Tom island near the Statue of Liberty where the immigration docks and train tracks are in ruins. I needed to know I was reading the right books to give context to his unique story. From photographs, Henry looked similar to Uncle Harry, but I imagined him more like Mom in his disposition who enjoyed being amidst people as his jobs were in sales and shops. Aunt Rita was very much like Agatha.

Chapter 13: Seeds and Songs

Jimmy (James Henry) Leahy grew up in the late 1800s in Elizabeth, New Jersey, the second oldest in a family of Irish immigrants who gardened for precious seeds, the wealth of any nation. His father, Timothy, employed Jimmy in the harvesting and bagging of seeds for food and flowers. Reluctantly, Jimmy worked side by side with his father, telling stories with a non-stop way of recounting his day, his friends, his world. "Just be sure you'll be counting twenty to a bag with your chatting consuming your brain power now, won't you?" Timothy kept close track of his harvest, his boy and his seeds. Where Jimmy shone was at the produce market near Union Station in Manhattan. With his deep dimples, parade of freckles across his nose and joyful blue eyes, Jimmy could sell a bag of compost to an apartment dweller. He was the apple of Timothy's eye, yet was not taken with gardening. Jimmy had a way of jumping into any group with both feet and steering its direction. He sang in the Catholic church chorus, enjoyed neighbors of all ages who stopped by the seed store and played a mean game of sandlot baseball.

Saturdays, he and his father rose before dawn to pack up the barrels and baskets of fresh vegetables, herbs and fruit in the back of their long, aged-cedar seed store, with its generous front porch. The Elizabeth road forked on both sides of the double storefront, with a row of framed windows. Chairs were clustered as an invitation for neighbors to rest awhile and share their news. The wagon was nearly loaded as the sun peeked over the well-established city of Elizabeth, New Jersey. Eighteenth-century red brick homes and municipal buildings had hosted George Washington on his travels between D.C. and New York.

Basil, tarragon, pepper, and carrot seeds in packages were in a basket in the front seat. Barrels of potato eyes, dried apples and pears kept each other upright in the back. Father and son drove the wagon of leafy greens, radishes and early carrots into Manhattan's 34th Street market through Elizabeth. Timothy and James passed the local church, a wooden sound box that carried the young boys' and girls' voices. Bleary eyed and silent, they arrived on 34th Street to set their wares at their regular farmer's market booth. While his father finished arranging his produce in the morning shade, Jimmy visited friends.

All of Europe was represented at the market. The salesmen shared a bit of loyalty to their homeland, especially about the current war, and strong opinions about President Wilson's policies. Europeans praised Wilson. As older men came to chinwag, younger men came for sparse day-jobs. Browsing and purchasing customers offered morsels of news to the local farmers. Jimmy and Timothy gathered enough information for a week of conversations on the store's front porch. With a full cash box, they gathered what was left of their groceries, handing some to the wanting homeless, packed the wagon and compared notes on what they'd heard and seen all the way back to Elizabeth. They unloaded at the seed shop and were home hungry for a hearty mid-afternoon supper. While Timothy napped, James went to find the afternoon baseball game or join a group of men on the front porch of the seed shop. He was home by dinnertime to rest before early morning choir at Sunday Mass.

When Mom's cousin, Mary Lou Greeley, showed me the Leahy seed store in 1978 I felt it was home. This is where my urge to garden originates. We are part Irish farmers. Since grade school, I had kept gardens, harvested seeds and grown vegetables from them the following year. I had grown seedlings by grow-light at Airdrie, cleared a patch of woods by the lake for corn, and planted tomatoes that were planted above nourishing alewives from the beach. I had worked at the St. Paul conservatory to understand grafting, rooting cuttings and transplanting while studying botany and hydroponics in college. In Oak Park, I grew a vertical berry-patch up the south side of my studio. An herb garden, leafy greens and tomatoes, while training a euonymus vine into a dragon on the west studio wall. Sophia and I took great pride in our pumpkin patch. The two apple trees couldn't keep our family in apple butter and pies, but I espaliered the branches and picked the fruit annually. I didn't inherit my grandfather's voice.

The choir was competing in the Elizabeth singing competition and preparing itself for the New Jersey rounds. It had perfected songs for the judges in the statewide competition. Jimmy didn't want to think any further than winning State. When he wasn't learning the choir church songs, Jimmy was busy learning Irish ballads. He had a way with the lilting rhythms and rising and falling cadences of ancient tales passed along like folk songs. Jimmy liked to talk almost as much as Jimmy liked to sing. He wanted to sing his best, yet the competition wasn't foremost on his mind. There was a lovely young girl in the choir for whom he sang. He and Michael Rogers hung around together as they both like to play ball and attended the same Catholic school. Michael was more reticent and watchful, while Jimmy found himself right in the middle of any mix.

As Jimmy got older and stepped out of the family more, his parents recognized he had other ambitions than being a farmer. His weeding left areas untouched, his mind wandered and a significant amount of seeds were left on the drying stalks. Timothy encouraged him to seek grocery sales at the dock, as younger Leahy sons were getting old enough to help with the harvests. Jimmy and Michael wandered the docks to see about selling produce for sailors heading overseas. It seemed the world walked these piers. Irish, right off the boat, labored to carry heavy parcels onto shore. Germans wheeled carts of goods to trains loaded by Spaniards. British lads tossed burlap bags to French boys on ships headed to Europe. Jimmy learned that the Germans knew which ships might need more provisions. They seemed to know schedules and everyone on the docks. He recognized Kristoff from the Manhattan farmers market and asked how to get in touch with ship's cooks. In no time, Jimmy was delivering produce to several nautical kitchens.

Jimmy took the train to the docks to sell his father's produce and helped with loading and unloading packages from far-off lands. His natural curiosity was triggered by exotic smells from the various parcels that arrived stamped with ligatures and languages from European ports labeled by far-away hands. Others' spirits were lifted to work a bit better when he sang while he hauled cargo. His heart was warmed by feeling closer to Ireland as the barrels of wheat, frozen crates of meat and giant parcels of oats were unloaded to feed America. Very little was sent back in the Irish empty ships. He enjoyed hearing tales from the old country. The Irish had an empathy with the Germans, who had lost tens of thousands of boys during the British battles in the Champagne region of France, and many in the Falkland Islands. If President Woodrow Wilson was neutral during the war, why did he detain German vessels along the Hudson? Interred German ships left sailors idle on the docks when they weren't scraping barnacles or repainting their hulls.

I told my brothers and sisters the amazing story of Elizabeth, New Jersey at the time our grandfather was a young boy there, before the first war. Working the docks might be how he acquired TB? It might have been the origin of their mother's scarred lungs. I will never know. I passed vegetables at the dinner table while telling my children how my grandfather Jimmy had learned the United States was selling bullets and bombs by the barrel load to England and France to fight Germany.

Jimmy listened to the firebrand, Jim Larkin, an Englishman and labor leader for the Irish, who spoke about Irish rights to a decent wage and urged America to stay out of the European war. Larkin organized protests to stop ammunition workers, who were underpaid for dangerous jobs, from loading armaments on ships. Explosions happened. Germans also wanted to stop the flow of munitions and paid Larkin to protest. Larkin moved to Chicago with no explanation. The dock workers gossiped and invented far-fetched reasons for the mysterious disappearance of an activist. Jimmy Leahy took note of Chicago as Michal Rogers' family had also moved there.

The New Jersey trains, filled with steel bullets and bombs, continued to pull in to a cat-shaped spit of land, just off the north New Jersey coast. Shockingly, three thousand trainloads of munitions in one year alone came to this spit of an island called Black Tom. Across the bay stood the Statue of Liberty. British and French ships pulled up to Black Tom and filled their ballasts with artillery, crossed the Atlantic Ocean, guarded by the British Navy, and used the artillery against Germans in WWI. The Germans were unhappy with America's product.

Kristoff was an unkempt Austrian immigrant, yet a fine fellow, who was usually looking for a day job. Not many people employed Kristoff though, as he was known for his short fuse. Kristoff, dressed in business attire, told Jimmy he was employed to be a travel companion for a German salesman Francis Graetnor. His aunt, whom Kristoff lived with, proudly exclaimed at Bayonne's weekly sewing bee, that Kristoff traveled the states by train with an official suitcase, to meetings at large factories. "Tickets always paid with cash," she announced with bursting pride. Kristoff didn't share that he was ordered to never open the suitcase. When he did, he saw glass pencil-size tubes, jars of sulphuric acid and chlorate of potash, copper sheets and blocks of soft wax. He thought little of it. What he noticed was factories, where they had meetings, suffered from explosions. There were lots of explosions at other chemical factories too. In fact, one hundred explosions in vessels and factories made them common. His was earning a good wage and he considered getting an apartment.

Kristoff liked Jimmy and they talked when he was in town, mostly at the pier. Neither of them wanted a factory job—it was too dangerous. The DuPont munitions and Anderson chemical companies had regular inexplicable flare-ups. Then Bridgeport's munitions factory caught fire. Kristoff was happy to be paid, enjoyed the fine suits and the lifestyle. Kristoff enjoyed the attention of important businessmen who recognized and greeted him wherever he went. Mr. Graetnor's motto was "Hide in plain sight," and he was affable everywhere. Kristoff's job was easy, his paycheck steady and honorable.

Everything went well with Jimmy and the choir competitions. After a tough battle and close vote-count, they earned the New Jersey State title for their singing and prepared for the boat ride to Brooklyn for regionals. He sang as he walked, sang as he loaded, sang as he sorted seeds. His step followed the lyrics as he traversed town to visit with the girl of his heart's desire.

That winter, he was home with a winter cold. A brother took over the selling of root vegetables while Jimmy recouped with teas and soups made by his dear mother. His cough remained steady throughout choir preparations. His father concocted dried garlic, peppermint and chamomile to suppress the cough for long enough to sing at the competition. Jimmy was on his way to Brooklyn with the choir. Twice a day he drank the concoction. He eased up practicing to perform a magnificent solo sung from his heart, for his love of singing and care of his loves.

He returned to Elizabeth with a trophy the size of a small child and a parade through the town square to cheers from children with their families. Jimmy felt whole, adult and welcomed in his town. In the crowd Jimmy waved to Kristoff, who was looking well-dressed despite his usually aggressive manner. He stood by himself, forced a smile and raised his hand to chest height for a jerked wave right. He looked tired and careless. His attention had already shifted to candy being tossed. Jimmy deliberated momentarily before returning to the revelry and celebrating with his girl.

His mother noticed that when he forgot to take the herbal concoction, the cough returned. It was wet and persistent. For Jimmy, the cough became a way of life. He covered his mouth with a sleeve and thought little of it. Jimmy focused on school, his singing and baseball as spring rolled around. If he hit a double, he panted when he reached second base. His triples and homeruns were non-existent this season. "It must be a growth spurt?" he mentioned to the pitcher. Even if he connected with the ball, he couldn't make the run without a coughing fit slowing his progress. Breathing deep for choir was nearly impossible and suppressing his cough was getting embarrassing. He planned to see the doctor.

Meanwhile, Kristoff visited Graetnor's offices in Manhattan. He carried the suitcase, as usual, and waited outside in the lobby while his boss met with another German behind the closed door. It wasn't a hard job, the pay good. His aunt was proud of him for having such an important position so he carried on, helped with his aunt's rent and occasionally thought of moving out, though wasn't home enough to look for an apartment. The view of Staten Island and the immigrant port caught his gaze. The busy unloading of ships reminded him of a simpler time. He wished he could have steady work and not be on the road so much. He had not played baseball in two seasons. Why had he been anxious to find employment and leave that life? He valued his life on that shore and missed it.

Jimmy returned from the doctor with a diagnosis of tuberculosis. A mild case. "Rest and stay away from the docks," the doctor had prescribed. "There have been cases of recovery. The herbal concoction probably suppressed the clearing of the lungs and could cause a pneumonia," he'd been told. Probably better not to aggravate the cough with running. Singing in a closed room with others is out of the question. Jimmy was contagious. Unless he got his TB under control he couldn't return to school. As an avid reader and good student, he accomplished a superior high school education. The toll of the diagnosis devastated his entire family. He ate alone, slept in his own room and saw no friends. Kristoff stopped by between trips. His mother was glad her son had company. Kristoff told great stories of his travels across the country; of mountains, of fields of corn, of great large lakes and busy cities.

Jimmy missed that a German submarine, the largest in its fleet, was docked on the Elizabeth shore. He might have noticed it the first or second day, before boats were docked around it on all sides, hiding it. The huge submarine was mostly forgotten. There were many German vessels retained along the port with bored German sailors wandering about not able to sail home. When it got too crowded, the German ships were towed to Hoboken. President Woodrow Wilson detained all German boats as his contribution to Britain and France, but otherwise refused to engage in Europe's war. Wilson was convinced the United States of America was above entering a war, yet made policies to favor America's British and French allies.

Seeing Germans around the docks was usual. Seeing Kristoff was usual too. The subversive Germans knew each of the dock workers on each of the shifts personally. Planning the explosions was easy. The Germans knew when the shipments of incendiaries filled the island called Black Tom, when the guards snoozed, or wandered off for a smoke, when the area was vacated. The submarine was nearly full of items to refuel the German necessities for war and needed to leave soon. Because it had been hidden, the sub was forgotten. President Wilson was sailing in Chesapeake Bay the week the submarine was filled. Graetnor decided, "Now is the moment!"

Kristoff had not been seen for days. Assuming he was on the road, Jimmy spent more time on the Seed Shop porch. Discussions swirled about the war in Europe and Wilson's hesitancy to get involved. "What is he waiting for?" Would their sons be involved? No one wanted to go to war. Late that night, Kristoff received the signal. The glass tube in his room was to be placed between barrels and crates on Black Tom. Then, he was to go home and have a quiet night's sleep. A row boat was already half way across the Hudson River. The rowers slipped cigar incendiaries into crates and barrels on the water side of Black Tom. Kristoff set a couple on the shore side. Second-generation Germans invented cigar-shaped glass bombs filled with two chemicals divided by a copper sheet. One of the chemicals ate through the copper in a matter of hours. Once the two chemicals combined, fire shot out the ends of the cigar tube, igniting nearby incendiaries. Another bomb was made to look like a piece of coal. Dow chemical plants, which made dynamite and bullet materials, were exploding into flames across the nation. The Germans wanted to stop the flow of bullets and bombs at their source. The boats around the submarine were moved and it slipped under the surface and out into open water.

The explosion of the tiny cigar-shaped bombs set off a chain reaction on an island full of bombs, bullets and hand grenades. The shrapnel pierced the Statue of Liberty, bounced a baby out of its crib onto the floor, killing it, broke every window from the tip of Manhattan to 42nd Street and reverberated as an unearthly earthquake, waking citizens all the way to Maryland. The explosions went on for hours as more and more bombs blasted from the fires of the first. The fire trucks and boats could not get close enough to the infernal shooting of bullets and shrapnel to penetrate the heat. The inferno burned and exploded past dawn.

President Wilson was summoned from vacation to Washington, where he announced the explosion was an accident. The relatively unknown island of Black Tom no longer existed. The death toll was unknown, he said, as the port was frequented by drifters, homeless and immigrated souls.

Kristoff never slept that night. The boxcar fire set off a domino effect of huge explosions hour after hour. He went insane with the realization of what he'd done. And, he'd only been paid $500! He ran around the house like an inconsolable crazy man. His aunt did not understand what he shouted. He ran into the street. He shouted as explosions added percussion to his irrational ranting. He jumped on a train with hundreds of other people, not knowing where to go. The train stopped in Elizabeth and he got off mechanically. He visited Jimmy, by habit.

Jimmy talked calmly, sang a bit to the crazed man, calmed him. Quiet enough to sit on the porch. Torpedo-like explosions sounded nearby. The shouts became sobbing as Kristoff's body slumped. "What have I done?" Jimmy thought he heard through the blubbering. "What did I do?" Kristoff whispered through the crying until exhaustion won and he was half-walked, half-carried to the couch for rest. Jimmy's mother sat with Kristoff as exhausted Jimmy caught some rest himself. Explosions lit the sky like daylight, sent shrapnel flying through walls. Windows were already blown out.

The Leahy family, with little sleep, rushed to Sunday Mass. The streets filled with families headed to services. It was as if Christmas, Easter and All Saints Day combined to fill each and every house of worship, of each and every religion, from Connecticut to Maryland with parishioners seeking solace from what sounded like the end of the world. Their ears were still ringing, their nerves frayed. Occasional explosions were still shooting off. Jimmy prayed at home after his family left. A knock on the door was not expected. The police. Jimmy was questioned. "No, I don't know his full name. Only Kristoff." He offered all he knew: the few cities Kristoff mentioned, the factories he'd talked about, his general travel schedule. They didn't ask if Kristoff was in the house. Jimmy did not offer. When he closed the door, he saw Kristoff was gone. His only option was to go the way of Larkin and the Rogers. Chicago beckoned.

"You've got your story, Jimmy, I mean Henry," Timothy guided him.

"Stick to your story that you are healing from a bad cough out west. You can build yourself a fine life as Henry Leahy outside the questioning you'll receive here." His parents gave him a long and powerful hug. His first stop would be Michael Rogers's family on Edgemont Avenue in Chicago, on his way to Hygiene, Colorado to cure his TB. With a leather suitcase and new suit, he set off to find fortune. In that transformative train trip, Jimmy introduced himself as Henry. Their one-time neighbors, the Rogers, had moved to Chicago a few years earlier. Henry and Michael Rogers were delighted to see each other. Henry was warmly greeted, name accepted without question, and given the extra sewing room to sleep. They adored his stories of New Jersey, his charming manner and the songs he roused around the piano. In the dry heat of his first Chicago winter, Henry's TB seemed to have healed.

Henry loved the Rogers family, his ease of feeling at home in a new city. Mostly, he loved Michael's sister, Agatha. Quick, spirited, engaging and beautiful, she blushed when he spoke and made him tea. He could not get over how nifty she was with the sewing machine, knitting needles, painted china and needlepoint pillows. It seemed the rooms showcased her workmanship everywhere. The others took the craftwork for granted as they became accustomed to her skills in everyday life. Her handiwork slipped into being part of their lives without fanfare or acknowledgment. Agatha's art symbolized all Henry had left behind of home, creativity and family. Agatha could cook and bake with perfection. Once a month she doubled her recipe and sent a meal, through the Basilica Women's Guild, to a family of six Franklin orphans, cared for by the eldest two sisters, in the same building. Henry's cough subsided as their romance flourished.

While his new suit was still fresh, Henry put his best foot forward for work. Irene worshiped his deep dimples and easygoing manner, his dark curly hair and personable nature. She loved his singing and the rhythmic lilt to his step. His stories of Elizabeth brought her quiet father into the conversation. The stories of singing competitions and parades for teenagers brightened her eyes with yearning. Elizabeth seemed idyllic. He loved her quiet yet fearless demeanor, her adept way of ruling the household while being a respectful daughter and younger sister. Her smile was quick and warm. Her eyes danced when he was near.

Agatha's parents respected him and the connection he brought to their beloved friends in New Jersey. The only disagreement was that Agatha cheered for the Cubs and Henry for the Yankees. They planned their wedding at Our Lady of Sorrows Basilica, where Agatha had attended elementary and high school. Before long he came home with a contract to work in an oil company that distributed heating oil for homes. That he was familiar with the New Jersey shipping docks and people did not hurt his prospects. He was in charge of scheduling train pick-ups and deliveries.

Chapter 14: Homework

In 1998, Dad looked the worse for wear. He was adrift without a rudder. He wasn't eating, barely slept and was working himself to the bone to finish his reportorial art. He had secrets, many of them, and I needed answers from the last remaining family member. It's not that I hadn't asked. Memories of morning sun pierced my eyes as I punched scan to change from the news to WXRT. Peter Gabriel and warm cornbread wafted, reminding me of when I had lived with my grandmother in high school and had grilled her with questions while writing the family genealogy. When my grandmother said, "Why do you want to know?" I backed off. I interviewed my father's cousin, who said, "Oh, you didn't know…" and escorted me out. I asked again. Gramma Mac said, "I hope you don't ever work as hard as I did at your age. Live forward, don't look back."

Only one ambiguous half-page of my father's family saga was written in that high school paper. I had questions to ask my Dad and dreaded his brushoff. Throughout my childhood he had traveled the world to capture the latest news events with drawing and painting on paper. The artwork was brought to life by panning the image with a movie camera for films. Mom captured sound for the movies by taping interviews and they wrote a weekly column of their explorations. "Rushing is not graceful," Mom had said. I slowed my minivan, slowed my breath and allowed my thoughts to wander.

Butternut squash soup had been simmering at dawn. Cornbread smelled nearly done, as our house woke with water running through the pipes. Daniel had already left for the train. Bailey, our terrier, watched my every move in expectation of the 7:40 walk to the bus stop. After a flurry of the kids eating crispy French Toast sticks, a leashed Bailey pulled Mahon and me to the arriving bus. "I've got a soccer game at 4:00," he reminded me. Sophia asked if a friend could play at noon. She and I talked about a new giraffe added to Sophia's beanie baby collection. I turned to see my crying toddler, Brie, in the sitter's arms through the back window. I waved, blew a kiss and started to walk back in. The sitter waved me away. The books say don't go back in or you will never leave in peace. Sophia and I turned to the mini-van in the garage. At the preschool drop-off, I arranged her playdate with her teacher.

Driving past Columbus Park, I turned onto the Eisenhower Expressway. The family pattern was to not ask our father about the past, but wait for him to tell about his latest painting of current events. I couldn't recall any stories about Dad's branch of the family tree. Mahon had brought home an assignment from school to fill out the family tree. I didn't know my grandparents' names for Mahon's questionnaire and I feared Dad's avoidance, but resolved to get the answers this afternoon. "Ask nothing. Say nothing. Our M.O.," I said out loud. I grabbed a tipping bag with soup as the minivan slowed, tossed a quarter and a dime into the toll basket. "Why don't I know anything?" I hollered into the toll basket. My heart was racing with an expectation of Dad's avoidance. As part of my teaching job, I had delivered slide shows on Italian Renaissance sculptors, their sexual preferences, quarries they carved stone from and techniques they invented. I know how old they were when they died. I had written a thesis on a French sculptor and his mistresses' art. Yet, I can't tell my six-year-old son my grandparents' names? At the next toll basket, I tossed thirty-five cents and vented my frustration, "Life is understood backwards!" The minivan careened, nearly on autopilot. I recalled how Mom's friend Madeline, who introduced my parents in high school, said at Mom's memorial, "It is all going to all fall to you, Margot."

I pulled into Dad's circular drive before a horizontal stone home in an oak clearing. The nearby roar of the highway triggered memories of the waves on Lake Michigan with a chronic rhythm that rose up the far side of the highway berm, arched then dropped in a wall of sound. Why did our family leave Ireland? They left before the Great Famine. Did they? Walking through the constant din, I chafed in jeans and a sweatshirt, too warm for the peaking 68 degrees. Where did they live between Ireland and Chicago? The asphalt driveway under my Tretorns steamed as I stepped through the highway hum.

My heartbeat matched the resonating crickets. I was calmed with the rhythms of the woods. A rustling of oak leaves caught the breeze, then the familiar clatter of cattails until a dense tranquility of nature filled my heart. I was soothed with the cicadas' cadences rising and falling, drowning the brightness of the sun in the shadow of the woods. The chirping, squawking, trilling of birds and clacking, rustling and creaking of branches stilled the chaos of my loss, reordering my life after burying my Mom several months before. I was further pacified as I passed between aromatic weeping cherry and fragrant crab apple trees before entering the side-door of Dad's mid-century modern home. The scent reminded me of Mom's making crab apple jelly with my kids. The momentary communion with nature entered my soul as a consoling friend. Remembering Dad was a man without a mooring, I turned the nickel nob and pushed open the wood door. Echoes of silence resounded through the long hallway. No familiar footsteps of Mom greeted me. A chair squeaked in Dad's studio.

"Good day," I broke the silence.

"Well, there you are. I'm glad you came," he said. "I'll just finish up here and be in." Damar varnish, turpentine and beeswax aroma whirled in the hallway. Smells like home. I stepped into his studio to see my Dad with three paint brushes in his mouth, and palette knives in either hand, before a vertical painting of a thistle in an ochre glow. A thistle patch grew outside his window. I knew not to interrupt, to wait for a lunch-time conversation.

"Looks good. I'll put lunch in the fridge and be in the living room, no hurry," I walked past my mother's empty office and down the narrow hall to the kitchen. A deer gazed at me, or at its reflection in the wide windows. I gazed back. This is the same sun-dappled, wooded yard in which Daniel and I met playing croquet several years before we celebrated our marriage. We jumped in that pool after our first date after a sweltering west side day. The deer twitched its tail, spooked and dashed into the buckthorn. This is the yard Dad and I raked, mowed and shoveled. We were building a reliance with each other there.

Tossing out the previous week's uneaten food, I placed fresh meals on the top shelf. In the living room, I sunk into the family's living room couch, realizing how tired I was. Was it only a year since my father, mother and I sat in this very room with my infant daughter? I had thought Mom was starting to age then. Nothing could have prepared me for her sudden death, other than if some explanation had been offered. *The more important it is, the less is told.* I had missed my mother's first stroke because no one told me at college. There was the unmentioned pneumonia, and no forewarning that my Mom had months to live. Until the night of her death, who knew she had a lung disease? I scanned my memory for clues. None.

Too big-boned for my mother's wedding dress, I learned in graduate school that I looked like my grandmother, which made we wonder, *Who was Gramma Mac?* Mac was an abbreviation of their last name. Adults called her "Bess". Mom had taken such delight in my high school family history, a definitive record. Tracking sons of sons of sons, daughters of daughters of daughters on my Mom's side, I searched for my father's history, then paused—for decades. My renewed quest for answers must have been a part of mourning Mom. As a high school senior, I had copied pages from her family bible; birth and death certificates were folded into thirds, then glued to my manually typed pages. Mom had lovingly opened and copied each certificate separately, glued them on pages for her nine sons' and daughters' 1975 Christmas gift. The hand-typed pages were stapled like a book, with a cover page, and placed in bubbly white folders with frayed gold cords tied around the spine. Leahy photographs showed generations of women with some likeness to me.

Conversely, Dad spent a decade cataloging and assigning each of his wide-ranging original artworks and copyrights to give to his nine children and thirteen grandchildren. His extensive body of art had been made for publications and to animate documentary films. For some cockamamie reason our oldest brothers argued so much about prints a third brother lobbied Dad to add a third trustee. Some thought keeping reproduced art in the public eye was beneficial with beneficiaries requested an accounting of prints that were sold. I, seven o' nine, held my position that original art was more valuable without reproductions. Our parents' will states clearly to divide all artwork equally. Dad suppressed our discord with a quiet calm.

"Have you seen this week's *New Yorker*?" Dad asked. He sat down in his rotating leather chair surrounded by two walls of windows.

"Only read the cartoons with the kids," I said. I braced myself, then asked if he can help answer some questions for Mahon's questionnaire.

"Maybe when we sit down to lunch," he said. "What does Mahon want to know?"

"It's a family history, asking for names and dates."

"Will you come to the back room for a minute?" he asked. "I want to show you a few things." We stepped down into the den, then up two steps single file then down two more steps into the narrow hallway lit by high, horizontal windows in the late morning sun. Turpentine and Damar varnish vapors faintly travelled with us down the hall.

"How is the painting going?" I asked. We passed my bedroom, with my sculptures on the low shelf. My family stays there often.

"It is winning," he said. I was annoyed at the way he deflected my questions. *That was the way it was.* We entered his bedroom, which my sisters had prepared for our mother's return with an oxygen pump and a wheelchair. My father opened his top drawer and pointed to a small box. He opened it.

"These are my Army Air Force medals."

"What, you have army medals! Why?" As if giving a tour, he walked over to a desk peninsula and pulled out a fireproof box. "These are important financial documents your mother kept." What an unprecedented moment. Dad is sharing secrets I have never been privy to. He's a decorated WWII vet? I couldn't imagine him with this pinned on his pocket. Was there a ceremony? Then he opened his deceased wife's closet door.

"It doesn't have to be today, but would you please empty her closet? All of it. And the vanity in the corner. I've taken care of the bathroom," he said. "I've lost the second bottom molar on the left. Now let's have some lunch."

I was amazed at the new information shared and took a deeper breath. A checklist of questions: Grandparents' names were deflected. Not even a clue about his army medals. Am I to take over the finances? Stick to the questionnaire. I needed to know more but was overwhelmed with the ask. That my Dad was sharing clues was heartwarming and disconcerting. I counted my free hours before being home for soccer. My daughter's playdate had started. The baby was napping. Breathe deep, I told myself. The closets will wait.

I warmed the soup and tossed a salad, mixed Lipton powdered iced tea and squeezed lemon on everything, barely noticing what I was doing. Patterns kept my actions automatic while I struggled to overcome my loss and the task ahead. I dreaded clearing Mom's closet. I had thank-you notes for the memorial service to finish and was behind on the sculpture due by Christmas. I set two plates at the end of the long table with a dozen empty chairs and sat facing the kitchen. My mother's vacant chair faced out toward the walls of windows and the oak grove. After sliding aside his nearly full bowl and plate and my empty dishes, I set the questionnaire between us. I caught my breath and slowly exhaled. "What is your father's name?"

"William F. McMahon, don't worry about the middle name. I'm not a junior." He was distracted thinking about his painting in the studio. I felt it.

"What is your mother's middle name?" I asked. He leaned into the questions.

"She never mentioned it," he said. "Put down Franklin, her maiden name." Dad was discombobulated by talking about his mother. "Elizabeth Franklin McMahon," he said. There, I am more informed already. His distress must be a part of mourning Mom. Churns up Gram too.

"When were they married?" The art kept me from getting impatient with the long, thoughtful silences.

"I don't know when," he answered. "There's a church in the Adirondacks where they were married. I've made a painting of the family farm there."

This might be as painful for him as it is for me. "When did your father die?"

"Have you told any of your brothers and sisters?" he asked. When I interviewed Margaret, his cousin, back in high school, she told me about my grandfather passing away in the 1960s.

"Why didn't I know I had a grandfather?" I flared at Dad then.

He stopped me in my tracks. "He was my father and I couldn't see him. Your grandmother's decision." Then he added, "Don't go telling everyone now. If they ask, tell them, but otherwise let it rest." I never asked any further questions and knew not to ask at that point.

"Only Patrick asked. I told him he could tell others, if they asked." We both leaned into the green sheets of questions.

"The year your mother died? I know that one—1974, at 88 years old." I was visibly pleased with myself as if I was a student in class who got one question right. That was the year I had lived with Gram.

"How old was my grandfather?"

"You do the math from her birthday and add five years for him—he was older."

"When were you born?" A long pause. "How about Mom?" I asked.

"September 9th, 1921, your mother in 1921 on May 27th. You can't go home again."

I jotted down the answers. He had longer delays between questions. I felt we were reaching his limit. The painting was winning his attention.

"Well, that's about it, thanks." I said. "I'll clean out the closet now." What a relief. Maybe not an A+, but answers enough to pass the assignment. A few details unsolved, a mountain of questions ahead, but not bad considering. My father was more open to talking about the past. *I might get more stories?*

"Take everything," he said.

"One more question. What were your WWII medals for?" He didn't change his outward expression, but looked deep within his memory. A cloud of fatigue past over his face. I got the feeling unlocking that answer took more energy than he was willing to divert. I had dived too far into territory not meant for me.

"Our book group just finished a book, I'll give you my copy. Also, read *The Great Escape* and *The Wooden Horse*," he said. "They are written about my P.O.W. camps. I'm headed back to my painting and will be taking some time off in an hour. Whatever you want to do, is fine."

P.O.W. camp, what is he talking about? "Can you explain P.O.W. camp please?" I asked.

"I was in several though I don't remember the names right now," he said. "*The Wooden Horse* tells about one of my camps and how everyone spent all their time trying to escape. They had a German name *Luftwaffe* because we were *Luft*, or aerial prisoners. They thought of us as terrorists. We were not!"

I wrote down the names of the books. "Can I check facts with you about these camps?"

"If you want. Read first." I could tell by his expression he was dubious I'd get around to reading the books.

No clothes were moved yet and I was exhausted already. How to start? Don't attempt stages. One fell swoop from closet to car—here we go! I pulled the empty van to the front door and lifted the rear hatch. Tidy, dry-cleaned, and still in the clear bags, dresses hung vertically and at attention. The bright colors and swatches of complementary colors shook as I separated out an armload. Mom's errands to make sure everything was cleaned and in order caused my tears. Just like Mom to have prepared her closet to make this move easier. The silver sequined dress that enhanced her gray hair at my wedding sunk my spirit. Each dress packed another memory of events we attended, holidays or watching her go out in the evening. I tossed the stockings in a garbage bag then folded blouses and skirts in a box. The comfy blouse and skirt she wrote in buoyed me. Better not to think about what you are doing—just get it done! The front screen door kept slamming as I summarized what I knew from the family history.

Mom wore turquoise and silver against the grey dresses. She wore silver pressed into squash blossoms when they went out at night. She wore a horizontal, double-diamond-shaped silver pin, with a turquoise stone over her heart on the herringbone jacket in the dry cleaner bag. She wore tooled, wide-banded silver bracelets with rows of coral and veined turquoise to art receptions. My sister Jean and I had organized her chest and divided the rings, bracelets, brooches and necklaces amongst her four daughters and in-laws. The legend that made-up Irene Leahy was that she was a trained art teacher who had two careers in travel: a WWII stewardess, then a travel writer after she raised her family. Mom saw only the best in people, created patterns that loosely controlled her kid's commotion and shepherded strays and all. Her elementary through high school years revolved around youth groups and singing at Our Lady of Sorrows Basilica that I, and my siblings, watched in the movie, *The Trouble with Angels*. She started writing again after we watched that movie. During high school, she attended after-church meetings and honed her natural organizing skills at Saul Alinsky's Catholic Workers. She emulated peaceful Dorothy Day until she became her. Then, Irene met Mac McMahon.

With the green dress, Mom and I had met with United Airlines designers to collaborate on an exhibit of early stewardesses for a United Terminal glass case. Her oral histories of stewardess friends were to be printed on large boards. I planned to sculpt portraits that gave insight into 1940s pioneering flights. Though the airlines cancelled the exhibit, Mom included her writings about early air travel in her weekly newspaper columns. Boxes of Mom's writings were loaded into the van. One box slipped off the pile of dry-cleaners bags and burst open onto the asphalt. A *Lake Forester* cover blared a headline: "Clipped Wings," with my mother's photograph amidst six children. The 1956 article described Mrs. Franklin McMahon with the sentence, "Whatever happened to those gorgeous stewardesses?"

"Do not quit your day job," Mom had told her daughters. The criteria for keeping her airlines job was to stay unmarried. From a league of her own, Mrs. Franklin McMahon was grounded after her wedding. Sidelined, she yearned for her paycheck and exploring the country. For her travel-writing career, Irene wrote a local newspaper column, gained a national audience through magazine articles and received a Mark Twain Travel

Writing Award for her acute and precise insights, bringing her easy-chair readers to far-away places, with remarkable clarity, and convincing detail.

Winded, I heaped more and more dresses and coats into the van. The next closet held shelves of knitted and woven jackets. Some clothes were memories from photographs of my mother's world travels. The red-sweater-coat brought back memories of my Mom coming back from Deerfield Library Writers' Group. She would quickly fix a pasta dinner and toss a salad in this jacket.

They are only clothes, I reminded myself. That's all that is left. Just a closet full of clothes. I was in great shape, yet increasingly weary. Each armload had the baggage of memory. I was breathless, sweating and wished I had dressed in shorts and a T-shirt. *C'est la vie!* As I tossed the red-knitted coat onto the pile, a pen slipped out of the pocket. I caught it before it hit the asphalt. A mahogany pen with cloisonné shimmered brightly in my hand. I gently set the pen in the glove compartment and took a break.

"Counting the screen door slams, I thought you might be done." Dad slumped into a folding chair at the kitchen table for a glass of lemonade. The two of us had picked up a length of the Lake Forest bowling alley in the early '60s for my childhood kitchen table. It was resized to fit this peninsula. Bowling ball dents are still visible in the surface. Original Formica cover the other counters that aren't stainless steel. I guzzled my second glass of lemonade.

"When did you and Mom fall in love?" I asked, stretching my back.

"Not sure about your mother. But it might have been my birthday at the ice cream parlor, when I fell in love with her." Without looking away, I grabbed the phone message notebook and scribbled furiously to catch his phrases and cadence. "The gang at the Esquire met for ice cream after school. I had just locked up my job at *Extensions* magazine as a cartoonist and was feeling pretty good about things. Irene and Charlotte stopped in, from the Madison Avenue bus. They were coming home from their first year at Teacher's College." I lost my sense of time in his story, which he recreated as if it happened yesterday.

Chapter 15: Yearning to Fly

I'd really like to fly in one of those!" Mac mentioned to his friend Jack at the Esquire ice cream shop and pointed up as a plane roared over. Irene was behind Mac, ordering her regular hot fudge sundae with peanuts. She had always wanted to fly! The pastel pink-and-blue booths were mostly filled with Trinity and Fenwick students. Mac nibbled a macaroon cookie and sat with his cousin and a few friends around a circular table on his and Jack's birthday. It was 1938 and airplanes were all anyone was talking about.

"Oh! So would I!" Irene said loudly. Jack and Mac looked over. "Traveling, seeing new cities, living elsewhere is my dream. I can live anywhere once I get my teacher's license."

"I would like to fly to D.C. and New York, with you." Mac surprised himself with his awkward boldness. It was his birthday celebration after all.

"Sky's the limit," she agreed. "I'd like to see St. Louis and Atlanta, Miami and Santa Fe."

"How about around the world?" he asked.

"Why… (not!)" Another propeller plane flew over, drowning out the "not." "That one is headed to Denver," she said. So began their guessing-the-destination as planes propelled through the skies. Jack watched them then he and the friends melted away.

"So when do you think Mom fell in love with you?" I asked. Another glass of lemonade. He looked at the surface in the glass, watching ripples settle.

"I may have started to have a chance with your Mother during a *Porgy and Bess* song at a Sienna Dance," my Dad said.

"Mom loved Gershwin's *Porgy and Bess* at the Fourth of July concerts," I said.

"Here's the book we just read for book group." Dad handed me *Monuments Men*.

"OK, I look forward to reading it," I said, feeling overwhelmed with another assignment. I wish he would just tell his story. What does

Monuments Men have to do with anything? Stretched in too many directions, I was weary of wanting more history, moving clothes. I debated with myself while observing my fatigued father. His hands were covered in paint. He slumped in his chair with bloodshot eyes.

"How's the painting going, Dad? You look tired," I said.

"Don't worry about little ol' me. It'll be an hour before I call it quits," he said.

"I've got just a few boxes left," I said. "Do you want me to take all the boxes?"

"Yes, please take everything. I've let this go too long."

"A pen dropped out of the sweater," I said.

"Take the pen. I've got troubles with the painting," he said.

We stepped out of the kitchen. He walked back down the hall to his studio. I walked past the dining table, thrilled to have heard the story told about their young love. It felt like a gift. The Till Trial drawings on my right haunted me. After loading more boxes, I bid my father goodbye and headed home.

The clothes in the van shifted as I turned off the Eisenhower Expressway onto Austin Boulevard, eager to be home and watch Mahon's soccer game. It had been decades since I gathered oral histories of my family. Why had Dad's history caught me by the horns then? I absolutely need to know more. I set Monuments Men in my studio. Dad gave the book to me for a reason.

Mahon's soccer game was over by 5:00 at the neighborhood park, one block away. After dinner, the five of us walked to the other end of the block for Daniel's basketball game at St. Catherine of Sienna-St. Lucy parish's gym. Daniel hurried ahead to warm up. Inside the pea-green tile gym, the kids and I climbed up the wooden stands. Sophia chattered about her friend's treasure hunt with hidden peanuts. They each had a water bottle and a Ziploc bag of Cheerios. Brie straddled my leg while Mahon and Sophia dangled their Converse sneakers off the edge.

"Your dad's basketball nickname is MX missile for attempting, and sometimes sinking, the three-point shot from outside the paint," I explained with a vocabulary focusing them on new words. "His team is called 'Short, but Slow.'" They got the joke. My thoughts wandered to this being the same gym where my parents had met, where my mother had fallen in love with my father. Remembering what Catholic school dances were like, I imagined the scene. My father was a senior in high school. My mother already had started teacher's college with Charlotte and Madeline. I knew their high school friends from annual picnics.

Twisted crepe-paper streamers and balloons were taped from the basketball net to the walls. A teen chatted with two friends, a boy and girl. Another girl walked in their direction. Her hair was held in a flip with hairspray or tied tight in a ponytail. One was Mom, just like in her high school photographs. She glanced at a boy who looked like my brother. Irene cannot break away from the conversation with another boy and his harebrained plan to join the army.

"Len, why not divert your civic drive to helping poor children who go to school hungry?" Irene said after she finished an explanation of what Dorothy Day might say against anything but pacifist action. "Let's feed them before school."

"I'd rather be a lieutenant than a jail bird," Len said.

"Have you ever seen navy polka dotted scarves?" Irene asked Madeline.

"I love the shoes. So many heels to choose from," Madeline said.

"Why would you enlist, Len, it's not America's problem?" Charlotte begged for a purpose.

"What's bigger than a world war?" Len asked, in his riddling way, to divert the question.

"Lo and behold! If it isn't a long-drink-of-water!" Irene smiled at a young man who walked up to the group. A magazine was rolled in his back pocket. A redhead, Clarence MacDonald, the Fenwick class math-mind, joined them and listened. Len asked quiet Clarence about his summer job in the University of Chicago physics lab. Clarence shrugged.

"Hi, Mac," Madeline and Charlotte said at the same time.

"Hey, Mac, what's bigger than a world war and smaller than a thumb?" Len asked again.

"The bullet you dodge," Mac replied, a bit peeved to be conversing about Europe's war.

"That's it, Mac! Better than the one I had… I was going to say the bullet that gets you." Len laughed. Several teens chuckled. Mac opened the *Colliers* magazine and showed Irene his published cartoon. They all leaned in to look. Pride from a friend, jealousy from another, a glow from Irene and dismay from another. Emotions muddled in their huddle. Mac was learning to deal with reactions to his art. Just then, Billie Holiday's rendition of "Summertim*e*" from *Porgy and Bess* began.

"Irene, would you like to dance?" Mac took her gloved hand in his and they disappeared onto the dance floor. Her hand lightly, gracefully, welcomed his. His hand gently, shyly, supported hers. Their two sets of blue eyes met. They turned and dipped to their living that was easy, becoming increasingly oblivious to their summertime surroundings. Chaos erupted as the DJ called out another Billie Holiday rendition of a jazz tune. Even though Leonard Cohen's song was written decades later, this was the jazz tune sung by Billie Holiday, I imagined to sum up the moment my parents fell in love.

"Dance to your beauty with a burning violin," Billie Holiday would have sung. The record skipped over its grooves. "Dance me through the panic, until I'm safely gathered in. Lift me like an olive branch and be my homeward dove…" Mac twirled Irene, who lightly spun on her right toe. The world was just the two of them. She was caught by her waist in his arm, his right drawing arm. "…show me slowly what I only know the limits of… Dance me to the end of love." Their graduations from high school melted away, the giddy expectations of what they'd do next evaporated into a misty future. This moment was their entire life. Each reached the sheer precipice of childhood's plateau at the same time. Hand in hand, they leaped into embracing caresses and gentle kisses. The music faded to an announcer who called the last dance, "…and it will be a slooooow one."

"Good night, Irene… Good night Irene," Louie Armstrong's rendition played the last tune of Sienna Night as they walked arm-in-arm to the Washington Street trolley. "Good night Irene, good night, Irene… I'll see you in my dreams…" As the song faded with distance and amplified in their minds, Mac escorted Irene to Central Park Boulevard in Austin, cognizant to walk on the street side in case a car splashed puddles. His handkerchief was tucked into his shirt pocket.

"That is so Dad," I said out loud. "He still does that kind of thing."

"What, Mom?" Mahon asked.

"Uh, oh. That is so Dad. Did you see him sink the three-pointer? It was just before the slam dunk." They returned to being glued to the game.

The morning after the basketball game, it was all I could do to give the older kids a warm breakfast of pancakes and orange juice. We missed the school bus, so I drove the kids to school. I had a tight deadline for three twice-life-size sculptures of the Holy Family by Christmas; Jesus, Mary and Joseph. Waiting in the pre-school drop-off line, I planned my structural strategies, figuring out how to hold the weight of two figures on a rolling platform. I looked for a pen to draw my plans. The cloisonné pen was still in the glove compartment. I jotted a few notes and sketched the plan. What is this pen! It writes like I'm driving a luxury car. The ink flows like honey. The pen inspired writing. The pen was carefully placed in a pocket of my purse.

I was reading *The Wooden Horse,* a book about WWII P.O.W.s tunneling beneath a wooden box or "horse". Other men jumped over the horse all day while one dug a tunnel below. The dust they dug was sprinkled from bags inside their pant legs or dumped and shoveled into the garden soil. When Mahon and his friend took an interest in WWII, I called Dad to see if he would tell them his story. During a half-day off school, he sat at his dining room table with the two boys and told his story with amazing detail. Why hadn't I been told the story?

I sat at the far end with a video camera running. Why hadn't I asked before?

Chapter 16: Parachuting Artist

Mac spiraled into his hero's journey with the Navy June 19, 1942, with a kiss-charmed photo of Irene in his pocket, his constant mother's encouragement and a rare paternal handshake. At Iowa State University, he was elated to be flying in giant churning clouds, flying with his eyes in the nose of a plane. He continued his training at Glenview Airbase while Irene graduated from Francis Parker with an art teaching degree. Mac was on top of the world. He had just flown solo his first time, flew and landed on January 1st, 1943. It had been a rocky landing.

"The plane was flying me," he told his friends at dinner. "It might have something to do with I've never driven a car? Don't know how to swim either."

"Why did you enlist in the Navy?" Nate asked.

"It was recommended, but I was misinformed," he replied with regret. The plane landed me too high, I washed out of Navy training." He enlisted with the Army Air Corps on June 1, 1943 and was assigned to Latrobe, Pennsylvania. Mac was later promoted to Lieutenant and stationed near the industrial plumes of Pittsburgh where he spent a month or two in dull, uninspiring mathematics classes.

"As if math was going to get me out of there," he joked with his mother and Irene during their visit. Irene and Bess had driven from Chicago to celebrate her college degree. Irene was applying to United Airlines after Congress cut education funding. Briefly, they'd forgotten a war was going on amidst October's glow of changing leaves. Mac was promoted Commander of a student group. "They found out I was pretty good at navigation," he told them. If the plane's navigation went down, he was trained to guide his plane back home by the northern star constellations. After celebrating, he said goodbye to his mother, then Irene. That was how it was.

In July 1944, Mac was transferred by train to warmer Randolph Field in Texas with the other lieutenants. Train after train passed by, filled with whooping army troops waving hats. Mac was humbled, while being made larger, in the enormousness of the nation's war effort.

In Texas, he and the aviation cadets graduated from flight school on August 7, 1944 with a crisp and orderly ceremony and new knowledge that a *G.I. can* was a garbage can, a *'24* was a B-24, a *Liberator* was a bomber built like a semi. The *C.Q.* was the guy in Charge of Quarters and counting. "Numbers were everything," he said.

Back in my studio, I looked at Mom's *cloisonné* pen in amazement. Gold lines made a pattern, with precious-metal powders sifting between them, blue, sea green, gold and ember red. These had been fused in a kiln with precision timing. A dusting of gold balls in leaf patterns further outlined the intricate design. How was that accomplished with a cylinder and formed around a mahogany pen? Not to worry, the pen wrote like a possessed wizard. Who cared how it was made, the pen streamed ink like liquid gold*!* It seemed to tell me Mom's story.

Every flight was a reminder of Irene's first time flying in a Boeing 307 airplane. It was exhilarating to step up the metal steps of an airplane at Chicago Municipal Airport. Careful not to allow her new Navy heels to poke through the opening of the stairs, she took them on her toes. The four propellers spluttered, coughed like a waking uncle, then caught as each propeller whirred into invisibility. The wooden chocks were being removed from the wheels as the crew stepped back to wave. Irene peeked out the tiny window of the passenger seat to see the grounding crew wave. She fastened her seat belt as the plane was pulled forward by the propellers onto a runway that intersected at its midpoint with another perpendicular airstrip. Speed built as the plane met and used the wind. Flares on either side of the runway blurred away as the air took the plane into its realm of atmosphere. The air lifted the steel bird over downtown Chicago, the rippling Lake Michigan and past flocks of soaring seagulls. It banked left over Grant Park and Navy Pier, then over Garfield Park to head west to pan America.

Irene recalled Mac and their game of spotting planes above and guessing where they were going. The rumbling of the splitting of air spoke to her through her feet. The churning of wires, sparks and pounding pistons filled her head with blinding excitement. The plane entered the clouds. Irene felt alive and one with the plane. It murmured in the gray, bucked and bumped on the turbulence. The captain veered to the left then right to find the smoothest path through the clouds.

Just four years before, a flight to Seattle would have required seven refuel stops. Irene was flying to Los Angeles with one stop in Denver to pick up mail and seven more passengers in about 15 hours. The pressurized cabin system was taken out to all the weight of fuel tanks but that meant the planes flew in the whims of weather and winds. It was not lost on Irene that Mac was training to fly a B-17 adapted from this Boeing 307. Her thrill was uniquely hers, but also tied to what Mac must be experiencing, to what they had dreamed. Just as she was getting up to serve her passengers their meals, her headache hit. Her stomach lurched and a dizziness consumed her thoughts. She remembered where the hot drinks and cups were stored, but the cold sandwiches and eating utensils confounded her as she was knocked nearly over by the turbulence. A passenger was upchucking from the unpressurized cabin and motion sickness; she had been told by the nurse.

"Watch that you don't turn an ankle," the nurse advised. She found the ginger ale and cool compress for his forehead. Though thirty-three seats were lining the curved fuselage of the plane, there were only a dozen passengers. She would get through this.

If Irene looked forward to find the horizon through the pilot's window to calm her stomach, she could hear what was being said on the radio about weather in unlimited visibility.

"Denver is clear with no precipitation." Looking out the passenger windows while delivering drinks gave a vision of the expanse of open farmland sectioned into squares like one of her mother's quilt patterns. The lush valley surrounding the fat, flat Mississippi River twinkled up like the magic of transportation and commerce it offered Midwestern cities. A few tributaries sent rays from this spine of the country. Dust puffs sprung up suddenly from the expanse of fields west of the river. As the dust dissipated tiny dots of bands of bovines ran as if bewitched by their fear of the sound of the four engines and propellers. The swaying billow of dust blocked the sea of grasses indicating wind direction. Imagine Mac and me looking up pointing and guessing "Denver, that one is headed to Denver!" After the metal cups, utensils and plates were stored for washing, the scraps tossed into the bin, Irene looked through the pilot's door to see the Rocky Mountains abruptly rise from the flat vastness. We were already preparing to land! We just flew over what would take three days to drive assuming no flat tires or breakdowns, overheated engines or motion sickness stops.

I remembered Mom's excitement when she drove us to O'Hare Airport to pick up Dad. Even on a school night she would bring a van load of us, park by the doors to United, Pan Am, or Continental and go through the lobby to the waiting room on the second floor above the tarmac where his plane would come to a halt. Everywhere was a playground for us, even in the blinding fluorescent light above the rows of seats. We ran, slid on the waxed floors, went to the bathrooms twice, drank from the water fountains. Mom beamed with her nearness to the adventure of flight. Steel stairs were rolled to the opening of the small jet. Dad was easily spotted ducking through the arched door with his brown paper package under his arm. Sometimes, the guard allowed us to run out to him on the tarmac. His smile was tired from an overseas trip; he watched the controlled chaos of life surround him again. Mom and Dad kissed and hugged. We grabbed his aviator bag between two of us and rumbled around the two of them.

I was reading *The Great Escape,* which revealed how prisoners escaped from Stalag III, Dad's first camp. Intuitively, I trusted my judgment on which facts jumped off the page and which details to skim. These notes I strung together into sentences, paragraphs, pages for Dad to review. That he confirmed my guesses propelled me on to define his experiences. Time ticked like sparks at the end of a fuse. Dad and I shared the intensity of capturing his story while he aged. Ink flowed like hot lava through the pen as I filled notebook after notebook. *Now, his eyes lit up!* It was not so much the verbal response I wrote for; it was the moments he was lost in his memory. That's when I knew I was onto something. That's what kept me writing. The more I wrote, the more I read for the treasure of gems, experiences of what he couldn't tell. I followed the intuitive bread crumbs of an innate memory I hadn't recognized, to discover what he had lived. Dad started to ask for my stories and to remember more of his. He checked my narratives, giving both of us more confidence. When I brought my next section to read, I was nervous to see his reaction.

"So, what have you been writing?" Dad asked.

"I thought you'd never ask." I handed him my notebook. As his story came to life, he relaxed.

After more transport by boats, buses and trains, Mac was stationed in November 1944 at Molesworth, England, north of Cambridge, to navigate B-17 bomber missions over Germany. It took guts to start up the ignition of a plane filled with gasoline and packed with bombs. They accelerated into an intersecting star pattern with eighteen-year-old pilots crisscrossing on take-off. Ten planes lifted off simultaneously into close-flying formations. Battalions flew mission after mission into the breathless hazards of the morning sky. His plane skimmed over a gliding sea far below. Rising sunlight glinted off the tips of patterned whitecaps. Tips or hulls of dark ship carcasses, some with smoky plumes, interrupted the repeated glistening pattern of wind and waves. It wasn't long before he could get a glimpse of Belgium along the horizon. His intercom crackled. "Pilots, check status." "Set," the co-pilot replied. "Set" was repeated by each crew member. Two small aircraft lined the target. The bombardier counted to twenty. The lead bomber dropped his load on the witch-hat shapes that loomed below in stone. Eleven other planes unloaded. Strangers shot at them with cannons of exploding flak. A blackened cloud of rounded metal like feathers dropped at the same diagonal. Forty bombs per plane. Ten planes, seventy-two thousand pounds of explosives, downed. Turn-out in formation. They returned to base. They'd defied the angel of death again. Triumph in life! Exaltation of nearness to death brought everything alive! The smell of grass mixed with burnt fuel.

"Pilots, man your planes!" blared over the speaker, followed by a sound like a giant's jews harp. Everything went as planned. The German Luftwaffe was nearly defeated and Allied planes roamed at will. Mac's 16th mission was with the 303 Bomber Group of the 8th Airforce in a plane called "Red." Like a kid on a first sleepover, he woke with jitters. His battalion was family. He took orders to fly with another Group at 0800. "At attention! Your assignment: fly to Merseberg, Germany. Target Mannheim. Prepare to take over for a visual bomb-run." *Inhale.* "Operation cancelled." *Exhale.*

"Operation resumes." *Inhale.* "Take your place in formation."

In the plane, the co-pilot began the call: "Bomb bays, in the middle." "Set!" A catwalk between the bombs, and the bombardier was in front. "Bombardier." "Set!" He had a bomb sight to look through to mark the target. "Engineer." "Set!" He stood above in the Plexiglas ball on top. "Waste gunner." "Set!" He was on the side, half way back. "Radio operator." "Set!" He sat behind the bomb bay. A Plexiglas sphere underneath the belly, installed with two .50 caliber machine guns and one small framed and nimble. "Short ball gunner." "Set!" This gunner revolved, like a fetus in a womb, tracking fighter planes below with spiraling rapid fire. "Tail gunner." *"Set!"* Tail and Waste Gunners lined the fuselage. Ten men dressed in heavy leather jackets with fleece lining, electric suits and boots. "Navigator." "Set!" Mac plugged his suit into the unheated Plexiglas nose of the plane.

For courage, they sang: "Off we go into the wild blue yonder, climbing high into the sun. Here they come, zooming to meet our thunder. At 'em boys, give 'er the gun! (give 'er the gun now!) Down we dive, spouting our flame from under. Off with one heckuva roar! We live in fame, or go down in flames. Hey! Nothing'll stop the U.S. Air Force!"

Four engine planes ascended in tight box formation for maximum mutual protection from their machine guns, at a slow climb to a five-mile height. After flying low over the glistening sea, they climbed to frigid heights of ten thousand feet and donned oxygen masks and head phones. High enough to parachute out if the mission didn't go so well. No matter what—stay in formation. Often, Mac navigated while blinded by a vapor trail. The B-17 Flying Fortress, in close formation to an initial point, turned and banked down into the target. Bombardiers shifted into alertness. They counted to twenty. The lead plane dropped its bombs. Then, the planes behind dropped theirs. The sky blackened with bombs like broken rosary beads falling in diagonal lines. Precision bombing often missed. Some by a long shot. Bomber wings threw out thirty tons of steel a minute. American precision bombing only happened in daylight, which caused huge losses of airplanes and men.

Fatigue was setting in, the cold was exhausting. One plane in formation exploded. Another dove into tail spin, then righted and turned back to base. Flak shells burst all around. More flak exploded. They were getting close to the target. How could so many shells miss? Thunk! one struck. Bursts of explosions surrounded their plane named Red. Shrapnel pierced the thin metal. Above and below, steely calm voices called in the headsets. "Set," Mac called back from the nose. A shell pierced the belly of the plane, and burst ten feet above.

The target was near! The bombardier lined things up and counted into the headsets. Targets were sighted exactly. "Bombs Away!" the bombardier called. Bombs darkened the sky in diagonal charcoaled clouds. Flak exploded. Mac recalled when shrapnel hit his chest, slicing the speaker cord. He couldn't respond, "Set!" They didn't hear his repeated "Bombs Away!" and turned out of formation for the long trek home to find out it was merely a cut speaker cord. Another of his fifteen flights, he nearly passed out when his goggles slid under an edge of the oxygen mask mouthpiece. Woozy, not knowing, panic consumed him. Then, he shifted his mask. Regained his equilibrium. "Set!" he called back to the co-pilot's ten-minute check. The tail gunner was frantically firing. The squadron banked sharp right. Mac sited the plumes as targets. "Bomb's away!" was called. Bombs dropped. Shells lit up with an eerie green light that reflected in the falling snow. The formation continued to drop, then turned. Red was hit in the bomb bay. Smoke filled the plane. The instrument panel was obliterated with smoke and frost. The pilot turned Red out of formation. Red's right oxygen was out at twenty-five thousand feet. Anoxia took effect. Fatigue and exhaustion permeated the crew. Breathe, relax, keep your wits about you. Red took a hit under the turret chin. Ammunition exploded. Smoke filled the cockpit.

Flake Dyson, the engineer, was blown out of the fuselage and from turret position, ending up between co-pilots Jack Rose and John Cornyn. Then came the worst hit. In the right wing, behind engine number four. Flak left holes throughout the plane. The first warning bell rang. Chutes were grabbed. Flak suits removed. The explosions were deafening without the headphones. Red's crew prepared for bail-out. Mac was tying his boot. The ship nosedived in a spin. Mac faced down, spinning against his harness straps. He'd hit first of all the men, but only after a five mile drop. Keep your wits about you. "Our father, who art in heaven, hallowed be Thy name…" No one could parachute out. The force was too great. Wings turned over. "Thy kingdom come Thy will be done on earth as it is in heaven." He was whiplashed like the tail in crack the whip. "As we forgive those who trespassed against us…" Red wasn't responding to controls. Rose throttled back on engines one and two. The ship righted. "Navigator!" came in through the headsets. "Set!" Mac gave him a heading. We might make it! If only the fire blows out, we might make it! he thought. Second bell sounded. "Prepare to abandon ship."

Thought left. Mac's training kicked in. Fire in the wing was now burning near the waist gunner. It might blow out. By proper procedure, Mac was the first one out of the plane. He left the .45 pistol. "I'm not going to shoot my way out of Germany," he decided. The silk map of German terrain was pocketed. The bell rang. He kicked out the escape hatch. Mac looked through the flak and clouds four miles above the forest. The fire, the explosions, lack of oxygen, the guys behind, *God!* Mac jumped. "Jesus, Mary and Joseph, spare me," his cry exploded, in subzero air. Mac gasped a thin breath in a two-hundred-mile-per-hour whooshing blast. Frigid air kept him from passing out. Free fall amidst intense explosion, accurate flak. "One-one-thousand." Shrapnel sliced at his coat and face. "Two-one-thousand." Blood froze. "Three-one-thousand." Tears froze. "Four-one-thousand." Focus on the D-ring. Ach! Mac remembered those guys at Fort Meyers who'd packed them. Did the guy pack this chute right? Need oxygen—don't pass out. Focus. "Five-one-thousand." Guys free fall 10,000 feet for oxygen. Don't wait. Got to know if this will open. Clear Red. "Six-one-thousand, seven-one-thousand…eight-one thousand." Pull the D-ring! The parachute, Mae West they called it, unraveled in his face, hitting his nose, cheeks and ears. Silk straps flapped, slapped his cut face. A tremendous jolt stopped him silently amidst exploding flak.

Time passed slowly, and Mac floated within muffled detonations. The plane had dropped closer to oxygen. He could breathe. *Get your wits together.* Shroud lines were pulled to aim his landing. *My foot is frozen. No boot! No sock! Keep your wits!* He descended through the icy smoke, passed the smell of scorched metal. Cold humidity rose. Thin scents of farms, hay, manure. Winter forests and frozen streams outlined the Earth with whiffs of evergreens and wet, cold stones. Hearth fires triggered his longing for family. Tears of relief, and a strange joy. Vague memories churned of desire, home, warmth and food. A stew was being cooked in the village.

Chapter 17: Captured

Mac landed in broad daylight in a snowy soccer field in Pirmasens, Germany. Citizens, police, kids and stray dogs saw him and he saw them. They ran towards him shouting, *terrorflieger*! A "terror flyer." Frozen and scared, Mac struggled to release the parachute harness then sprinted with one wet foot. Woozy, Mac scrambled up a hill. Fast through the snow... Hide. There's a cave. They're not following.

In the cave, Mac ripped the inside of his jacket sleeve and stuffed the silk map and photo up higher behind his elbow. He knew that German propaganda ministers dropped leaflets from planes through the streets alerting civilians to report "any Allied air force soldiers." If caught by citizens, they might pull Mac apart limb from limb. Keep your wits about you. Wait for the guards. German soldiers arrived and Mac was hauled away.

Mac was marched past a red brick town hall with a towering clock. Soldiers who captured an officer knew their job was to get their prisoner to an interrogator. The soldiers barked commands in German, escalating Mac's fear.

The Germans had also captured co-pilots Jack Rose and John Cornyn. Cornyn's .45 pistol was confiscated by a *Hauptmann*, a Captain, an imposing figure.

"Gangster pistol," he said with a heavy accent.

Only one of Red's airmen—also captured—spoke German. On the plane, he had listened to the radio and told others what the broadcasts were saying. He told Mac that the airmen were considered *Kriegsgefangeners*, prisoners of war. After Red was crippled and flaming, Cornyn had decided to ditch the plane. One guy jumped, then another, then another. They landed spread out in various clearings or outcroppings. Two or three were captured nearby. None of them showed recognition of each other.

The POWs were marched through Bavarian-styled blocks of buildings on cobbled sidewalks of various colored four-story homes. Mac's heightened awareness of his surroundings inspired awe. Led by rifles in single file past medieval Romer and St Nicholas church, Mac felt the depth of history of this thousand year-old architecture.

In front of an armed guard, Mac didn't acknowledge his fellow airmen, nor did they show him recognition as they were marched through the center of the once medieval city center leveled by bombs. Trees were ripped to splintered shards next to crumbled stones with low walls that were once homes. A horrified pit rose in Mac's stomach. What was this war? Why are we here? No one showed any emotion. None of the prisoners talked to each other. Leafless trees and trunks were black with wet snow. The roads were cleared of cars and pedestrians for jeeps, troops, POWs and artillery to move through. Mac remembered what H.G. Wells had written of what a tank might look like. "In that flickering pallor, it had the effect of a large and clumsy black insect, an insect the size of an ironclad cruiser, crawling obliquely to the first line of trenches and firing shots out of portholes in its side." Not fear of the Third Reich, nothing, prepared Mac for the imposing Tiger Tanks as they rolled between beamed, double gables with colored stucco. Giant turret guns tipped into the sky from sleek, precision killing-machines on rotating tracks. Mac was awestruck with fear. Allied soldiers faced these engineering feats with .45s and war-torn gear.

Red's crew was transported into Frankfurt by train and then by tram to nearby *Durchgangslager der Luftwaffe* or *Luftwaffe Dulag Luft*, for collection. From previous bombings, framework metal was twisted and shards of glass fell from the canopy onto platforms and tracks. Angry civilians shouted, "*Luftgangster!*" ("Gangster") and "Murderer" in German and English. Outside, troops of German soldiers marched in unison, like automatons, down what was left of the cobblestone streets. Expressionless German soldiers marched in step; the loud, steady rhythm of boots rained down heavily on hard stones. Everything about them gleamed: buttons, boots, those metal coal-scuttled hats. Their blank stares were scarier than the rifles slung over their shoulders.

Mac and the crew were transported via a twenty-minute tram to Oberusel. After being given his new ID card and fingerprinted, Mac was put into a tiny six-feet by six-feet cement cell with fleas for company. At Auswertestelle West, the Interrogation and Evaluation Center, interrogations were carried out: temperature fluctuations and solitary confinement. The air carried the odor of a pail in the corner of the cell that served as a bathroom. A small opaque window, never opened, allow almost no light. Only a single lightbulb hung from the ceiling and burned day and night. Exhausted, the men slept fitfully on a flea-infested straw mattress. Meager meals were delivered by German staff. From time to time, they were taken to an interrogator, who spoke perfect English and greeted them warmly. In the meantime, Mac paced three feet back and forth with his shoeless foot colder than the other. He wore the same clothes he had been shot down in, and that would not change for many weeks.

Guards clicked the heat on and "forgot" it was on; the cells were extremely hot for hours before they switched it off again. Mac learned that this was the *Luftwaffe*, not the SS, the hated "rival." *Luftwaffe* interrogators were "polite," and in the early days, took some POWs to the local bar, for walks in the mountains and even called home for some of them. The master interrogator there used a form of "kindness" rather than torture to get what he wanted.

Mac stomped about in his cell as he grappled with the moral complexities of war. Holy Mary, Mother of God. Pray for our sins… Mac mentally listed his belongings: one boot, the map, a blanket, an empty canteen, his coat, his pants, his prayers. POW 9324 William F. McMahon, 2nd Lieutenant of the Army Air Corp, 02065589. Name, rank and serial number were all they would get from him.

Generals called this a war of nerves. Guards tried to make him uncomfortable. The nuns at his childhood St. Itas entered his consciousness, repeating, "*Do not kill.*" The "etiquette" of war didn't make sense to Mac. He had not fired a shot at a person. Was I excused in God's eyes from murder? What was war about? Anger arose within Mac. Everyone at home was comfortable. Why was I here alone, trapped, hungry?

With an imaginary pencil, Mac captured the look, the likeness, that strange wildness in his guard's eyes. Draw it again. Thickness to thinness of line gave depth to nostrils, eye corners, ears. This kept the committee of a thousand voices and fears at bay. Mac sketched for a tomorrow he could not yet see. Strength, purpose and true faith emerged from those dark shadows by tracing likenesses in his memory. In between interrogations Mac gathered more details for mind-drawing. He checked his proportions. Insights into gestures and expressions kept him observing intently. The drawing gave a purpose to his unearthly hell.

The cell door rattled open and a guard took Mac to be interrogated. He was greeted with, "Come in, I am your interrogator," by a tall man in an immaculate blue Luftwaffe uniform. He spoke perfect English, having lived in the U.S. before the war. He offered Mac a cigarette and smoked one himself. He spread out folders and papers on his desk. Mac sat across from him on a chair.

The interrogator knew about the plane, Red, where it crashed and more facts about Red's crew than Mac knew. He knew Mac's parent's names, where he went to high school, and where the military trained him. His questions to Mac were answered by only name, rank, and serial number, but Mac had to hide his astonishment at what the man knew and wondered how he knew it.

"What was his target?" the interrogator asked. "What kind of bombs were you carrying? What do you know about the Norden bombsight?"

Mac was not forthcoming, so he was returned to his cell.

Back in his cell, Mac made images with no pencil or paper; it organized and calmed his mind. Unlike most men who looked outward, Mac had a way of looking inward to reflect the impressions that this astonishing world flung upon him. He was determined to look closer and closer at his surroundings, then reflect as he processed an impression of himself from within.

Dulag Luft days tested Mac's hard-earned endurance. He had parachuted into a place at the bottom of Dante's Inferno, to the bottom of life itself. Repetition in tasks made a new world order. He was taken to his interrogator again.

"Why are you fighting against Germany? You should not even be in this war."

Name rank and serial number—careful. After a few more "soft" interrogations, a guard arrived to take Mac to the transition center where he joined other prisoners who had finished their interrogations. The Red Cross served a hot meal. Mac was able to shower and sleep in a bed.

Mac was presented his first Red Cross Packet parcel that was eaten before he left the center. He and Red's crewmembers were marched to the train station with over a hundred other prisoners for a three-day train trip to Stalag Luft III in Sagan, Poland. At the train station, they parted with their enlisted waist gunner, who was sent to an enlisted men's camp.

They took the tram to the Frankfurt train station, where Hitler Youth sang spirited marching songs until they saw the airmen and started yelling lewd obscenities with all the hatred they could rally.

The air raid siren blasted the icy air. The officer-prisoners were strong-armed into a bomb shelter by guards. Allied planes dropped their payload. Screaming avalanches shadowed the terrified crowd racing for cover. The station shook, glass cascaded, then tinkled. Explosions pierced their eardrums. Walls vibrated and crumbled and Mac looked upward. *We could be buried alive!* Screams, moans, howls and sobs erupted then, and roaring loudness reverberated. Furious, panicked, civilians dove into the shelter. The *kriegies* huddled, trembling, tightly cramped with the Germans. Not every German felt good about Hitler, but hatred for Allied airmen fueled the villagers' stares directed at the American troublemakers that bombed civilians. Mac squirmed. Everything was inaudible. His eyes adjusted to the dark, and he glanced about, momentarily deaf, but aware.

An indigo-eyed nine-year-old boy in a Hitler Youth uniform stared at Mac. A row of stoic, uniformed boys, one straw-blonde with sapphire eyes, one white-blonde with azure eyes, a cerulean-eyed platinum blonde and another with sandy hair and cyan eyes staunchly poised on a bench. The boy shared his anxiety. They shared the silence. No one could hear.

Mac found being a *kriegie* demoralizing. An overwhelming hopelessness settled in his heart. Hope was only a dim shadow tucked in a far dark corner of this crumbling confines. At first, it was easy for Mac to sit back and follow orders. The "promise" of survival numbed any instinct to escape. The captors kept a close eye on their prized officers, each a potential fount of information. The prodding, poking, and commanding resumed when the air raid siren went silent. The boys were harshly commanded to leave their shelter first. One spit at the *kriegies.* Citizens were directed to leave next. Prisoners were then prodded by pointy rifles.

Mac jumped down from the big, hissing train at Sagan station onto frozen stones. His eyes took time to adjust to the gray clouded haze. Mac was taken to a room at the station and given a blanket. With foreboding, the *kriegies* filed past a tall lean brick guard house where their IDs were checked. They slogged up the sandy road for a quarter mile to the camp. Tall trees planted in symmetrical rows lined the road like sentinels secreting a pleasant pine smell as they witnessed their captivity. Through the pines Mac got a view of the camp as he passed the ten-foot rustic fence made of split pine saplings nailed closely together leading ahead to the main gate. A huge Crimson sign emblazoned with a black *swastika* hung limply from a pole near the *Vorlager,* the German administrative building, a small hospital, and cooler at the entrance of the camp. Through the enormous gate on his left, Mac could see clusters of green-gray weathered barracks, a barbed wire fence and elevated wooden guard towers. Stumpy trunks sat between the maze of barbed wire between compounds and the forest. Guards swung open the gate and peremptorily checked papers. The cluster of men were paraded through with low spirits as the gate shut abruptly behind them.

Warily, Mac looked around at his compound, three hundred yards with two fences about ten feet high and five feet apart around it. Each fence was strung with twenty closed strands of rusted barbed wire. About fifty yards behind those fences stood the "goon-boxes" on stilts fifteen feet high, with guards behind with search lights, machine guns and phones. German guards pointed their weapons from towers in greeting. Thirty feet inside the barbed wire was a warning wire about eighteen inches high. Everything was gray. Gray earth and aged barracks, gray clothes and worn floors. New *kriegies* were herded into a forecourt of a stark one-story building. Each man was led in for processing and given a metal identification tag stamped "Stalag Luft III" and his POW number. The men showered and were dusted for fleas and lice from a Nescafe can punched with holes over a cold water pipe. Mac was issued bedding—a thin wool blanket, one sheet, one mattress filled with wood shavings, one pillowcase, one small linen towel and one pillow filled with straw. Also, a two-quart mixing bowl, one cup, knife, fork, spoon, given once and not replaced; all tied with a cotton string in a knot. This, the silk map still up his sleeve, and his clothes, minus one boot, was Mac's list of items owned.

Mac tossed his mattress and pillow onto the wooden surface. It was more of a wooden shelf built of four-by-fours, three platforms high. He saw the other POWs had woven together pads of scavenged paper, like scout campfire pads, to cover the straw mattress. That first night, with the stoves flickering, he considered what he'd become in two short weeks. *Will my foot fester with infection?* Listening to the conversations around the stove, Mac picked up a burnt stick. Unconsciously, he sketched the faces across from him with the burnt tip on the wooden floor.

So many bodies in one room barely warmed the drafty, cold night. Days and time swirled in the gray freezing murkiness. The corner stove was not enough to warm the barracks.

"Hey, do you have a smoke?" Barney asked a guy by the fire. No one ever did. That was the way it was. The blankets were not long enough or warm enough. A distant owl hooted. Mac slept.

Aufstechen! Like a stone, the foreign command fell to the bottom of his soul. Chilled gusts of winter blew into his Silesian barrack. The illusion of a warm blanket and night's sleep shattered around him. Mac learned to eat to live rather than live to eat, with his heart melting as he spread Red Cross orange marmalade over torn bread slabs. Bread seemed huge in another's hand. His own, tiny enough to make him quiver. If he traded his ration, the illusion was inverted: his portion was undersized and the other was generous. Dawn offered glimmers of color. Distant artillery explosions looked like summer heat lightening with no thunder. Rumbles reverberated over the hills. Then shot were heard nearby. Mac's arm was knocked while in line.

"Hand over the frickin' map. We'll show you the ropes and give you some work."

"I need my map," Mac said.

"Just give us the frickin' map. You'll get it back, if you're lucky."

"Do you have a left boot? Size nine." Mac said.

"We'll get you a frickin' boot, just give us the frickin' map."

"I want it back. And a sock," Mac said.

With an ill-fitting worn boot, Mac was welcomed into the smoke-filled room of the underground political system that had been organized into an intricate pattern of underground patronage and cunning. Carl Holmstrom handed out YMCA art supplies. He heard the twelve surviving Tuskegee airmen were divvied up in different barracks including Lt. Alexander Jefferson from Detroit. What would be called the Lost Airmen of Buchenwald had told their story that traveled through the barracks. Barney gabbed about the seventy-six escapees from Stalag Luft III via an elaborate tunnel, civilian clothes and false identifications.

"That's where our slats went—to shore up the sandy tunnel," he said. To prove it, Barney and Mac fought the biting cold to visit a stone memorial built to honor the 50 murdered escapees from the *Great Escape*, as signed on a cartoon by 1st Lt. Alex Cassie.

Mac nurtured his compassion. He drew ideas for cartoons, which he mailed back to *Extensions* magazine in Chicago that somehow bypassed the censors. He drew a guard, then another and another. Reality was restored, purpose achieved, freedom in art discovered. His heart and soul relaxed.

The *Reveille* sounded as the first signs of a rose-colored dawn arose from distant knolls. Mac was awake in his bunk. *Well, I'm alive.* He wasn't dead, but he wasn't alive. For a few moments at waking, that's when the soul lives, when a moment of something enjoyable entered existence. It was better not to think of something I love. The early bird gets the worm. Mac jumped up, dressed, tightened the cotton string on his newish boot. It snapped. He adjusted paper pads in his jacket to keep the cold from penetrating. Pencils and a razor, strips of metal fashioned into a fork and a spoon. A wayward wire threaded his boot eyelets over its tongue that pinched his arch. He loosened the wire. The razor, mirror, bar of soap were wrapped in a cloth. These were his daily count of possessions. He stepped into the dawn besieged already by barking commands, inciting spasms of oppositional defiance. The rush to the latrine with hundreds of men panicked before *bread-brot-broid-lechem-keyner* was distributed. If you've ever known hunger—real hunger, then you'll understand our lack of contentment with German hospitality.

"If Germany loses the war, Hitler's orders are to shoot you all," the guard said.

Mac's purpose of drawing cartoons helped him stay human. Compassion sprung from observation. During those long days, weeks and months his purpose was to capture a likeness of each and every *Fuehrer,* goon, *Unteroffizier, Grenzpolizei, Kommandant* and "ferret" he could portray. In the moments they weren't looking, he caught expressions in the stroke of a pencil line on coarse paper. He snagged expressions made solid in lines of what was neither hidden nor lost. By looking closer at a German, he saw a humanity in the men that were missing their families.

Mac barely had time to dry his ink wash when they were alerted to a possible relocation. The humming of ten thousand men in five compounds of quiet activity with distant intervals of artillery exchanges awakened the chilly wind. Drawings were organized, exchanged, and packed in tin boxes.

By January 20th, the POWs could hear Russian guns firing. By January 25th, the camp's loudspeakers reported the Russians had advanced through Poland and were 48 miles from Sagan. That the Red Cross distributed two D-bars, a quarter pound of cheese, half a pound of oatmeal, half a loaf of bread and sugar indicated they would be evacuated soon.

It's only me... Mac started a letter to Irene asking for her hand in marriage. He carefully folded his allotted 24 lines of airmail weight paper and addressed it to 421 Central Park, Chicago, Illinois, USA with a licked 40 *pfennig* stamp. From the west, a louder, sustained artillery exploded. Lightning-like explosions merged at twilight. Large machines rumbled the vibrating ground. Windows rattled. Thousands of feet above Mac, in the blue spaces between gray clouds, the complex hope of aerial duels filled the skies. High above, helpless and unarmed comrades sought reciprocal death with the most precise and refined machines of destruction the world had ever known. Mac listed his gains every morning: two short pencils, three scraps of paper, four sticks of charcoal, a short wire, a role of string, seven rubber-bands, a blanket, coat, pants, three socks, a shirt, a flat-edged razor for shaving and a bar of soap, four packs of cigarettes, a toothbrush and comb, drawings. Russian tanks could be heard in the distance, then their bullets.

Mac's Red Cross parcel arrived in a caravan of white trucks. The prisoners knew Red Cross parcels came from the neutral country of Switzerland. *Moses can talk about manna all he wants.* He's never tasted anything like a D-bar. Mac listed again its contents in his head like a mantra whenever his hunger hankered: 8 oz. raisins, 10 oz. salmon, 4 oz. cheese, 2 oz. tinned milk, 15 oz. marmalade, 5 oz. of sardines, 6 oz. prunes, 1 oz. each salt/pepper, 6 oz. chocolate, tea, 6 oz. sugar, 20 oz. biscuits, 20 oz. butter, 13 oz. Spam, 1 tablet of soap. And always a big chocolate D-bar bar—bitter chocolate with nuts. Jelly, bread, Klim (milk spelled backwards), cigarettes, soap. He folded his returned silk map and slipped it in his sleeve. Everything was useful—a wire to lace shoes, and paper to weave a pad to insulate a jacket. These precious crafted utensils were squirreled into jacket pockets, slept on and inventoried every morning. Mac listed what he could eat and what he could pack for trade: *cigarettes, pepper, biscuits and soap accessible on top.*

On January 27th, Berlin sent a notice the prisoners were to be evacuated immediately. Colonel Goodrich interrupted the South Compound's theater production "You Can't Take it With You" to say the goons announced they had thirty minutes to pack their things and be at the gate.

"Things could get worse before they get better," he said. "We leave at 11:00 p.m."

"Hey, you got a smoke?" Barney had been in sick bay. "Looks like we're headed out." Mac was relieved Barney would be making the long one-day march. Thinning hair caught in the teeth of Mac's new comb.

"It must be the soap," he half-joked.

South Compound *kriegies* left at 11:00 p.m. and Mac's West Compound followed at 1:00 a.m. on January 28th. It took eight hours to evacuate the whole camp. Flanking guards had counted ten thousand men who filed out of Stalag III.

Mac and his fellow *kriegies* were marched south then west out the gates of the gray camp into two feet of drifting snow followed by two dogs and a horse-drawn cart of brown bread. Be careful what you wish for, it could get worse. A grim trip lay ahead. Every thirty minutes, the column stopped to adjust bedrolls and packs. In a few hours, half-loaves of bread were issued to ease the gasping horses' load. Mac moved the Red Cross jelly, biscuit mix and cigarettes on top of his pack. He traded these with the *volks* along the way for eggs and vegetables. Don't confuse the volks with the volkisch, or racial-nationalists who shaped the perpetrators. Mac marched a fifteen-hour day and tasted the freshest provisions he'd eaten since becoming a *kriegie*. In the night, they trudged through Hermsdorf and the tiny village of Halbau.

Mac perceived the want and sorrow that rushed over the outside world like a deluge. The narrow road wound through Barau, Friewaldau and turned west to the larger town of Priebus. His exchange with refugees moving from the Russian army offered connection with people other than prisoners. They were hungry, too. This is the best food I've had since I landed in Germany. His woolen sock was his main concern. It kept embedding in the numb blister at the back of his heel. The sock ripped open scabs each night. Tomorrow I'll try a piece of cotton undershirt between the sock and the foot.

Mac's first leg of March in frigid cold weather allowed little rest because the intense cold froze their sweat to chilling ice. A long rest might freeze his trousers to the road surface. South Compound men, a mile-long column, had trampled the snow ahead of West Compound. We'll cross that bridge when we get to it. Mac's replacement boot didn't fit well but was merely troublesome up to then. Fifteen hours of daily trudging pinched his toes and chafed at his insole to the ball of his foot. Painful sores blistered. Might get fatally infected. The boot opened the blistering wounds every morning; they bled all day. Thank God I packed soap. Frostbite threatened and frozen bread couldn't be eaten.

Mac hadn't received a response from Irene. Had she received my marriage proposal? Had her response gotten mailed to Stalag III? Would she agree? I wish I'd never sent it. He fought the worry to sustain his optimism. Drawings were in his right sleeve with his silk map. The men marched further and further toward an unknown camp, hoping it was better than the last. The line stretched out like an accordion. Items that became too heavy to carry were discarded along the littered trail. Men marched in small groups at a leisurely rate, trading along the way. Mac shivered in the biting cold during silent reflections while marching. One meal of barley soup each day was inadequate. Trading cigarettes for eggs was Mac's lifesaver. Snow was their water source. Just being outside of the fence was tougher. Ghostly shadows of German refugees joined his evacuation march from to Sternberg in brutal cold. Article Seven of the Geneva Convention that said no prisoner should be marched more than twelve-and-a-half-miles a day was broken.

In Sternberg, they boarded a cramped boxcar train to Nuremberg that was even more difficult and colder than the march. Their day-long train traveled through Dresden a couple weeks before it was destroyed. Mac heard that Allied forces were closing in. His train stopped near the

Nuremberg station where Mac disembarked on frozen gravel by the tracks. "*Fertig machen!*" [Get Ready!] older guards ordered, counted, and urged on tired, starving *kriegies*, who helped carry the elder guards' loads who said "*Muede, muede!*" [tired].

Chapter 18: A New Lease on Life

Every morning, "*Raus! Raus! Appell! Appell!*" German *unteroffiziers* belted commands. Officers filed from the filthy barracks, squared up in five appells, in rows of ten by ten men, to make hundreds of prisoners into quadrangles on exercise areas surrounded by frozen mud. The German *obergefreiter* went down the rank and counted: *eins, zwei, drei* and so forth… One morning, an officer announced: "I think we have a bad boy here!" Orders were momentarily silenced. The senior officer checked the number against the German guard's, and the count began again. Sometimes the POWs would not come to order quickly and that was when an escape had taken place. Prisoners wanted to delay the guards to give the escapee a head start. Mac was never sure what happened to that guy. Probably got the cooler. He wasn't sure what happened to Barney, either. Maybe escaped along the road?

"*Eins, zwei, drei...*" The POWs disrupted the count, so it began again. Grayish blocks of freezing men endured. Bone-whipping wind blew through him. The cold dried their will into wispy leaves. They stomped in place in cesspools from overflowing latrines, exhausted muscles gripping them with pain. The hypnosis of endless rhythms deadened into this monstrous rite . . . *einhundert, einhundert eins, einhundret zwei . . .* They stripped wood from the latrines to burn for warmth. Mac's entire barracks shared one loaf of brown bread with sawdust filler each day. Everything they had needed washing. In warm weather, he slept outside. The radio informed them the Russians had reached Sagan camp by February 16th and that General Eisenhower told Patton his plan, "to halt the First and Ninth Armies to await the Red Army. Patton's Third Army would drive south, liberating camps while conquering German territory, to Czechoslovakia."

There wasn't enough soap to keep clean—not the clothes, not the barracks, not the POWs. Skin diseases pustuled. Scabies resulted from burrowing mites that bit relentlessly. Nightly rituals of pinching lice from clothing seams filled their evenings. Bartered soap and coveted razors filled their days and conversations. The guys bartered or shared weekly Red Cross packaged food. It was every man for himself. Mac's demeanor transformed when his map revealed how close the Allied soldiers were. The constantly monitored radios shared daily changes. Friendly Allied fighter planes flew over the camp regularly. Mac could hear Allied tanks rumbling across the field. The goons left the watch towers. A jet plane thundered overhead. The bellow shook the whole camp. Mac dove into a muddy, hastily dug trench—he had never heard a jet fighter. He tried to convince himself this overcrowded filthy camp was better than being shot at in the air.

After his colonel complained about the conditions of one hundred calories a day, they were evacuated from the camp, which was within three kilometers of a bombing target, the Nuremberg train station, and that defied the Geneva Convention. The POW request was to march the men to Switzerland while influenza and pneumonia ran rampant. April 4th, 1945, Stalag XIIID was evacuated and the *kriegies* marched for a couple days with weakened bodies, hunger and heavy packs until delirium descended. Mac watched while Allied P-47s dive bombed a freight marshaling yard while the column of POWs passed, killing two American and a British airman; he counted his lucky stars. They were transferring to VIIA.

The everlasting sun shone its blinding brilliance from a resplendent blue sky onto the white, reflective puddles of wet snow. Sunspots pierced their yellow-skinned headaches. Red noses were runny above wet shoes and feet. Mac jumped into ditches when the Army Air Corps and German fighters swooped over and sprayed fire. From behind, friendly fire bullets rained down alongside the gray-faced marchers from fighter planes that splashed Mac with slimy mud. Still, the friendly fire was a reminder that the war's end was near. The Germans knew they had lost the war. Men were nearly hit, the landscape blasted. Continual icy rains turned the rotting earth into slime. It decomposed his socks into slippery webs that pulled the pickled flesh from his feet. His ears were still ringing from the gun blasts. Fatigue ruled. His body is not his own.

Through the fuzzy, blinding, cold rainy mist, Mac saw a Todt worker, just a boy in ragged clothes, crawl into a garden for a leftover potato or perhaps a spring garlic. Just under the fence, the boy collapsed. He laid there, thin, wasted and covered in squirming vermin. That poor boy couldn't feel the lice and maggots crawling in his hair, over his eyelids and down his face. To do this to mere boys! That was the way it was. A hungry German soldier caught a feral cat by the tail. The cat wailed meaaaaAAW! Then screamed MEAAAAAW as the soldier whipped it around to hit its head against a tree trunk. Loud, childlike echos of meaaws reverberated through the twilight. The cat had been decapitated.

"Pass' auf, pass' auf," the guards shouted. Someone had run. Guns fired. Keep your eyes peeled! Mac cautioned himself. Mac marched with his favorite guards. Their camaraderie was forming at the end of the war; a blending of German and English was used for jokes. Both German guards and American prisoners knew it could be every man for himself. Germans hopes were to become an American, rather than a Russian prisoner. Of the rest of his comrades, seventy percent were sick. Each had shaved off thirty pounds with no spare weight from the start. Men collapsed. Some, merely missing. Maybe escaped? Maybe shot? Mac's group settled onto a damp pile of hay beside a barn for the night.

He felt his inner sleeve for his heart's compass, a cryptic, military-anodyne telegram from Irene, "I'll see you in my dreams," and his silk map. Keep your wits about you. He peered at the sky for his location in the universe and inward for his heart's guiding purpose. Stars were his pilots in space and time. The night sky was a calendar, tides and seasons, day and night, dreams and visual reminders of an essential harmony and values that transcended culture. Star patterns let him know he was headed southeast. Mac cleaned his raw foot in a small pond. The reflection of Orion's Belt briefly shone its twinkling brilliance from a dark moonless sky confirming he was headed southeast. No radios informed them that Allied Forces had crossed the Rhine. They didn't know Patton had pissed in the river as the

Third Army surged towards them. They trailed onward. Himmler's orders were to be eliminated from possibility of war crime's testimony by utilizing both exhaustion and hunger.

They marched to Stalag VIIA at Moosberg that would land Mac close to the gas chambers at Dachau. Once the column reached Moosberg, they trudged another half mile through another gate that smelled like a stockyard. Horse stalls, barns, and a sixty-foot toilet trench greeted them. Mid-April, Stalag III's West Compound from Nuremberg entered a camp that was beyond its breaking point. Mac was led to a desolate wire enclosure with two empty sheds and only floor space they dubbed "The Snake Pit." Overcrowding, cold and mud was their new reality in barracks for two hundred men filled with four hundred *kriegies*. Stalag VIIA camp, a Werhmacht, held over 120,000 international POWs in a facility originally made to hold ten thousand. The luxurious relief was Mac had his first warm shower with soap. Mac learned to channel his rage into stoicism.

"About face! March!" In the barracks, spare possessions and fitted bunks were shamefully inspected. The overcrowding was so severe many men slept on the floor where walking through the barracks was treacherous. In the middle of the night on April 12th, a prisoner woke to wind his watch and checked the time on the BBC. President Roosevelt had died. President Harry S. Truman was announced Commander in Chief. April 15th, a VIIA memorial service was held. On April 22nd a new Allied Agreement was accepted, but the German told the *kriegies* to line up at the gate on April 23rd. Lt. Colonel Clark said, "You'd better check, there's been a new deal, and we ain't going."

Mac focused to conserve his strength. Patton's Third Army continued their drive as Allied aircraft whizzed over the camp continuously, some doing barrel rolls. The guards' visceral anxiety skyrocketed. Some became friendlier hoping for American supporters. Mac was one of the 120,000 prisoners in the camp. One of 14,891 Americans. One of 300 Chicagoans. Allied tanks skirmished to the west. Russian tanks resounded from the east. Keep your wits about you.

On April 27th, tanks were on the crest of the hill north of Moosberg. On April 28th, it rained all day, but American fighters flew over VIIA waggling their wings, dipping dangerously into the camp. Allied soldiers went out into the fields around the camp. Germans were required to submit an unconditional surrender to be attacked at 9:00 a.m. Germans left in trucks during the night of the 28th. On April 29th at 6:00 a.m., the men heard booms of heavy cannons and guns nearby. Germans blew up two bridges over the Isar River. By 9:45 a.m., *kriegies* were gathered for church service at 10:00. Planes flew over with rapid fire and chatter of machine guns. The ground shook with one collective THUD from thousands of prisoners hitting the ground at the same time. Bullets zinged through the camp. At 10:00, two American P-51s roared low shooting up the camp. Guards shot back from towers. Allied planes spit bullets that ripped the wooden guard tower to shreds. Two mortar shells landed in Moosberg. *Kriegies* dove into trenches and fox holes below strafing. SS troops fiercely battled for Moosberg in the woods, then demanded German guards to join them. The guards refused. SS threw grenades into the guards barracks, killing some. Most of the SS were shot on the road and in the fields, some were brought to a lazaretto. Miraculously, no *kriegie* was seriously injured. Camoflauged Sherman tanks of General George Patton's Third Army came over the northwest hills at 11:00 a.m. Puffs of smoke rose from their tanks. The American 14th Armored Infantry Division of the U.S. Third Army was nicknamed "The Liberators." The celebration in VIIA was explosive.

Grown men cried. Complete chaos ensued with thousands of men shouting, praying, laughing, hugging and dancing with unrestrained joy. K rations and C rations were passed around by tank drivers. They were overcome with great emotion so long pent up. By 12:30 p.m, Old Glory was hoisted up the flagpole. The American Flag was raised on the church steeples of St. Kastulus at the edge of camp. Eight thousand American kriegies came to attention at the church and saluted. Mac entered the church doors to give thanks.

American Army troops and Red Cross nurses entered the camp. Donuts and coffee were offered, but their stomachs revolted. Speakers were put up, and American music played, including "Don't Fence Me In" and "At Last." Two days later, Mac watched General George S. Patton, with his ivory handled pistol, his polished riding boots, his shiny helmet and full-dress uniform, rode in a Jeep into Stalag VIIA. Seemed like he should be riding a bronze horse. Prisoners sobbed with relief. They did not know he was coming and looked more like a bunch of surprised hobos. Liberation by the 14th Armored Division of StalagVIIA was an event anyone there would never forget. Soon after, General Patton entered the camp getting the POWS, then called RAMPS, and asked which guards had treated them badly. Within a week they were trucked to the local German airfield and flown up to Camp Lucky Strike in LeHavre, France, to be processed for home. They received back pay, new uniforms, showers, food (after standing in very long lines) and slept on cots in tents. Mac, a lieutenant, a trainee, a *kriegie* and a RAMP, received a new pair of boots. He was not sorry to toss his old boot away.

Eventually, they were taken to the harbor by trucks and put on their ships to make the journey home, traveling in convoys for safety. U-boats still lurked in the Atlantic, so the ships had to zigzag just to be safe. The weather was stormy and many of the men got sea sick. Mac entered New York and was surrounded by men who cried when they saw the Statue of Liberty. When Mac disembarked, American flags flew and bands played. They were home!

Chapter 19: Second Chances

Daniel, my kids and I visited my Dad more often with new summaries and quick jottings of what we pieced together from the books he'd passed along, frantic to get the story straight in case he didn't bounce back so quickly from TIAs. Dad did bounce back from the large strokes and the small barely noticed ones. Each occurrence allowed the rehabilitation of synapses so he was able to sign Mahon's birthday card in June and walk to breakfast. He became more dedicated to checking my facts and filling in gaps in the story of what happened to him after the war. It was sad that he had to give up drawing, but he was in his late eighties, and he had created a piece of artwork every day since long before I was born. I read to him in the hospital and the intensive care unit starting with his return to the United States in May, 1945, before the war ended in the

Pacific. He was terribly thin, with an intense wide-eyed wonder. The only clue to what he'd experienced was a stiff way of turning his left shoulder and a new silent and grave intensity in his smile. He was quiet, stronger in character, yet leery of noises and unexpected car backfire. Fireworks were out of the question. It would be months, maybe years, before he unwound enough to allow the nightmares and interrupted sleep to leave his life.

"No complaints," he said. "I came out unscathed."

He returned to an America that had out-fought and out-produced every country. American soldiers ended the war and were the best on the planet—highly committed, superior in morale and morals, superbly led. The military worked together like a family. The rest of a nation at home had done the same. When the U.S. called up a workforce, women responded. When the men returned home, the women returned to run households. It was a cohesive splendid can-do country, and Mac and Irene reunited as changed twenty-five year-olds.

When they greeted they shook hands. Mac knew he'd come out of it OK. No one asked about his life as a camp survivor. If he did tell them, they wouldn't comprehend. Mac learned to shrug, to put the war out of his mind. He drew and painted to escape. The GI bill helped him transfer his purpose to an education and a few vittles and vice in their new neighborhood.

He landed safely on Elm Street in an exuberant Chicago that hosted a beehive of thousands of GIs traveling home by train, plane and boat. Ex-soldiers flooded into a vibrant Chicago, this wealthy industrial city as the most hospitable in the country. Apartments and houses filled to near bursting as men explored Chicago's music, restaurants and schools to prepare for new jobs. The celebratory openness of the Midwest absorbed thousands of students eager to create a new world.

Mac was eager to make a long-term commitment to his city and his hometown dove, Irene. She was still flying the country as a United stewardess, nursing soldiers who were limping home with lightly packed duffels of souvenirs. She saw the broken spirits, the missing arms and bandaged heads of her wounded generation. Irene's sisterhood of Teacher's College forged a camaraderie with art teachers with a social justice message.

Her community was reformed in her sisterhood of stewardesses for United Airlines. Irene wanted to be part of traversing the country with Chicago as the main hub.

Irene lifted Mac's spirits like a leafing olive branch. Her voice calmed his unease like a cooing dove. She had sent a telegram response agreeing to his marriage proposal, but it was never found. Now they were actualizing their love together. Each had yearned to be together, yet it might take time for their new selves to meld. Irene and Mac were engaged.

After a bacon, lettuce and tomato lunch on Michigan Avenue, they walked to the river to watch the glistening gray-blue water flow past. The tour guide announced facts about the Wrigley building as the boat rippled a path beneath them. At close range, their faces showed tension. They were too polite with each other, too thoughtful. Mac postured self-assurance with poise. Irene tread lightly on their fragility. They pretended nothing like a world war had come between them. Conversations flowed about their upcoming wedding, their reception at the Knickerbocker, flower colors, table cloths. How many children they would have. How would their passion for travel fit with family? Would they live in Chicago? Of course, travel was their priority. Maybe a house in the suburbs? The artists were all moving to the northern suburbs. Guests lists, press photos filled their awkward space. Their smiles were too intense. Their jokes strained. They held hands too tightly and hugged liked they never wanted to let go. They had dared fate in the newest aircraft technology. They learned to walk together again, understanding they had a shared dream no one else would know. They flowed like water through the dark.

Mac and Irene seemed the happiest couple in the world. Dining, they rekindled their long-imagined love, at Chez Paree and Chez Paul, Armandos, the Erie Cafe, and Riccardo's. Free at last to be together, they reminisced about high school friends and discussed work. They planned their honeymoon and danced on and on to their wedding dance on July 27th, 1945, at Our Lady of Sorrows Basilica. Our Lady of Sorrows ceremoniously gave the couple scapulas with advice to pray to Blessed Mary, *My Mother, my confidence.* Mac dressed in his Army Lieutenant's uniform that morning in his accustomed ritual steps, wishing for good luck while he shaved with a new razor. So sharp, it nicked his jaw. None of the invited guests could know his kind of satisfaction. He was alive and marrying Irene. This exuberance was a form of greatness in itself. His mother set down his packed leather aviator's bag to pin a carnation to his lapel. He jolted as a camera flashed.

When the catch on the garter caused a run, Irene asked her sister, Rita and friend, Charlotte for new stockings. She'd barely had time from her last air flight to pack for the honeymoon. Rita gathered their best sweaters, blouses and skirts. The sisters exchanged clothing which caused them to look more alike. In a hanging bag was her post-wedding dress for the Knickerbocker Hotel reception. Bess' neighbor arranged for the reception room. In another bag she held the borrowed wedding train which would be attach to her dress at the basilica.

Irene had purchased a simple ivory dress. Long sleeved, embroidered and gathered at her thin waist, the skirt gracefully flowed around her tall heels. In the flurry of scurrying into Our Lady of Sorrow's chamber with her hair intact, the head piece was pinned and second application of powder patted on her cheeks and glistening forehead. She paused to catch her breath. Entrance organ music echoed throughout the vaulted ceiling. Not many soldiers had returned. Several of her stewardess friends were flying this weekend. Her uncle-in-law would escort her down a very long and almost empty aisle. An organ began "Here comes the bride . . ." Charlotte and Rita stood beside her. Irene was the first to marry. The press arrived with their cameras.

Irene felt the desire, love and envy of those around her. She held herself gracefully with a straight back and head lifted proudly. Though many of her friends had written to several beaus there had not been many relationships for any of them in years. Chicago was a hub of military men passing through. Women were anxious to get on with life in their waning twenties. They were anxious to know who, and how, boyfriends would return.

Irene winked in the photographs that ran in the *Chicago Tribune*, *News*

Sun and *Daily Herald*. Mac attempted to calm the adrenaline triggered from the camera flashes. Only his eyes penetrated into the terror he squelched inside. The scapula hung under Mac's shirt; Irene's was in her clutch. All were celebrating the end of the war, rations, separation and coming together. Whoops and hoots, cascading rice as they ducked arm-in-arm through the gathered group of family friends on the Basilica steps. Irene's parents had been married here in quieter, but just as uncertain times. Her grandparents on both sides had been married in New Jersey.

Mac was gazing into Irene's gray hazy-blue eyes. She had a solemn, warm, girl-like calm face. There was something ethereal about her, as if she always gracefully carried a bouquet of fresh flowers. Irene looked into his sky-blue wide and excited eyes. She handed him her suitcase. He had the keys to Bess's Buick. They were giddy with their plans for a road trip. She watched his agile, delicate hands, artist's hands, take the steering wheel.

They drove to the Knickerbocker with tin cans rattling behind them. Only recently, tin had been rationed. Soap was flagrantly wasted to write *Just Married* on the back window. They passed the sound of waves on the outer drive. Combining food stamps, Mac's GI bill salary and a reduced-price reception hall, they celebrated a glorious wedding. Capturing every posed moment of cake cutting and feeding each other forkloads of Gram's whipped cream frosted angel food cake, Bess' brown-sugar dipped figs, dark-chocolate macaroons and William's pineapples from California.

Free at last! Together finally! They settled into their suite in the Knickerbocker while the celebration continued below. Calming waves were still breaking along the Streeterville embankment. In a few weeks or months this would be the kind of quite ordinary thing young people would do, but for that day, they were celebrating one of Chicago's first post-war weddings. Past, present and future transported them into a oneness. After postponing Mac's military check-in, they traversed the states by car to honeymoon in Niagara Falls, then north to Alderbrook, New York. Their compromise was to honeymoon in the Adirondacks with the Franklin and McKillip cousins.

As a redefined, eager housewife, Irene concocted a home of two birds of flight who had landed into a life of nesting. She stirred the wedding-gift pot with a new wooden ladle and the lemonade with a silver spoon. While she seasoned the food, the phone always seemed to ring. She stopped whipping the cream to answer the revolving door. Her service in the air was fine-tuned to elegantly buff the marital silver and china, and charmed a life with a table of friends around a dish of parsley'd potatoes. She longed for travel.

"When I was flying, I felt on the edge of my life," she said. "The closest I'd ever felt to being me in the fear of the unknown. I could feel my blood moving in my skin, my fingernails growing. My hair and face were full of electricity! I glowed silver. When I was flying, I was in control of myself. I knew who I was." After marriage, stewardesses weren't allowed to work, to fly, to earn.

Mac and his new bride flew together for the first time to Miami for a week at the Army Air Force Separation Base to be released from service. There were health tests and medical advice before he returned to civilian life. A hurricane blew in after they landed and rather than shorten their honeymoon, they rode out the storm with another young couple in their hotel room.

Back in Chicago, Irene and Mac walked home from Institute of Design (ID) lectures along Clark Street, known as the street of missing persons, with not all of them dead. Here, he happened upon Casey with the Cleats, who shuffled because he couldn't walk or run. His legs didn't move up, down, forward or backwards more than an inch or two. Casey covered the soles of his shoes with cleats that he struck against the sidewalk to give sparks and a rhythm to the song he hummed to himself. Mac paused, sat down and drew Casey who pocketed coins. An organ-grinder named Annie picked a cold corner to grind out a cacophonous "O Sole Mio" for a few coins. With a world of wonderful characters to draw here, why live anywhere else?

Mac polished his philosophy and persuasions in these years, to witness his time through images and moments of humanity. He wanted to be more than just himself, a continuation of impression and expression without the

-isms. He knew Art was as old as humans. A desire to create was the hand on the cave wall to say *I existed*. Art always had been, still was, and would always will be a necessity of life. At ID, they heard art was an indispensable means of merging the person with the community to create a perpetual equilibrium with everyone's surrounding world. Mac learned the process to seize the moment, transform his impression into memory and express that memory into material form and project onto society from Lazlo Maholy Nagy. Emotional expression happens in the immediacy. In this process, he took possession of what nature imposed on the social order, worked his magic with pencil and paper and gave us a new insight. Irene got it. She saw art's importance to reshaping society. Irene and Mac dreamed of a mid-century life designed to redefine post-war chaos.

What Mac called *the 95% sweat* was to know his trade, enjoy it, understand the rules, skills, forms and conventions and tame the subject into a symphony of lines and color on paper. This process of reasoning purified his creativity. His rhythm of lines delighted his viewers to look into the difficult imagery he had witnessed. Moholy Nagy invented, taught branding and packed a lunch to draw on the street. Mac's first big break was to draw images for a new cookbook, *Vittles and Vice.*

The week both cars were in for repair Daniel flew to England for his brother's birthday. Bailey, our dog and I walked Sophia and Mahon, with lunch boxes and backpacks, to the bus stop corner. Djibril ran up and announced, "A plane flew into one of the twin towers in New York!" as he walked up with his mother, Shira.

"Yes, we saw a plane fly into one of the towers. It may have been an accident," she explained. The big yellow bus slowed, flipped out its stop sign and opened the accordion fold doors as the line of neighbors eagerly climbed up.

Half an hour later, Bailey and Brie fed, we scooted to Pilgrim preschool, one of her first half-hour days. Parents met for coffee upstairs.

"The first tower was collapsing." Daniel had called last night to say he was moving his flight up.

"Daniel is over the Atlantic now. Where would he be landing?" Kellyn asked.

"He'll probably land in Canada and be there several days," Peggy, a travel agent replied.

"A plane is downed in Pennsylvania," Julie just arrived. "Reports say it was headed for Sears Tower." Are they shooting planes out of the air? Stay calm.

After hours of calling United, searching the web for Daniel's flight, the kids came home from their playdate and school. I showed the older two the plane causing the collapsing tower once, but not my three-year-old. We were settling into dinner again without Daniel when the phone rang. No one was there at first.

"I've only a few seconds, but want you to know I'm fine. In Neufinlung. We've landed and waiting on the plane. I have to go!" Daniel called.

"I've waited a day for your call. Give it one minute and tell me where you are?

"We landed in Newfoundland with hundreds of other planes. I'm on UA929. We'll be here for a few days. I've got to pass the phone on. What does "US Airways closed mean?" Daniel was calling from the pilot's cell phone in the cockpit and noticed a teletype paper message on the control panel: "Company aircraft is under attack, divert to Gander immediately. All planes down immediately." They spent their first day in Newfoundland in the airplane.

"Planes have flown into the Trade Towers in NYC. They've collapsed. No planes are flying nationwide. Another plane is downed in Pennsylvania but we don't know why." Over several days of short phone calls, I heard what happened.

The United pilot announced, "We will be landing immediately. Flight attendants, please take your seats." Daniel liked to watch the planes fly across the globe on the screen and noted their plane nosed down and descended like a rocket ship angles up, descending numbers flipped frantically. The screen went blank. There was nothing but water on UA929. His seatmate and he grabbed each other. "This must be what pilots say when our plane is going to crash." He wrote a note to the kids saying everything was going to be fine. There was no more information given. Airplanes, now defined as bombs, landed in a quick succession on the tiny airfield of Gander.

Some of the planes had finally opened to let their passengers out after 24 hours. Most still didn't know what had happened, none had seen the television images of the collapsing towers.

"Welcome to the Rock," they were greeted. "You are on the edge of the Atlantic where the river meets the sea. Wherever you are, know you are here." Daniel's flight was led through a throwback to the Cold War airport to school buses and driven to a church basement; he had his wallet, an airplane blanket and pillow. "Your luggage will remain on the plane. Please load onto your bus." British musician Julian Dawson, a guitarist and singer, who knew thousands of songs from the Beatles to David Bowie, was on their flight. He'd already pulled out his guitar for a sing-along on the plane. Dawson strummed his guitar and began a round of John Lennon's "Let it Be". They sang their way to the church. A television was set up in the basement. Flight 929 watched the images of the towers collapsing for hours, over and over again. All wanted cell phones and internet to write to family members, to check if they were okay. Computers arrived; WiFi was set up.

Flight 929 was driven to a Moose Lodge to hear a local band and have a few beers. They downed screech and kissed a cod and were designated official Newfoundlanders. The kids and I rushed home from apple picking with friends when Daniel arrived home at O'Hare five days later.

"Where there is darkness, let there be light; where there is sadness, let there be joy," was sung at our Sunday Family Mass. Daniel sang "Imagine all the people, living life in peace..." and "I want to hold your hand..."

Part III: Settlers in a Foreign Land

In the last two years of Dad's life, Jean discovered our family genealogy online. She discovered two large families with two branches from Grandma Mac's lineage. Jean and I dove into online searches and asked Dad more questions while he recovered.

Chapter 20: The Grey Lady of the Dark Hedges

Our great-great-grandfather, John McKillip, grew into his bearings in Antrim, Ireland in the 1830s. It doesn't matter where you start the subjugation of Irish culture: the twelfth century Normans, or the sixteenth century Tudors. For as far back as the island could remember, Northeast Ireland and Northwest Scotland were part of the same tenor. Lowland Protestants and Highland Catholics migrated to and from Scotland to Ireland voluntarily and fluidly until the Protestants from Scotland/England established vassal plantations of Gaelic-speaking Irish who tilled their land. Generations of Irish were born of Catholics loyal to English values where Catholicism was no longer allowed. British structuring of shifting land and business interests locked in a British-owned Ireland.

In this turbulence over the meaning of communion, John's parents grew up together and courted in Cushendall in the Barony of Glenarm. Here, the formative United Irish rebellion attempted to ease Protestant fears and accomplish Catholic Emancipation while Margaret Murray MacGormac and Daniel McKillip sat next to each other in first grade. Over the years, their friendship bloomed into a love for each other that evolved with secrets, sacrifices and tendencies to look the other way in the case of conflict. Allegedly, Daniel grew up working in his father's lucrative soda ash business. They harvested and extracted sodium carbonate from kelp and sent it to England to staunch the bleeding of Europe's wars. Brits sent back a tall black hat and suit for Daniel's father, who voted just-so, and wore his hat raggedy. Daniel raised his family in a rambling stucco house overlooking the Bush River's flow into Lough Neagh, near to his boats in Cushendall and Ballymena school where a systemic discrimination against

Irish Catholics was perpetuated.

As a child, John, with his younger brothers, Hugh, Patrick and Archibald, and sisters, Mary Jean and Bridget Elizabeth had intuited that, in matters of catechism, not everything in their family was harmonious. Their world was made in the picture perfect Armoy Presbyterian Parish of County Antrim. The long-suffering Church of Ireland's minister was perpetually perplexed during their summers in the Layd Church of Cushendall to find the words to his Sunday sermon, to address his papal-leaning Catholics, and his Reform-leaning Protestants, and those leaning towards Anglican communion. He found the less words used, the better.

When the Americans defied the British parliament with a Revolution, Ireland knew they were fighting the same battle. Some colonists were Daniel's Irish emigrant friends from Ulster, so he watched the Revolution closely. Some fought beside George Washington in early battles opposing the French. Like America, volunteer militia became the fashion in Ireland. The McKillips' booming kelp business stayed flush with profits until Napoleon's wars subsided. John learned the trade from his practical, sprite and nimble father.

The Glens of Antrim are at the heart of Ulster. John grew to young adulthood amidst this world of folktales and scripture, the small murmuring music of the hens, hills, politics and tiny passages into knowing what was Irish. As the oldest son teetering in a schismatic culture, he learned to be an edge-walker at the religious divide. He enjoyed tales about Legendary Fionn mac Cumhaill who was told to build the steps to fight the Scottish giant Benanadonner, allowing the giant to flee back to Scotland destroying the steps on his way. John and his brothers found and collected flint arrowheads and tools in their wanderings through the glens. These connected him and piqued his curiosity in Ireland's ancient Celtic ways. He grew up visiting the town square for the *seanchai* tales in English intermixed with Ulster Gaelic. He picked up a wee bit of Gaelic in the adventures told of small mischievous sprites in lyrical Irish tales, not taught at his Ballymena high school. *Seanchais* brought to life ancient rhythms, cadences to sustain folk songs, belief in fairies, tales and lore.

John, with his friend Erin, listened intently but knew to keep the Irish quest for independence from their classmates. It was their secret world.

John didn't consider much about religion, but noticed their mother had something to hide around portions of the family. John realized over time his mother had converted to Protestantism to marry his father, but continued her Catholic ways including attending fifteen-minute Mass, confession and taking Communion privately in rotating homes. He was aware he'd been baptized Catholic in a hushed, tiny ceremony. John walked his girlfriend Erin home from school. They wandered into the square in search of *Seanchais* storytelling, chatting about classmates.

"Irish Catholics were struggling for rights to own our native land, learn our native Gaelic, practice Catholicism and be represented in government! Aren't we now?" was shouted from the podium. "Congratulations to the new Catholic Association, expanding from a club to a massive movement and their extraordinary triumphs, including electing the first Catholic M.P., Daniel O'Connell to British Parliament! Won't we be celebrating Daniel?" The crowd erupted with cheers and hoots. "Furthermore, Catholic Emancipation has become law! Don't ye know it is?" The speech was punctuated with the uniformed flutes and drums blaring of an Orange Order Parade, its cacophonous marching band that entered the corner of the square to scatter the crowd. John's Anglican father conflicted with his Mother's silent religious practice. Erin grew furious with the Catholics shouting at the band and her growing sense of trepidation.

"Ascendency of a new world view, won't ye believe it?" John said to Erin while walking from school. They passed under the arching Dark Hedges and felt the spectral presence of its ancient Gray Lady. "Might we be enjoying the bit of shade for a bit?" John said.

"John, this is an ill subject for jesting?" she said. "Your tongue is bold."

"If you are concerned for me," John said, "I am neither of those people, nor these people." Erin looked at him quizzically. "You and I have enjoyed listening to the Gaelic songs and stories and tapping to the Irish dance," he said. "But owning land and a business matters."

"Yes, John, but the stories and dance lets the spirit of people express their family's traditions. The poor Irish people here are dying of cholera, don't mix with them. *They* don't even speak Gaelic. Ya' must be aware of it?"

"Erin, it's necessary to raise the status of ordinary people. There is a need for justice. Don't you know?" said John. "Farmers need to feed their children from their own harvest."

"And shiftin' ken happen with literature, plays, songs and music. Don't you be guessing that is truth?" said Erin. "Change'll be dangerous, John McKillip."

"Cluinim beachd," he said obediently, then paused. "Erin, change can happen so people can work in other than a pub. Fathers can own their father's parcel of land again. The innocent surely come before the guilty?"

"John McKillip, I'm earnest. Do as I say, for your life!" Erin turned down the lane.

"Eiteogai" he spoke quietly to himself. "Wings. Don't ya know it?" While John was grasping at the hatchling ideas lilting amidst the breeze distinguishing between Catholic aspirations and a valid nature of a true-born Irishman blurred his definitions. What happened to a seventeen-year-old's repositioning himself amidst politics and signing Erin's dance card?

"Everything seemed strange at first, then very quickly normal existence seems strange," John said as he cleaned fish at Glengormley.

"You don't aim to stay here John, do you now?" Hugh asked. "Wouldn't you know, the States are a profane, irreligious pagan country of gross materialism." Hugh swooped in what breath he could as he cleaned fish tangled in kelp. Ships of Irish grown grain, oats and meat were being loaded for export on the docks behind their table.

"I love her, but I'm finding no peace with O'Connell's refusing to sit in Parliament or gather a protest." John said. "I met with her Da' who wouldn't say a word of our lives together as one. What good would it do me to stay now?"

"John, I'm going to marry Maggie and follow you." Hugh said. "Please know we'll be trailing your footsteps." The following year, eighteen-year-old John McKillip squeezed out from under the Imperial British thumb, boarded the Brig Joseph Hume at Belfast and headed to Scotland, then

Montreal to begin an emigrant family chain. Right away, he found eighteen-year-olds destined for distant shores. Of their past, they said nothing.

Saturday afternoon the phone blasted a call from the emergency room desk that Dad was ambulanced in after a stroke. I was in a condolence line for a friend's mother's memorial, gave him a hug and raced to the hospital berating myself for my irrational driving speed in a sputtering rain. My distressed excitement peaked as I walked through the emergency room doors. Once I penetrated his uber-white curtained space I entered an ethereal calm, a meditative place of mere breathing. Blurring medics swarmed the bed to raise Dad onto a gurney while I covered his gown with my artisan jacket broad enough for his shoulders. Andrew was there and saw my clothing on his father. We hugged stiffly and chatted with worried brows as we exited the sliding door into a shivering chill, then said goodbye and that we'd each call half the family.

Everyone cared for and visited Dad at his rehab center over the following months. We started a spiral notebook to leave messages about medicine, treatment changes and physical therapy "We could improve the art in these halls," I always said and he grinned as he pushed a walker in front of him. "Dad everyone is out buying you a red electric scooter."

"Why don't you tell them I'm walking just fine," he said. I texted everyone the nurse's photo of us walking to lunch and cringed as I pressed send. That photo stopped the scooter chat and stirred their rivalry for his love. By pecking order, four siblings were skipped when I, seven o' nine, was asked to be a trustee. Not all of Dad bounced back. He'd been to a deeper world and prevailed in a vertigo stage of life. Walking was to lean forward, hold handrails to remind himself he was going *onward*. To where? From here. He was leaning into getting to what he had lost. By walking forward, he would arrive at his past and his loss would be regained. Here was a weary stage of watching his adult children circle around for selfies in cell phones where he floated as a reflection on the screen. His adult children came wanting, longing for something he did not know. He never understood our rivalry. He only saw the spaces between his gray-haired children and grown grandchildren. The shadow of them told him more that the clothing, dogs they brought to visit, or coats they slid onto chair backs. The flowers set on his side table was less than the action of how they set them down.

Seagulls swooped and screamed. Songbirds filled the empty spaces of sound. The lake was like glass with nary a ripple at the sandy shore. The beach was deep, built by the current from the southwest. The water was too clear for a Great Lake. We retreated to this beach house often after 9/11 to connect with water and wind. Sandpipers ran along the edges of the tiny strips of foam at the water's edge. The screen door slammed and slammed. Dodge ball began as the sleepover boys played. Breakfast was served with piping hot coffee, peppermint tea and lemonade. The yard filled with celebrating families; the little kids jumped into the icy lake while the older boys continued dodge ball. The grill was started, the tea was consumed and the coffee pot was refilled and emptied. Parents stationed themselves to watch the water, the balls being tossed. The burgers and brats sizzled.

"Mom, the beach ball's blown in the lake!!" Mahon called.

"Quick, get life jackets, the canoe—let's go!" I heralded a "call for action" reenacting our family's favorite lifeguard game of saving beach toys on a glassy calm lake day... yet an irrational gust of wind took the toddler-height ball spiraling strangely over the calm surface of turquoise water.

"Mahon, put on the lifejacket and take the bow!" I captained with a flourish of the sea adventure.

"Mom, I want to go!" Tiny Brie put on a life jacket. She was already in a wetsuit. Ethan, a second-grade friend who had been swimming, jumped in the canoe. I tossed him a lifejacket as the bow sliced through the lapping ripples. So caught up in explaining how to paddle, I lost track of the shore. The beach ball skittered across the surface of the water very fast.

"Pull hard! It's getting away!" I called in my playful skipper's command under a white wide-brimmed cotton hat.

"We're getting closer, Mom!" Mahon called from the bow. The ball had slowed. Fog descended. Perplexed, white caps lapped around us.

"White caps! We're turning back, pull hard Mahon, don't reach for the ball!" With a sweeping motion of the paddle the canoe took a sharp left turn to the far distant shore and we capsized with a wave. My white hat dripped in my face and I threw it away. The canoe's bottom faced the cloudless sky. Brie started to cry. Ethan looked terrified. Mahon gasped for direction. The cold June water seeped into our chilling lifejackets.

"Grab the two sides of the canoe and hold on!" My *uber* calm had no hint of frolic.

"We can't use the energy to cry now, we must stay calm, hold onto the canoe and swim the canoe into shore—everyone kick!" This action focused their panic and offered a moment for me to assess our situation. The shore was too far. *What have I done? They are too little. The water is too cold. I must stay calm. Focus, we will get out of this. I just don't know how. Sarah, Brett... I'm so sorry I have your son in this water. I will get him back.*

"We are going to be okay," I said. "Keep kicking."

"HELLLOoooo!!!!" we all shouted to passing motor boats that sped by. They couldn't hear us. *Where's my hat?*

"New plan. We're going to conserve our energy. Hold hands over the canoe and tread water. Hey look, a Coast Guard helicopter!"

"Will we get a ride in a helicopter, too?" Ethan asked, perking up. It gave hope.

"Let's wave and see if they see us. Wouldn't a helicopter ride be fun!"

"Mahon, take Ethan's and Aubrey's hands and hold tight." I let go of the tiny, barely-know-how-to-read-hands and grasped two paddles floating nearby at their ends and waved the broad ends to cross like a college logo. *These three are going to college.* A motor boat turned.

"How long have you been in the water?" the man in the boat asked while leaning over the back to lift up the kids and wrap them in towels.

"Thirteen minutes." Time had crumpled and bent.

While preparing for his Atlantic passage in Scotland, John caught word of the fate of the Highland set of McKillips. "Wouldn't ye know I'm a McKillip," his new friend, imposter or cousin said. They raised their hot coffees to cheer and retold old myths of their clan barely surviving old wars. Just then, the fisherman next to John stood and sang a clear, lyrical, compelling version of the Elfin Knight, a song of impossible tasks. The thunderous pub went silent. A bodhràn, uilleann pipes, tin whistle and fiddle accompanied his clairvoyant legendary tune. John's looming voyage was graced with the Scottish tune:

"Tell her to make me a cambric shirt, For thou must shape a sark to me, Without any cut, or heme" quoth he, "Then she'll be a true love of mine, Tell her to find me an acre of land, Between salt water and the sea strands, Tell her to reap a sickle of leather, and gather it all in a bunch of heather, then she'll be a true love of mine. Parsley, Sage, Rosemary and Thyme, Remember me to one who lives there, She once was a true love of mine."

When the brig *Joseph Hume* set off from Grenoch for Montreal, John shook for leaving behind the parceled land from which goodness vegetated, an inalterable pattern of seasons to sow, tend and harvest. The moody, perpetually shifting sea offered reckless ever-changing transformations of his circadian rhythm. Hungry Irish, squeezed away from their kin, assumed everyone was either a devil in disguise or an angel in wolf's clothing. Generosity and goodness were apparent, but desperation whittled most down to deception and an occasional underhanded back-stabbing.

He chatted with the Captain about the winds, moon and waves or sailors to learn a knot. Evolving into a self-made man fluidly shifting with the storms and calm of the rollicking water, John developed his cadence with the constant harmony of the Elfin Knight and impossible tasks. Occasions of solitude found him unwrapping his arrow and tool-head collection that he re-ordered on deck. The ancient tool makers harkened a time long ago. A glint of sunshine glittered from the faceted flint… or was it a teardrop? After the uprising, Daniel O'Connell exemplified the importance to win the hearts and minds of the people. In his turbulence, John wrapped his collection and found friends.

On day two, John fell in with the few young men and sat down with their Catholic group looking for something to sort through his loss and to keep the contents of his stomach and tears from spilling about. They showed him community, like parts of a circle, that balanced each other.

Their strange yet comforting prayers calmed his fearful dread of this uncertain life. Vague memories of their curious chanting ways comforted him. Longing for the hint of reminiscent traditions strained his memory of the few brief Masses he'd attended. He barely recalled the rituals, incense, candles, cups of wine, chants that filled aching voids. Camaraderie steadied his rocking ship. Catholics welcomed him into a collective life. Something familiar resonated in the Apostles Creed, "*I believe in one God the father almighty, the Creator of heaven and earth…*" The shrouded blessing in Latin of the host and wine, and the unified chorus of *"Bless us O Lord and these thy gifts which we are about to receive…"* intermixed with sage incense, in burners that clanked against chains, drove away frightening entities. Once strange faithful prayer began to sink in and calm him.

By the fourth day and higher seas, the stench of illness and a staccato of hacking coughs overwhelmed the bunks from diseases with no names. The seas brought up the contents of sparsely filled stomachs. John stayed on the deck with the fresher air in his ever-present transformation of an abstraction of his land-locked self. He joined the working sailors and learned some sailing craft to keep his mind and body in tune, all the while humming *"she once was a true love of mine…"* The sailors did not answer to nobility, religious or sovereign guides. They had no privileged or traditional bonds. Skidding about on sea-drenched decks meant the boldest and luckiest survived.

About twelve days into the voyage, the waves swelled prodigiously and excessive motion sickness was added to his aching heart, empty stomach and troubled spirit. With the waves, John was confined below while the brig made three knots per hour. The storm heaved the ship from side to side below, producing the utmost confusion with beds and chests that slid to and fro. The contents were strewn everywhere. His alienation of leaving behind land's patterns to depend on this heaving wooden vessel was compounded by the chaos of strewn and broken items from home. Mild hysteria broke out below deck as injured and hungry passengers were separated from their known treasures and nature. "*…Tell her to reap a sickle of leather and gather it all in a bunch of heather,*" John hummed to create his own calming ceremony. He was transforming, but wanted nothing else than to be rooted to the land with its patterns of sowing, threshing and Erin.

It took a few days for his stomach to seek out the provisions aboard and his companions. His beloved oatmeal breakfast was accompanied by curlings with molasses, potatoes, salt, hung pork, bacon and ham. Salted veal was made into soup. Coffee was much preferred to tea as the water was stale. Bottled ale was good for thirst, but in his opinion cider mixed with water was cooler and better for the stomach. Eggs, pan bread and port wine helped his constitution. To preserve raw milk for the voyage, he had put it in a clean jar that was boiled over glowing embers. The cultured clabber was wrapped in brown paper to keep for the whole voyage. He and his fellows learned to keep the fragile ceramic packed and to use wooden noggins or tin porringers due to the lurching of the ship. The voyage of eight weeks, tightly nestled in an uprooted humanity with possessions that shifted from one trunk to another by both envy and gifting.

"May you stay out of the lion's den in your new start in life John," the priest blessed him with oils on his forehead at his Confirmation ceremony. John chose Saint Daniel for his patron saint who had guided his Da' and MP Daniel O'Connell. "In the name of the Father, the Son and the Holy Ghost, you may go in peace." During his religious passage John transformed from a child into a young man and now a soldier of Christ. John's pack became heavier and fuller with the gifts bestowed, including a peat carved Celtic cross at his Confirmation ceremony into the Catholic Church. John shared prayers, songs, stories, illness, food, ale and joys until they all reached calmer waters and the port of Quebec where the brig cast anchor in the great battery.

After a quarantine, he wobbled then strolled in Quebec to regain land-legs and earn some food. He peered intently at the British soldiers hovering at the border for their chance to win back America's immense, uncharted expanse of unknown forest, mountains and minerals. When British guards traversed the hill, John crossed the road, then overcame his reluctance to board a steamboat for Montreal. These years formed land-loving John in compassionate ways as he guarded his adopted definitions of becoming American while remaining true to home. His father's kelp business was wanting with waning battles in Europe and his help was needed.

John and his friends kept an eagle's eye on ways to enter the United States.

"Meet me in Burlington!" John leapt at a job on a steam ship that sailed along Saint-Jean-sur-Richelieu down the Chermin de Portriotes into the United States. Dazed with fatigue, he was overwhelmed with the excitement of Lake Champlain, bustling with ships brimming with lumber and coal. Daunting remnants of Lake Champlain's engagement in the Revolutionary war was still evident with bullet pierced war craft at Crown Point's Fort Amherst at the foot of a mountain range that felt familiar. He envied the luxurious paddle wheel steamers but his yearning was with the land. Wide-eyed, John knew those mountains were his new home.

Chapter 21: Bark Eaters in the Mountains

John sprung from steamship planting his well-worn shoes in Burlington, Vermont, giddy with the thrill he'd finally landed. "May this be my last watery voyage ever," he said as he steadied his seaworthy legs on solid Burlington soil, picked up a *New York Sun* and read, "James Madison, who inspired the non-secular aspects of the U.S. Constitution to avert tyranny through religion, passed away." Was he killed? John wondered.

The Irish exodus of young men seeking a future or squished out from a tightening of the British fist around their prospects for a livelihood. Prosperous lads were coming from nutritious beginnings, loving families with a moral, academic upbringing, John joined some lads from Antrim and his Atlantic passage to Quebec and Montreal. None of them asked or told their stories to protect each other. The less said the better. Cornelius, James, Martin, Owen changed faster together in the Whig endangered streets of Burlington. Irish Catholics were under fire with their beliefs denounced, convents attacked and churches burned from Maine to Texas. Lost in angry thoughts, John nearly passed by St. Mary's Church emptying after Mass and Father Jeremiah O'Callaghan's lilting Kerry accent. Father O'Callaghan greeted John with the thoughtful answer that old age had taken our last Founder, James Madison.

John agreed to attend next Sunday's Mass. It was as if Madison's beliefs, swirling in the air, were inhaled as John breathed into the very marrow of his bones and rooted a seedling of hope in his brain and becoming part of a definition of "American." Was America at a hinge of history stepping forward as a graft of the oppression of the world? God may have looked away for a bit, but might glance back at the likes of us and grant grace? John prayed as he looked for work. Land was the answer as his changing terrain that still felt like the sea under his feet. To still his growling belly, he entered a local pub and spotted Cornelius. While he and the rest of the Irish lads tried to make sense of Madison and the other founders, as well as the North-South debate of this new country, John eventually secured work as a logger. John noted that older men on the coal ships coughed uncontrollably while lumberjacks merely walked with a limp. Bosses talked about newspapers being printed for everyone, maybe even daily, and they needed wood to make the paper. The Hoe type printer would revolutionize mass printing and John wanted to be a part of it. West of Lake Champlain was unchartered wilderness and a visibly inexhaustible supply of trees.

John hopped onto J&J Rogers' logging wagon with Cornelius, Martin and James. New boots, wool shirt and jacket, deer leather gloves and rabbit skin hat remade the young man into a logger with an advance paycheck. Trees took no notice of the men silenced by looking small under the black mighty arches far overhead. When they threw bark on a campfire, light was swallowed up before spreading into a dozen trunks of dark aisles that stretched to the St. Lawrence River. The trees' cones offered pine nuts, roots to break up the rocks into soil by reaching roots, and scent to redeem health. Logging trips familiarized John with the wooded New York mountain roads as they rode wagons deeper into the Adirondacks to cut, then float logs to Burlington along the Ausable River. Huge lichen-covered, folded granite cliffs sheared from billion-year-old tectonic uplift, once as high as the Himalayas, warmed, then softened John's achy heart. Brooks flowed in radial patterns, like wagon wheel spokes, from mountains, cutting granite into gorges. This feels like home.

Stretched and broken rock faces directed cascading waterfalls into the North East. Week-long trips of sawed and chopped white pine and red spruce were loaded onto wagons then slipped into the river near Ausable Forks. John revealed his affinity for horses, the way he could beguile them to pull the heaviest of loads. "I'd rather be planting the trees than annihilating them, wouldn't I now," he said as his natural ability to drive a horse-team became his job. "We were never lost, we just didn't always know where we were," he told Father O'Callaghan after Sunday Mass.

"Watch for injury, for it will, as sure as my brogue, interrupt your plans. Do you have a specialty yet? Find your talent and make your way," the priest advised. A bright bluebird reflected the blue sky in its wing, the earth on its belly, as it flickered by to avert John's attention one morning after Mass. That's when he noticed her strong and slender forbearance, with a calm, graceful common-sense way about her. Her profile might have been on a coin. She was sorting peaches in a bright tin pan with a gentle, round, rosy face and strong nose that touched others to brighten their day. Her clear, honest hazel eyes caught his sky-blue eyes for a moment's gaze. He captured, in a flash, a vision that reached to the very bottom of his trusting heart. Her heartbeat throbbed, good and true beneath a cornflowered cotton dress fit snugly over her square, thin shoulders and bosom. John glanced about to see if others woke to the beauty of his vision.

"You might be needing a hand with those peaches." He'd set his heart on winning her.

"Now why would you be wanting to know?" she asked with a wrenlike voice when John inquired. "They'd be bruised and not fit for eating with the tar pitch on your fingers, would they?" She noticed his kind and strong demeanor.

"I'll not argue that. John McKillip is my name. County Antrim was my home. Always something new to learn." Now he was talking her language.

"What would you be wanting ta learn?" she showed a tiny smile.

"Your name for beginning our romance, so I get in the habit of calling you what your mother prefers?"

"Well aren't you sure of yourself, John McKillip from Antrim." She moved the dish of peaches to the table. John intercepted her, set the bowl down, brushed her hand and caused a slight blush in her cheeks. His heart quivered. Long logging trips intensified their longing for each other and time together. Betsy Goff taught third grade in the St Mary's school and was from Father O'Callaghan's parish in Kerry, but he could forgive her for being from southwest Ireland. "I now pronounce you man and wife." Father O'Callaghan blessed the couple. Parishioners gathered on a drizzly Saturday to celebrate the union of a younger herself and older himself in a Catholic Holy Matrimony at St Mary's church. They frugally saved their salaries for a piece of this land while getting to know each other over long winters as the snow clogged sleigh paths and froze the Au Sable river.

In my studio, I was sculpting *Hawk and Dove* for our family burial site. I wanted the whitest granite possible and remembered the quarries on either side of the Franklin Farm that Jean told me were still in use. Our great-great-grandfather, an 1880's Franklin relative, was a miner, maybe for stone, coal or garnets. The Franklins had a fertile farm along the river bed between the quarries. I wanted the stone from there for Mom and Dad's tombstone. I made my way to the Adirondacks to find white granite. I rose before dawn to drive from Cotuit on Cape Cod to the Adirondacks. I was looking for Alderbrook, once a vibrant crossroads settlement, that no longer existed. My only clue is that it lay west of Au Sable Forks on Fort Hopkinton Turnpike. In Burlington, I boarded the car ferry across Lake Champlain, drove along the Au Sable River valley to Au Sable Forks, and the Franklin's farm in the later afternoon. Franklins' farm thrives between the forks of the river where sediment settled into rich soil. Dairy awards were still posted on the barn walls. Nearby stood a covered bridge in North Jay, the only one in the area. Margaret and James might have swum in this river! I was excited to find rapids with pools. I photographed the welcome sign and river that carried logs to Burlington, and the historical marker at an Au Sable Forks sugar shack. I found white granite for the carvings, but they didn't have the saw to cut two silhouettes.

I followed my paper map, uphill five miles, through Blackbrook, and then traveled fifteen miles through Franklin County to the intersection of Rock Road and Alderbrook Road as the sun was setting. How could they have met? James and Margaret lived twenty miles apart? A fox ran past my headlights. There was a cabin at the intersection. At long last I saw the sign for my family's parish! This is the Alderbrook intersection. I walked in St. Rose of Lima graveyard, where the parish foundation rests amongst tombstones. I was elated and nervous to be at the site Gram had mentioned over 35 years-ago. My parents came here on their honeymoon.

Daniel called on my cell phone to check in. "Can I call you later? I have a half-hour until dark."

"Get a hotel room, you won't make it tonight. I've got the kids," Daniel said.

Two grand Maple trees stood outside the graveyard, and several hundred-year-old maple stumps lined Alderbrook Road. They must have planted them. If only trees could talk. The tombstones from the 1800s brought my family's names alive. Cornelius was the oldest stone. Several graves had freshly planted flowers. American flags fluttered. Later, afternoon shadows stretched long between the mountains. I checked online maps for directions and saw McKillip Mountain was just behind the cemetery. I had found it! It took decades to find Alderbrook, a name I hadn't known before Jean found the documents. Now I could inhale the pine scented air and sift the needles for stories. I drove down to see a brook and a cast iron sign for the Port Kent-Hopkinton Turnpike which existed since the 1830s. Maybe paved for the stage coach to get through? A sign for McKillip Mountain drew my attention as an eight-prong whitetail buck held a stance in front of the mountain named for my family. I took a photograph of my great-great-grandfather's spirit animal as it looked back to the brook with McKillip Mountain behind. A family of quail slowed my drive along Rock Road to Franklin Falls, as total darkness fell and emotions rose.

I drove forward rather than retrace my route. *All roads must lead through the river valley.* I drove on a dark winding road with no lights and worried a deer might leap out. In the headlights, swaths of spindly pines suffered from acid rain. At *World Book Encyclopedia,* I described rain from the industrial Midwest's exhaust, being carried by dominant winds to rain down and contaminate lakes, fish, trees, and people in the North-East states. Here, decades later, I drove through the same images published 30 years before as a warning. Logging roads covered in asphalt wound for hours through the dark within a valley of skeletal trees. The acid rain contaminated these lakes, mutated the fish and the dinners of the locals. When did protecting the earth become political? The map was useless. With no cell phone reception, I was lost.

Finally, a sign to an unfamiliar town. At the gas station, I wrote down directions to Au Sable Forks and imagined I could get back to Burlington from there. *Damn! I missed the turnoff.* Making a U-turn my headlights lit the glow of several sets of yellow eyes in the shadows of trees. I panicked as they stared, captured and stilled by the beam. With shaking hands, I reversed, inched forward, reversed on the narrow asphalt above deep ditches, and skidded away. Getting so close left more unanswered questions. Everything about Alderbrook was a question. Where was that grocery store? The cabin? The church? Why did it burn? Flying shadows swooped before the car. Finally, the lights of Au Sable Forks! I had reached a recognizable place and could find my way. A hotel room in Au Sable Forks would do. From a log lobby with braided rugs and wooden Adirondack chairs, I called Daniel to say I would be back the next evening. I needed to get more answers. Pen in hand I dissolved into the darkness of the pine scented cabin where 1834 came alive.

A soaring fish hawk was merely a dot in the sky as it dipped in and out of the low clouds, peering intently on the travelers along the terraced shore. Mountains stepped up, like a grandstand, cut by the Au Sable River flowing into Lake Champlain. The geology of Northeast Ireland is the same as this area. Sixty-two million years ago, Ireland was connected to the Northeast corner of the United States. Similar granite and basalt can be found in both terrains. As the continents separated from Pangea, Ireland spun around clockwise to echo the northeastern United States. In Antrim, the hexagonal formation of the Giant's Causeway. This majestic basalt rock formation warmed John's homesick heart. He drove the lumber wagon, with its crew, upstream along a rutted dirt road beside the rapidly moving river lined by ancient pines rising up the mountains. The gum trees flew their colored rags and were the first to lose their leaves. "Take the first right turn onto the Port Kent-Hopkinton Turnpike," his boss had told him. "Clear the woods west of Union Falls. It's the second lake along Silver Lake Road." Regarding supplies, the woods were for their getting. The loggers traipsed for chestnuts to berries, pine gum and acorns for flour. He chewed the sweet amber-colored gum sliced from spruce. The hawk floated down watching for prey in the heavenly, cornflower-blue of chicory, black-eyed Susans, the burnt orange of hawkweed interspersed with Queen Ann's lace.

After emptying a wagon of logs at Union Falls, John led the horses along the dirt turnpike to a clear brook to quench their lathered thirst and then grazed in the tall grass. He could smell aging autumn. He dropped a fishing line into the ice-lined brook and tied the other end to a flaming maple sapling. In a flash, the hawk floated out of the crown of an old alder, retracted into an arrow and dove in the grassy edge. A high scream erupted from its arched wings. The hawk rose again with a plump rabbit in its talon. A fish quivered the line. The pine-studded terrain of rock outcroppings echoed County Antrim.

He was nearly twenty-two-years-old. John's boot sunk deeply into this shady mire. He shook himself and gazed at the bird, who cautiously peered about before tearing into its meal. The trout trembled the line, the sapling juddered, bent horizontal then was pulled out of the soft ground. John grabbed the wiry stem, pulled in the fish, before disentangling the sprout. In his soft footprint, he scraped a deeper hole and rooted the tree along the road where the maple could grow straight and tall out of the alder's shade. He'd survived by the grace of God so far, if only for a moment's pause.

John took up the reins and drove along the icy creek through the field. A twelve-point buck sauntered, on promenade, glanced with haughty, brazen curiosity. Only his tail twitched. What was this place? The buck bolted away through a clearing, below a mountain. John sensed waters running deep. This land beckoned his heart to a calm. He returned to the Silver Lake campsite enthusiastic about this remarkable discovery.

Once they knew of the brook, the crew of Irish lads camped there so often it began to feel like home. With an uncharacteristic impulse, John claimed plots 26 and 27 for a homestead under the mountain. The other lumbermen were heartened to do the same. After brushing down the horses with frow and auger and tethering them near fresh grass. he cautiously joined the logging crew, surprised to see visitors. What are they doing this deep in the woods? Cornelius was striking fusils to cook fish. A gourd of bear fat fueled the damp wood. It was peculiar that two scraggly strangers had joined the logging crew around the cook's fire. John glanced over at his maple sapling not yet eaten by a deer. *Must be well fed*, he reckoned as he sat on a log. Why does a trapper sound like a college professor? John wondered.

"Greetings, Ebenezer Emmons, Williams College geologist," he reached out a hand.

"John McKillip, Burlington logger, wouldn't you know." John noted his gentle handshake and lightened his firm grip. Ebenezer's companion nearly sprained his hand with a robust handshake. "This large, domed area was a volcanic hotspot," explained the gentleman in trapper's clothing with worn deerskin boots. "Hot lava pushed up the earth's crust. Mile-thick glacial ice sheets advanced and retreated over worn mountain-ranges, carving lakes."

"Wind rushes from yonder with bogwaft, treesmell or elkspray."

"I don't suppose there's a chance of eruption?" Martin said.

"Not in the next million years or so," Ebenezer said. "*Adirondack* is a Mohawk name for Algonquin 'bark eaters'. The Algonquians chewed bark for nutrition at the winter's end. Only the Algonquians could survive there. Not the Mohawks, who lived along the fringe of this spectacular and sparsely soiled terrain." The other visitor remained silent.

James then said, "I'm ecstatic we found Ireland's soil, lads. We intend to grow a livelihood in this rocky soil."

"Did you hear of deviltry afoot, or were they hatching to match, the settlers and Indians?" Cornelius asked. Ebenezer lectured on, earning their admiration. He carried on as though he was organizing his thoughts or trying to forget about dinner. Ebenezer told them that the first Europeans were French Catholic missionaries, Father Isaac Joques, and the explorer Samuel de Champlain. From the early 17th century, these two settlers established a lucrative fur trade, encouraging 18th Century settlements and military posts—mostly along the big lakes named George and Champlain. Mohawks, Algonquians, and Europeans lived together peacefully. A sordid story evolved. Pequot battled Puritans, Narraganset were annihilated for relating with Puritans. French were defeated by the Iroquois' seven nations.

Skirmishes peaked between colonists and the Canadian British military that lapped at Lake Champlain shores and left politics an open debate.

The fish and roasted cattail hearts were passed on birch bark with two-tined forks whittled from sassafras twigs. Icy brook-water was poured from an oiled haversack into whittled quaiches. Cornelius' sassafras fork flipped the fish.

"Colonists decimated the Iroquois and pushed the Brits back over the northern border," Ebenezer continued. "The Yanks and British had a battleship each in Lake Champlain. Americans chased them back to Canada and the area has prospered since."

"How'd they get battleships into the land-locked lake?" Owen asked.

"Built them there with your lumber." Ebenezer replied.

"So we loggers are the reason for the final battle for U.S. independence?" said a teamster.

"We deserve more acclaim than camping out eating fish," Cornelius said.

"Imagine, we Irish lads!" Owen exclaimed. "Founders of a mere shadow under an alder by a brook." The raised their quaiches in a toast to themselves.

"Well, there you have it." John smiled. "Let's call this place "Alderbrook." Laughter erupted—they barely considered it a campsite.

Ebenezer recognized they were at the limits of what man can do and reached into his bag for a jar of ink, pen and his map. He carefully wrote "Alderbrook" at this spot on the turnpike. In that act, he solidified what each man had barely dreamed. Each man felt a swelling of their own audacity. As he packed up, John said he'd like to give a mountain his name. "I've got a claim on that one there." John pointed up the brook to McKillip Mountain, the tallest peak north of the Turnpike. Ebenezer recognized the importance of this ensemble of loggers and wrote the name "McKillip Mountain". Then he wrote, "Law Mountain" with James' request and "Ryan Mountain" with Cornelius, who still needed to make his claim.

John and his bride Betsy visited their new homestead for the weekend, enjoying their scarce solitary time, in balancing her teaching in Burlington and John's logging trips. The waning snows of Alderbrook captured their ambition while the pine scent offered them hope. John and Betsy spent weekends in a tent under their mountain while he laid the homestead foundation and she planted fruit trees.

"I mentioned the naming of the mountain McKillip to Professor Ebenezer Emmons, a college geologist. He wrote it on his survey. Is it fitting for you?" John asked. She nodded as it fit with her creating a legacy for their imagined family. "We'll see if Professor Emmons and his map make it back to the registry," John said.

Betsy stewed a venison hock with carrots, onions and herbs from her school garden at St Mary's. A fresh deerskin was wrapped for the tannery to be finished into a coat and leggings for winter. A generous bundle of stripped hemlock bark was his exchange for tanning the hide. John kindled new businesses. Betsy envisioned an earl or nobleman in John's face, which showed no hint of time passing, though he was ten years her senior. She liked that he was never rushed but was always occupied. She liked that he was not much for small talk, yet said what was important. She liked, no, loved, that about him.

"There's plans to build a single-room schoolhouse on the corner. We will need a teacher. Would you consider that?" John lifted a brow in Betsy's direction, knowing she adored her Burlington students.

"If you'll be the grocer," Betsy replied. "To have children for a school we need a working community, a church, a place to share harvests, skills and potluck conversations. John, if you were the grocer, this pie-in-the-sky idea of a town could be a reality." A grocer arranges land exchanges, mediates barters for crops, disputes between land borders, runs the post office, the stage coach stop, the conversations amongst those who need to be heard.

"I've grander ideas than being a mere grocer," John told her.

"Of the lot of you Irish blokes, you're the pick of the bushel," she said.

"Well now, that's quite a compliment. Bushel of what?" he said.

Bleary-eyed I finished a second cup of lobby coffee to chase down an apple cupcake. I was going back to the Alderbrook corner and wait. Not knowing what might happen, I rushed to get there. On the drive up the dome, a slapping rain started. As I sat in my car at Alderbrook, a woman came out of the only cabin on the corner. I waved hello and was invited into her cabin.

"I'm related to the McKillips," I said.

"Oh, this was the schoolhouse cabin from the McKillip's farm up Coldstream Road," she said. "Hugh Law moved the cabin and planned to live in it, but sold it to us years ago. The foundation to the grocery store is across the road and next to it was the Hall. Just a minute, I'll show you," she said as we stepped out.

"Oh, there is the apple tree I've written about," I said, knowing it was too young, but a descendent of where Eliza's pie was praised. "What's in your garden?"

"Those are rutabagas and squash, beans and sunflowers," she pointed. "The stone wall behind it was the buttery."

"I'm going to put rutabagas back into my writing, I switched it to turnips last week," I said.

"I grow turnips too," she said. We walked the grocery and hall foundations together, then down the Turnpike to Betsy's white schoolhouse with a collapsed roof. I was given Hugh Law's phone number. When she called Hugh, he arranged to meet me later that day at a cemetery in a wilderness still dripping with rain. Hugh took me to see McKillip and Law family tombstones. Four children died in the 1919 Spanish Flu and were etched as angels in stone. I was delighted to see the gravesites, to walk through their history with military markings on family graves. Fresh flowers were by our McKillip graves and war medals, and weathered flags fluttered. I discovered the name of the regiment Johnny, Betsy and John's oldest son served in when had been injured at the end of the Civil War. Months later, that led to a description of that battle on Griffen's Farm at the Newberry Library. Johnny must have lied about his age to travel back to the South with the Adirondack regiment and been injured just before the end of the war. The McKillip brothers, Patrick, John and Hugh, shared my brother's names. My oldest brother was named Franklin like the county. Our sisters, Elizabeth, Mary, Jean, Margaret and Ann's names were etched into these tombstones making me, Margot Ann, feel welcome.

Because his name was Hugh, I got in a stranger's car to tour our family homes and had lunch in his cabin. We drove to the still-lived-in Ryan's home that was our connecting relative. "Law Mountain was taller, on the other side of the Turnpike from Eddie McKillip's Mountain. That's what we called it." Hugh used to help Eddie post the homestead's "Private, Keep Off!" signs in the fall. In Hugh's cabin, overlooking Franklin Falls, were homestead maps, measured in chains, from the late 1880s. The McKillips owned 1500 acres and a home overlooking Franklin Falls. Another 1910 map listed Eddie McKillip as the homestead owner.

Hugh drove me past my great-great Uncle Hugh's yellow frame house, the first framed house in Alderbrook. He married Catherine Ryan, had a large family and was widowed. Hugh's County Antrim sweetheart Maggie and he were married and moved to Goldsmith to raise their combined family. John, who had started the immigration chain, remained the grocer at the intersection and hub of the community. Hugh and I walked through rock foundations of the grocery store and Uncle Hugh's Hall, which served as the church until Saint Rose of Lima was built. We drove up to my great-great grandfather's second home, across the street from his Uncle Hugh's frame house, both above Franklin Lake, high above Grassy Bay. John had a clear view of McKillip Mountain from his still-standing barn and log home. It started to get dark. Hugh pointed to a path in the woods and said, "Eddie McKillip's homestead is down that municipal road. The raised bed of the path had creeks on either side that flowed in different directions. We'll bring you back there when you return."

Gramma Mac's uncle Eddie had kept up the original homestead from 1834 to the mid-1970s. The Franklin County Historical Society had the records of St. Rose of Lima Parish. There I found the marriage certificate of my grandparents and that my grandmother Bess' name was Elizabeth Margaret Franklin. My name derived from Gram's, her mother's and her grandmother's names! I hummed in the car ride, "I'm Margaret the Fourth

I am, Margaret the Fourth I am I am." Then, I realized my high school interview in Pullman was with Gram's niece, Margaret Franklin. "I'm Margaret the Fifth I am, Margaret the Fifth I am I am…" until I wondered who these Margarets were?

Mahon, Sophia, Brie and I returned to Alderbrook to meet with Hugh Law after a Cape Cod Burke reunion. The roots of birch, spruce, maple, pine, oak, butternut, hackberry, fir and gum trees grew together for five generations of growth underground, ever since the woods were clear cut. Aboveground, Ryans, Laws, Franklins, McKillips and Caseys returned to mourn their ancestors for five generations, sharing their potluck dinners, ceremonies and sacraments. At the cemetery, Hugh handed each of us a walking stick after pointing out the maple stumps on either side of the cemetery entrance. "See the trunks along the Turnpike. Alderbrook founders planted maples here that were only cut down a few years ago. The municipal road had been overgrown for decades, though drywall stone walls lined the edges. Trunks crossed their path, streams gurgled on either side. Moss ruled. We hiked over an hour up the lichen-line, boreal-forested mountain. We passed the community butter churn on a horse harness, wagon wheels tipped over where the wagon bed had decayed into the ground, a collapsed shingled roof and sugar shack and barn basements. Shed rafters were covered in moss. A bucket was still tipped over by the sugar shack. The collapsed carcass of a Hupmobile with wood chassis and rubber tires rusted under a spruce. A wagon rested its metal rims by the shed foundation. We walked on past the outhouse and garden clearing. A creek flowed behind us.

"Don't follow the flow of water," Hugh cautioned us.

"It flows off McKillip Mountain," I noticed.

"Eddie McKillip's Mountain," Hugh corrected me. I watched the awed expression of my children as they entered the clearing of where the cabin had stood. I ran my fingers over the carefully stacked stones. Absolutely remarkable that these stones held so well for over a century. Stones, stacked one by one in 1834, by my great-great grandfather still stood, holding back the slope and the water. I stepped through the threshold and into the house's foundation.

"The log cabins were burned to keep the taxes down," Hugh explained. "John McKillip was a good stoneworker who laid drywall foundations all over Alderbrook."

I could have visited this cabin if my grandmother had let me know. I could have purchased it from Eddie. Instead, my college roommate and I had purchased ten acres of boreal forest in Minnesota on the Northshore of Lake Superior. We built a drywall foundation and fireplace with the twelve-foot chimney being the most difficult. We cut logs for the walls that notches were sawed and hand-chiseled near the end to stack at corners. Each pine timber was measured and cut where it fell, dragged by chains to the foundation with a truck we called *Simba*. Besides our cabin building instruction book, the Lincoln Logs child's game by Frank Lloyd Wright's son was my only reference. We framed in a door and laid floor planks from the sawmill down the road.

"The state park takes any land a family member doesn't claim," Hugh said. This is where my family lived for one hundred years! In college, I had worked hard for this life not knowing it was my heritage. My family thought I was making a big mistake by building a cabin in a boreal forest. We climbed up to the raspberry patch that had spread across the bulging plateau with thin, uncared-for canes. "There's the apple orchard," Hugh pointed out. "Every family had an orchard." What I would give to hear what these trees witnessed.

"What did you bring to leave for them?" Hugh asked. "Not many make it this far. They want to hear from you." I thought of the Reiki master and the room of relatives who waited for Dad. I wrote them a letter on the back of a dry-cleaner receipt with a pencil, Zip-locked it in a plastic bag and tucked it into the rock crevices near where the doorknob would have been. Hugh and I shared mailing addresses (he doesn't use the internet) and promised to write. We have been sending Christmas and St. Patrick's Day cards since. I was beyond excited to tell Jean all I had learned.

Chapter 22: Hill of the Ward

Exhaling a long and loud sigh, Betsy and John arranged their hopes and aspirations to plan a just-so log cabin in the woods, by a brook, under a mountain with their name. They walked a lichen-covered plateau, as the sun shone through the clouds, envisioning the berry patch on the left and apple orchard on the right. "Look, this terrace could be the back of the stables and hay storage," John pointed just below the plateau. "I'll lay stones for only three walls." A gurgling brook that flowed from the mountain, slowed with a crescent of stones to pool by what could be the kitchen.

"Let's put the house above the brook," Betsy said. They stepped back, seeing their home in this forest glade. Terraced above the brook was an imagined cabin, and above that, a lean-to for hay, grain and a horse barn. Terraced above that was a glade for a vegetable garden, apple orchard and raspberry patch. Several trees needed to be cleared. When he wasn't logging, John tilled the soil for hops and oats, milked a dairy cow and harnessed an enviable pair of dappled grays. The animals offered heavy labor and nutrients for the meager soil. Their quiet cabin in a boreal forest was a mile wagon ride on a municipal road. Heavy snow required a sleigh to the turnpike. Where the roads met was a parcel for one building. Betsy imagined her schoolhouse.

Early on, John milled and smoothed a small fag-bottom oak rocking-chair for the cabin's kitchen corner by the only window. Betsy fashioned a patchwork cushion of scraps from her mother's dresses. The chair invited a gentle swaying back and forth with its wide welcoming arms and down-feather cushion. She was still teaching in Burlington, but the rocker let her know this was home. Above the rocker, John nailed a board with his flint tool and arrowhead collection from Ireland to remind him of its ancient Celtic culture. Betsy contacted the school superintendent of the district to alert him of her decided interest to teach on the turnpike. He indicated a District 1 school house was planned for the Alderbrook intersection and a committee was interviewing for a teacher.

"Would the school be supplying a piano? The settlement has procured string instruments, *bodhráns* and tin whistles, but an understanding of chords, intervals and octaves on a piano would be foundational to all the student's musical education." She was uneasy to make a request before procuring a position, but wanted to create opportunities for a well-rounded education. John offered to oversee and build the schoolhouse at the Turnpike.

The settlement neighbors transplanted sugar maple saplings alongside the sunny shoulders of the Turnpike. Nestled in their tiny cabin, John staked out lots 50 and 51 up the south hills where the snow was cleared along Cold Stream by the settlement. He began building a barn for his horses there, near the Union Falls side of the road, with a thrice-as-big log cabin. His brother Hugh built the first frame house on his larger stone foundation across the road.

John grew enough excess herbs, vegetables, milk, butter and preserves to sell to passing stagecoach and Pony Express riders at the corner. Extra cash was sent to Antrim for his siblings' fare to America. John made claims for Lot 31 by Sweeny Brook and Lot 73 on the top of the next hill, each 50 chains by 50 chains. The members of the logging crew were becoming citizens, with meetings at the corner tavern to agree on lots, boundaries and use. They drew plans for a grocery, blacksmith shop, school, churchyard and butter factory up the Turnpike from the original campsite.

John claimed several furlong lengths of land at the corner for his stick and stucco grocery and planted apple trees. The village men built with a wrap-around roofed porch extending the store by five feet. Horizontal sapling banisters were three-feet high with crisscrossing bent branch. Eight chairs were built of spruce branches roped together so the seats dipped down in the back and swung a bit. At the back of the knees the seat raised up to a bull-nosed front, lifting the knees to stretch and relax the logger's weary backs. Lengths of milled pine were toe'd together with butterfly joints into benches that lined the walls under two windows.

The grocery store was stacked with pickled vegetables, canned fruit, pine nuts, acorn flour and chicory root. The McKillips carried haversacks over their shoulders to forage as they worked their fields. John sowed his cleared acres of uninterrupted fields of every variety of oats he could find and hay. His two gray mares that could clear a field or haul a wagon of stones without breaking a sweat. With a bull and cow, he started his herd, which grazed by the commonly shared field at the brook. Betsy started her flock of chickens up the hill and sold eggs. John's not-so-well-kept secret was to feed them all oats. After harvest, he and his neighbors forded posted signs: "Property of John McKillip." If they didn't, their claim could be lost.

The tidy Alderbrook corner had a blacksmith shop, a designated church yard, a tavern and a newly finished grocery amidst towering spruce and white pines, an orchard of apple trees at the corner and rows of maple saplings along the Turnpike. Beneath the surface, the web of roots of these trees grew around rocks for water and nourishment, intertwining to exchange alerts of drought, cold, excessive heat and invasive bacteria. In the shops and homes above ground, the settlers shared skills and harvests, seeds, knowledge and tips to survive a colder winter.

"Did I see John limp a bit?" Winnifred asked Betsy as they cooked in the grocery.

"That's likely, between the grocery and logging, John's been working long hours." This roomy, brightly painted kitchen with a glossy green floor was swept dustless. A prim well-blacked cooking stove was the focus of their attention, with shiny pots steaming full for a festive midday meal. Betsy's large wood table, surrounded by glossy green chairs, was covered in flour handprints from their biscuit making. Her rocker was set up in the bright corner of two windows. John's arrowhead and stone tool collection from Antrim hung above the rocker. This quiet scene of homey contentment countered the hammering, sawing and shouting that was giving rise to a butter factory across the road. Parish women were on their way from St.

Matthews with bread, salads and news of the day.

"In Oregon territory, women have the right to own land," Winnifred said.

"That's because no woman wants to live there," Betsy said.

"The states want equal representation and need more votes," Winnifred said. "Babies ensure more people and more votes for the territories."

She poured dried chicory root into a mortar to pestle it to powder and stretch the coffee. "One scoop for me and one for the pot. I hear Kansas might allow women to own land soon." They thoughtfully skinned and quartered apples for pie. The back door opened and a screen door slammed. The parish women arrived with a potluck of fresh baked bread, steaming turnips and green beans. These women preferred to visit on the back porch.

On the front porch, the spruce chairs squeaked as John and his friends rested their weary backs. The lot was filled with teams of horses hitched to carriages and wagons, de-bridled and tethered to mow the grocery yard's brush and grass. Each family had a freshly built home and a sprouting vegetable garden. Most had smoked venison in their attics, stretched rabbit and fox skins on their back porches. None wanted to see Ireland again yet all missed their families.

"To welcome Hugh and Patrick to our cornucopia!" Cornelius cheered. Chicory-coffee was lifted, celebrating the day of rest as well as the relief of John's brothers who'd arrived safely from County Antrim. The brothers had soaked hay in pine tar to stuff cracks between logs and chinked fireplace stones of John and Betsy's homestead cabin.

"Thank you for the welcome." Hugh stood. "I'd like to earn my keep by building a hall for Mass to be served and the lot of us to gather in the space next door." Hugh had his heart set on the foundation John had laid for a house across from John's new home and cow barn overlooking Franklin Lake. No matter the brothers' generational struggle, each had a genetic memory that guided them to a common sensibility of home looking over a lake. Patrick was happy in the cabin with the terraced gardens and barns while he staked out and built his home on Grassy Bay.

"I'd like a collie myself," Hugh said.

"I'd like a hound dog more," Patrick responded.

"Yes, a hound makes a good hunting dog. It's like anything else. Some people like one thing, some like the other. I've always liked blunt-toed shoes. Well, I know fellas that like pointed-toed shoes," Jim said and took a sip.

"Doesn't make much difference to me about my shoes. Wouldn't you know I like boots?" Hugh said. Hugh had just finished a chair more upright than the low chairs so it sat higher than the others.

"I'd like a coy-dog," John said. "Half-wild and half-tamed." He was feeling more at home with his brothers.

Betsy called from inside, "John!"

"Oh, hello." He looked up.

"Kin ya' give a moment?" Betsy retreated into brogue.

"Sure." He loved her brogue that was waning since she had become an American citizen.

"Come on inside, please." Betsy opened the front door. "You makin' out all right, Patrick?" She and John stepped into the grocery.

"Say, Betsy," Patrick called after her, "you were all wrong in that argument we had yesterday. I looked up the information in the encyclopedia an' it said..."

Betsy tried to cut him off. "Patrick! Watch yourself."

Patrick continued "...rutabagas had just as much nourishment, any day of the week, as parsnips. If you didn't hear it?"

Once inside, Betsy looked about and said quietly, "John, you should know right away. I'm with child. I know we're not ready. I haven't settled in my teaching job, but here we are!" She threw up her hands, and John swept her off her feet and gently spun her around.

"I've nothing but joy! It'll mean our child is native to this free country that seems like it'll be here awhile." He hugged his beautiful bride. "We will have a citizen born in America!" They hugged and kissed again before Betsy returned to the back porch. On his way to the front porch, John saw through the window a group of families laughing under the apple tree.

He recognized the Catholic parishioners who worshipped at St. Matthew's Parish in Black Brook. After their midday meal, he saw some continue on the Turnpike to Loon Lake and others travel south on Sorrel Road to a Saranac Lake community that would be called Timbuctoo. These few found Sunday solace and food at this intersection under the apple tree's shade with their breakfast wrapped in kerchiefs around clay pots to keep warm. A ceramic jar of coffee was still steaming from the center of their picnic table.

Betsy returned to the back porch. "Well, I did want to tell you something today." She took a serious tone. "John and I are to have a child." And they all sighed a breath of relief. What they'd mostly guessed was out in the open. Congratulations and hugs were shared; advice assailed her from all directions until the cry of one-year-old Nicholas, who'd caught a splinter, caused Winnifred to run to the side porch. Winnifred nearly tripped on wood blocks that were stacked high before they tumbled and skittered to a heap. Older girls swapped news while they cared for the tiny ones, or ran a haw comb through their hair. Littlest ones lay on a quilt. Older boys high-jacked all over the place, wrestling, racing, climbing trees and yelling without listening. Wooden trucks, soft dolls and little log cabins littered the puncheon.

The opposite side of the house was for checkers, reading and music. Adults taught children to play the *bodhrán* or fiddle. Tin-whistle fingerings and breathing were taught to a group of kindergarten-aged children by young adults. Friday evenings, that side of the house was used for a gathering of musicians that made up a band. If teens could keep up, they could join the adults. Autumn weather cooled to a spectacular array of maples boasting health. Men met around the potbelly stove in the grocery. Women gathered in the kitchen around the cooking stove and the children played noisily in the post office. Rules and regulations of the community were discussed by the folks who gathered in these rooms. Time, skills and labor were measured and traded. John mediated disputes. Betsy tempered injustices with an extra cup of flour or tapped the weights on the steelyard favorably when measuring butter at the counter. Their survival depended on the community.

In no time, Betsy and John's first born, Annie, was nearly running the homestead and Betsy's classroom in District 1 frame schoolhouse on the Turnpike. Annie gobbled spoonfuls of cooked oats to entice her baby brother, Johnny, who surveyed the grocery kitchen happenings from the confines of his high chair. From there, he gained an understanding of the way nods, smiles and lilting conversations that were exchanged. The rough texture of his father's shaven face, to the soft caress of his mother's smooth hand, became his knowledge of father in relation to mother. As his uncles immigrated from Ireland, he looked hard for the differences in their similar profiles.

"With the wars of Europe subsiding down there's not a much need in Ireland or England for Da's kelp. His business is limping along," Hugh said as he glanced along the Turnpike. "Seems a dozen Irish are coming through by the hour to empty the Erin island into Alderbrook."

"Seven of the thirty-nine signers of the Constitution were foreign born," John said. "Respect is what the new citizens are seeking. Nourishment, lodging and respect." The brothers looked up to see a calm, handsome and strong man on the bottom porch step holding Annie in his arms. Just then, a frantic Betsy came running around the corner of the house with a basket of basil and tomatoes.

"Oh, thank you! I was gathering tomatoes and she scooted away so fast I couldn't see where she'd gone. Thank you!" Betsy nervously hugged her little darling. "Thank you." She brought Annie inside while still trying to catch her breath. She was with child.

"Good morning, please have a seat." John recognized the man from the Sunday group that ate under the apple tree and invited him onto the porch. Cornelius moved over a chair and offered him one. "Thank you for helping with Annie, she's a pistol, that girl." The young man looked sharply at John.

"I mean she's always energetic and running here and there—as soon as she was up on both feet she was off like an arrow," John explained. The young man nodded while silent.

"I'm John!" he said.

"Hello, Master John, I'm Harris."

"Hello, Harris, you can call me John. And this is Hugh and Patrick."

Then Martin, Cornelius, Michael, Darby and Owen introduced themselves and Harris began to visibly relax a bit but remained silent until he was called on to briefly answer a question. When John stepped away to tend to the cows, Harris quietly followed and silently handed him a milk bucket or hay fork just as John needed it. Seamlessly, Harris worked his way into assisting John on his farm each day until the peeper frogs started up at dusk. John offered him a share of the oats and use of the oxen with a weekly wage. Betsy continued to stock the grocery shelves with preserves of apple and nut butters and dried chicory with Eliza's help.

Set back from the Turnpike and behind the schoolhouse, the thrice-abandoned log cabin glowed from the firelight within. The constant hum of crickets, cicadas and frogs enveloped a patch along a grassy creek, with a tidy fenced vegetable garden in front. A silhouetted figure walked past the light, momentarily eclipsing the flicker. Peeking through the single-paned window, a young boy played by the hearth with wooden blocks. Beneath his knees were braided rags coiled and stitched into a rug. The blocks bent and swayed on a rough-hewn floor, worn by boots and stained by spilled, boiled sap. Mouse-chewed holes were carefully covered with hemlock shingles. Hanging on two pegs above the mantel was a Sharps rifle. The rafters of this one room had been swept clear of webs and strong boards now stretched to store-bought belongings—an apple picker, a rake and shovel, heavy blankets and extra flour. In the far back corner of the loft was a two-pound tin coffee can of hope, nailed to a rafter, heavy with coins. The tin contained the confidence of Harris, the father, the grace of Eliza, the mother, and the joy of a clever child named George.

Harris now had a dirt floor to sweep clean and a hearth to keep lit. He had steady work since he'd been offered a chair by the men on John's porch, and he found his way there every Sunday to catch the lilt of the Irishmen's talk. Eliza brought partridge pie and fish soup for Betsy while Nicholas Fox and Annie McKillip took turns swinging under the maple tree. Eliza was paid with egg cash and Betsy's teaching salary to help with the grocery, children and garden.

1844 Hill of Ward & Alderbrook, New York

Mary Jean, Bridget Elizabeth and Archibald McKillip arrived at Catholic Corner emptying of the home at Lake Lough in County Antrim of children. The Alderbrook grocery kitchen filled with all the brothers and sister lilting syllables of overseas-hills.

"Betsy, it's hard to imagine a million Irish moving like a sea upwards in bands with banners flying all up and down the hill of Tara. T'was the first rally of Daniel O'Connell that rose the people of Ireland to unite. T'was like a landscape engulfed in vertically moving floodwaters," Mary Jean said. "We raised the spirits of the High Kings with our hum of humanity in our striving."

"We've a stream of Irish here flowing up Irish Hill near Elizabethtown," Betsy said. "We're watching out for the ones that come by the grocery, but so many Irish are in need of work and housing." One wee frog went peep, then another and another, until the entire valley reverberated with their echoing, deafening oneness.

On the front porch, the brotherhood of family and parish continued to imagine the spired cathedral they hoped to build with the county priest, Father Keveny.

"Why don't we build the church after our cabins are built?" Patrick asked.

"Because, each Sunday I harness the tired horses and drive my family ten miles to St. Matthews in Blackbrook to stand through an increasingly overcrowded Mass," John said. Just then, the peepers went silent. John rose to check on the horses. Hugh joined him, and their contrasting oneness made a long shadow on the tall clover. John had brown leather boots and a deerskin jacket. Hugh wore tall black boots and a black and gray herringbone wool coat that flapped against his thighs. Their footsteps bent down the damp, glistening clover and grass, leaving divots in their misty path.

Hugh said, "there's a shortage of housin' for the Irish and you've given the sugar shack to George's family." John saw a wren going in and out of a hole in the foundation wall of the grocery. As he glanced up the mountain, he spotted the fish eagle warming in the sun.

"I don't have a spare roof, Hugh," John said.

In the grocery kitchen, Betsy and Winifred were preparing for a meeting. Winifred nervously opened the gathering with Proceedings of the Women's Rights Convention from Seneca Falls. Elizabeth Cady Stanton and Lecretia Mott had just presented the Eighteen Grievances of Women of which Elizabeth authored from her experience as wife, mother and widow. There were a few grievances that required attention.

"'Number 4: Women are denied the first right of citizens of the elective franchise thereby leaving her without representation in the halls of legislature. Women should have the right to vote. Number 5: He has made her in the eye of the law, if married, civilly dead. Number 6: He has taken from her all rights in property, even the wages she earns. Number 9: After depriving her of all rights as a married woman, she is taxed if she becomes single.' These Eighteen Grievances were presented in text by Elizabeth and Lecretia to the Connecticut Senate. Of all the states asked, Connecticut was the only state senate that accepted, considered and responded to a written presentation request," Winifred said.

At the intersection of Franklin Falls and Alderbrook Road, McKillip brothers John, Patrick, Hugh and Andrew fulfilled their dream to build Saint Rose of Lima Church in 1852. Necessity became stronger than desire as the United States grew that year in population by one percent, with the flow of Irish Catholics over the Canadian Border.

John's calm and strong gray mares easily took on the brunt of the work patiently pulling up the pentagon ribs. John and Hugh tied a long rope to the roof's apex and the horses' harness. John coaxed his horses who heaved into the weight of lifting the end walls. Quickly, men lifted long pine braces that were pinned diagonally with nails to support the vertical ends until the constructed siding were doweled at the corners. Two men were readied to hammer long nails through angled cross bars to balance the walls.

John and Betsy's baby boys Patrick, Archibald and Hugh were born in two-year intervals and baptized in the freshly hewn church. Ann was by her mother's side reading to and watching this passel of boys while Eliza helped with the garden, mending and cooking. Betsy's egg money went towards Eliza's salary so it wouldn't be counted as Betsy's own. Betsy was constantly aware of the dangers of farm life for her children. Grassy Bay, down a path from Sorrell Road, was forbidden without her supervision, as were the pasture and stable across Sorrel Road, the plow shed where the tools were kept. She sat more as she worked and napped on the couch in the afternoons while Annie entertained Hughie and Patrick with wooden blocks by her side. Betsy grew heavier and walked slower, then, she waddled with her toes pointing out. "Oh, you pretty, pretty boy," she cooed to wide-eyed Hughie. Her tummy bumped the high chair when she leaned over him and rubbed the kicking baby within.

"Mom, can you explain what Abraham Lincoln and Senator Douglas are debating about?" Annie asked while she flipped the potato pancakes.

"This is how candidate Lincoln described his thinking," her mother said. "If A. can prove, however conclusively, that he may, of right, enslave B.—why may not B. snatch the same argument, and prove equally; that he may enslave A.? You say A. is white, and B. is black. It is color then, the lighter having to enslave the darker? Take care. By this rule, you are to be slave to the first man you meet, with a fairer skin that your own."

Betsy continued explaining President Lincoln's theory. "You do not mean *color* exactly? —You mean the whites are intellectually the superior of the blacks, and therefore have the right to enslave them? Take care again. By this rule, you are to be slave to the first man you meet, with an intellect superior to your own. But, say you, it is a question of interest; and if you can make it your interest, you have the right to enslave another. Very well. And if he can make it his interest, he has the right to enslave you. It is causing a great grief Annie. So, Mr. Lincoln is an option for guiding this divided nation through troubled times." Her mother said. "But the stakes are high and the process ripe for problems."

"What do you mean, Mother?" Annie asked.

"Each state has the same number of electors in relation to senators and representatives," Betsy said. "I don't know much more about Mr. Lincoln other than he is called "Honest Abe" and splits rail fences."

In 1859, Winnifred visited Betsy one hazy afternoon with Nicolas. He and Annie took the boys fishing at Grassy Bay while the mist settled around the willows. They pointed out the ducklings waddling in a winding line behind their mother duck near some cattails. The boys had never gone to the lake without their mother or father and listened carefully to Ann's panicky, barking orders to stay back from the edge of the water. They watched the line of downy ducklings following their mother into the pond. One by one, the ducklings splashed into the water with boisterous quacks and squawks and buoyed away in a line of ripples. Nearby, a Bantam hen scolded her chicks into a single file line and herded them away from raucous splashing. One fluffy chick broke free from her clutch and leapt into the water after the ducklings. A downy flapping barely kept the chick above drowning. Hughie ran to fish the chick out of the turbulent water before Annie could catch him. Though Annie berated him for misbehaving, he beamed about having saved the chick and could hardly wait to tell his mother. He ran ahead to avoid Annie's harsh words. Hughie dashed through the back door and stopped in his tracks when he saw his mother was sitting in the rocker with a new baby in her arms. Hughie stared, then froze. He felt as if he'd been pushed off a limb and was in a free fall, floating without connection to heaven or earth.

"Ohhh Margaret, you are my little dear," Betsy cooed while adjusting to her baby's chosen name. Hughie sobbed with confusion as Annie ran up to hug her little sister Margaret. Hugh pounded his fists into Betsy's skirt while she smoothed his angry dark curls. He was too upset to remember to tell his mother about the chick.

1865 Father's Train, Annapolis, Maryland

The weeds had taken over Alderbrook, the garden, the church yard. Turkey vultures flourished and floated, circling above where passenger pigeons once clouded the alders. As soon as she lost her first tooth, Margaret, the seventh child, held her mother's worn docile hand in her tiny one as they walked along the brook path to the one-room schoolhouse at the end of their road. Margaret's long hair was pulled tight in pigtails that were twisted into buns above her ears and secured with a ribbon. They stopped often to pet the moss, the sage soft patches, the tall miniature forest above velvety green, the blue ones and the deep green moss. Margaret's skirt was buttoned from behind as was her white shirt. A collar with square corners dropped halfway down her front, was buttoned from behind, with the loving swiftness of her silent mother. Betsy found a smile in her sorrow as Margaret stood for inspection, all scrubbed with rosy cheeks and eager, excited eyes.

At the time, Margaret was thin as a wisp. Amidst her family's sorrowful ache and dark days, she became the promise of a bright and cheerful sprite that flitted about. A woman's name clung to Margaret and the community shared the burden of restarting a broken country. Allowed plenty of free time, Margaret liked to draw. She would hide these drawings carefully under the clothes in her lower drawer. No one cooed over her private sketches. She'd listened to the conversations to find the words that matched the sound until she was reading as well as the next. She clipped the extra newspaper to decipher the squiggles into sounds and sounds into words. It was still hard to understand the meaning of the words "attorney" and "Tawney." She repeated out loud, "Tawney" and "Dredd Scott," with two Ds. The names were whispered enough on the porches that she knew something happened. Something with a Supreme Court that was new.

When Margaret wasn't asking too many questions at school, she was acting up with mischief. Both interruptions caused her to be banished behind the wood stove. She drew on precious paper reserved for writing. She was often reprimanded for using school supplies and told to show the class that lined paper was for writing, not drawing.

In the turbulent Glens of Antrim, Ireland, Margaret MacGormack McKillip was laid to rest in the Layd Churchyard the very year John and Betsy's youngest, Daniel, was born. John sent home cash for his father to bury his dear mother and her library of stories. A tombstone was laid. A quarter-century had gone by since he'd seen her, but not a day had passed without his thinking of his mother. Had she been the hawk who pointed out this corner? Or the bluebird who pointed out Betsy? Had she kept him calm when the children were too noisy or he was too fatigued? Would she continue to be with him now? A slow-walking and sorrowful John McKillip mailed a sealed letter to his father and boarded the train in Burlington to NYC filled with other fathers in search of their battle-injured sons.

Quiet, mumbling conversations created a low hum above the rhythmic clatter of the moving train. The steel wheels rattled on the rails as the men in crumpled brown, black and blue holiday suits slept deeply, two by two, garnering strength before troubled searches for mere boys. In New York City, John transferred to a train to Washington, D.C., Annapolis and sat in the velvet seat by an impeccably dressed and distraught father.

There was a long silence.

"How's your son?" John asked.

"Three sons serve: two fighting in blue for the North, and my oldest son was killed fighting for the Confederacy. They grew up in South Carolina. I live in Washington."

"Where's your boy been serving'?" he asked.

"142nd regiment: New York. Was missing for a while."

"I'm John McKillip from New York." He extended his hand in greeting.

"Francis Lieber." He shook his hand heartily and winced as if injured. "I fought with Napoleon from Prussia."

"I'm sorry for your distress and loss. It's hard to imagine," John said. "I left dear Antrim, Ireland in 1832 after a bit of conflict. I will not return. Our family business is to make a medical staunch to stop the flow of blood."

"Ahhh, the blood did flow." Francis said. "I'm working on codes of conduct for *Laws and Usages of War*. Fight fast and furious, get it over with, and get whoever survives home to heal. The best wars last the shortest time. There has to be codes for captives as we are fighting for one country. Different codes apply to guerilla fighters captured. I want to reverse laws to ensure right to fight hard. Get it over with!" Francis said. "With sons on both sides, I want to get them home safe. If captured, I want them home intact and as healthy as possible."

"Has anyone thought of this before?"

"Maybe, but I'm writing it down. I'm including terms of truce and prisoner exchanges. I've got to include the Negro captives, just don't know yet if they are defined as fugitives or free men. We have no Negro prisoners now."

"Why is that?" John knew there were Negro recruits.

"Currently if captured, Negroes are executed." Francis Lieber's *Laws and Usages of War* was the adopted code for European wars. His code was adapted in Europe to become the Geneva Convention laws of combat, imprisonment, interrogation, and release for the World Wars. John was heartened that a compassionate and loving father had made order of what he was about to witness.

An agonizing and sleepless week ensued of searching through churches, schools, makeshift tent hospitals filled with amputated, wrapped and bloodied young bodies that looked decades older than their age. The revolting reek turned John's stomach. He grew accustomed to the stink and the fresh and clotted blood seeping through bandages. John again showed Johnny's tintype to a nurse, who pointed vague directions. With stalwart heart and seemingly lead-filled shoes, he strode carefully, examining bandaged heads and feverish shaking bodies for one son he might recognize as his own. As he trudged, he tried to remember that without the army's victories and grave losses, Lincoln's Emancipation Proclamation would not have been issued. Without the votes from the troops, Lincoln would not have been re-elected. The National Army in blue could be the heroes of the new nation. States had proven to be tyrannical as the Founders feared the federal government might be. Our original Constitution had failed. Now a central and federal government might be freedom's best friend.

There—he saw the back of Johnny's sleeping head. As he drew near, tears streamed down his face. His knees buckled and his body collapsed onto an emptied crate. His arms shook, then trembled. Johnny's wound was massive, with the stench of gangrene dripping from iodine soaked cloth. Who knows how many tears streamed or how much time passed before Johnny began to stir.

"How's everyone at home?" Johnny asked. "I've missed you all, deeply."

"Your mother reads your letters before going to sleep every night." John had to pause with a trembling chin. "You've a new baby brother, Danny. Everybody in Alderbrook and Au Sable is praying for your recovery. They asked that I say hello. Your brothers and sisters are shaking the mountains with hollering and hunting. Margaret has begun to make out letters and started school this year." They both knew to stop talking about home. Margaret has been the reason Johnny had stayed behind until the 142nd returned to reenlist.

"We skirmished at Chaffin's Farm, I nearly got out intact, but a bullet hit while we were in retreat." Johnny winced with the pain, but carried on. "The 142nd marched with Sherman before I got here. I missed most of it, father. I'm sorry I ran away with the regiment, Dad."

"Rest a bit, Johnny. I'm not going anywhere," John said. "Soon as you're better we're taking the train home. Rest a bit."

Johnny's hopeful, then wistful look told all. "Sure, Dad, I'll just rest a bit. Can't wait to see everyone. I love you, Dad," He dove headfirst into a deep sleep. John nodded off, but jolted awake at any murmur.

"What is the dripping red on the horse about, Margaret?" Annie, Betsy's oldest daughter and substitute teacher, asked her sister. Betsy was missing more and more days of school after Elizabeth and Edward were born. Though Annie was married, she helped her bedridden mother's recovery from childbirth by teaching. Margaret said that she was sure Johnny died while heroically riding on a white horse in war. "He brandished a ceremonial sword, and wore a very tall hat with a green feather," Margaret explained her colored pencil drawing to her class. "Johnny on a white horse rushed with his regiment up a hill on Chaffin's Farm. He was in a regiment charge! This is his white horse, with red blood pouring from a knife wound, that made his horse fall first." She gasped at his chivalry. "His best friend carried him to safety after another lance slid into my brother's hip. That cut got infected. That is how my brother died."

When the paper was stored elsewhere, Margaret practiced reading from a *McCall's* magazine the older girls shared. Margaret cut fashions and quotes to tuck away in her bottom drawer. Margaret imagined another place with big cities, with women in wide hats carrying parasols to protect their fashionable hair styles. Over the months of her being sent behind the stove, Margaret read primers: "Our New Constitution," "Founding Fathers," "Great New Frontier."

In the spring of her first year of school, Margaret listened for the sound of a heart breaking. It was a small and slight sound, quieter than silence. But with her father, it was louder than the peculiar eagle screaming above. John was being taken apart wheel by wheel and wire by wire as if there were instructions in how to dismantle him. There was no sense to putting them back together again for the pieces were now lost. There was no solace to offer her parents, as they lost the vision of their babies becoming children.

It may be that all things come in threes. This era was physically and psychologically ravaging young men and their parents through the landscape left littered with the wounded fragments of mere boy's evanescent souls. A nightmarish life rose from this bitterly scarred, vicious notion of a transformed ideal of manhood in the preposterous, foul-mouthed and murderous Jesse James. A fearless teen-veteran captured the idea of young manhood for fatherless and brotherless boys while he opposed restructuring one union. Brash antics of frightening and heart-gripping escapes entranced the spirited young sons of America. That climate consumed the 22-year-old lives of James and Archibald.

John and Betsy crumpled in this rancorous aftermath of war. Diatribes against the pernicious nature of young men's lives, continued to resound with a moral and religious fervor. Betsy passed away a year later, leaving little Eddie and Dannie McKillip to carry on the family name. Margaret, at thirteen years old, and Bethie, at ten, assumed keepers of the home and grocery. They were allowed to continue their schooling with Eliza's help. Dannie and Eddie went to live with Ann and Nicolas Fox. John ensured Betsy's dream of a high school education for his girls.

James Franklin drove his father to an Au Sable Valley meetings at the buttery across from Alderbrook's grocery store with milk deliveries. James and Margaret sat in two deep seated chairs with their feet dangling above the ground near the buttery and cold storage.

"I don't even know what I am missing at school," James said.

"I can help you keep up," Margaret said. "Mother has all the primers and I can tell you stories about U.S. history. We have to pass a test about the Founding Founders this school year. If you take that test you can graduate eighth grade."

And so began decades of James listening to Margaret synthesize her prolific reading. Practicing hard for the annual axe and saw competitions might allow him to get work with the logging company and help with income at home. His father had a hacking cough from working the mines and James would have none of it. Logging would get him out of thankless daily chores around the farm. What began as childhood churchyard romping in Blackbrook became hugs with cousin-like pecks on the cheek in Alderbrook. James' farm tasks included driving milk to the buttery once a week. After commiserating over chores, Margaret listened to James' family burdens.

Margaret and James' long lingering kisses on a Grassy Bay log one summer night, without a moon, led to consummating their desire for each other. Guilt, time together, time apart, blossomed into a unified love. A profound interwoven love. A neither-could-live-without-the-other kind of love.

Mining or logging were no longer options for a middle son to support James' and Margaret's hope for children. While he was toppling a tree, the cut trunk kicked back and wrenched his spine, leaving James fit for nothing but teamster work, driving the horses. Chicago's Columbia Exposition— and its need for deliveries—beckoned James to consider the ferocious growth of a teeming city and inspired his proposal to Margaret. Knowing there was none other than James for her, and confident that her younger brother, Eddie, and sister, Bethie, were old enough to help their father, she heartily agreed to marry James and discover Chicago together. They'd manage city life together, but absolutely wouldn't be alone.

"Margaret's the love of my life, but I've no future here with the state park halting logging. I'll be sure to care for her all my days," James said to John McKillip while asking for Margaret's hand in marriage. John had lost his wife, oldest son and daughter and three more sons after the Civil War. Now he was losing Margaret, the apple of his teary eye, But, he agreed to the marriage recognizing how she came alive when James was around.

No sacrament given in St. Rose of Lima was more magnificent than the marriage of Margaret McKillip of Alderbrook and James Franklin of North Jay. Fiddle, tin pipe, base and *bodhrán* music, with country singing, lilted them through a parish ceremony. The flower girls, Johanna and Bethie, carried larkspur and roses. John, her father, dropped another tear for his dear Antrim at the stanza *parsley sage, rosemary and thyme, she once was a true love of mine...*

A potluck dinner followed at McKillip's Grocery across the street. Tables under the apple trees were set with woolen cloths held in place by vases of black-eyed susans, daisies and Queen Anne's Lace. Margaret and Bethie prepared bread, beans, coleslaw and caramelized carrots for the celebration, kept cold in the next-door butter factory. Salads with sweet corn, watermelon sprinkled with mint, cheese and roasted hazelnuts filled the wooden bowls. When John washed his hands at the pump it signaled for everyone to wash and sit. They were starting to say grace when Winnifred arrived with venison roasts and a giant layered buttermilk cake. Margaret's own butter was in the middle of the table. She blushed when Aunt Bridget proclaimed "the best butter in the parish." James had hung two swings in the side yard for the grandkids to play. While waiting to swing, they took turns churning ice cream surrounded by ice and salt. Lichen covered boulders in the yard kept the boys busy for hours playing King of the Hill, sending oratories from on top.

At a glowing red dusk, James paused the music and announced, "Margaret and I will be moving to Chicago!" The news rippled rapidly through the friends and family. "Now, we are both available for harvest season, so please don't hesitate to call on us for help." His brother George Jr. stood up, a bit at a loss, and offered a teary toast. "Then I take my hat off to you two," he bowed low over the hat, "and pass my hat to the others for a fund for your safe travels. Wouldn't we all like to help now?" The hat was passed through the stymied reception, returning mostly-filled with coins and bills. Heartbroken, John could be found in the grocery kitchen, slightly rocking in Betsy's worn chair beneath his arrowhead collection and chatting with gray-haired Eliza. "We held such hopes for Alderbrook," he said. Once-vibrant, Catholic Corners of Alderbrook, Franklin County, New York, United States of America was losing another cornerstone couple seeking their future in an unknown city.

John discovered the fish hawk's nest in a Red Spruce. Three fluffy fledglings peeked over the stick nest with downy faces framing tiny, dark eyes. Parents regurgitated food into their open beaks. Within weeks, they were awkwardly feathered out with veins sticking straight out of the soft down in a constant state of surprise. A few flaps of wings sent old unwanted fluff through the high forest of reaching branches. One feathered early and practiced its flight in laps across the three-foot-wide nest. She jumped up on a branch and plucked tufts of infant down, in adolescent defiance, from her belly, to flutter in the wind. Gliding back to the safety of the nest, she flapped again to another branch. The other two peered from their downy pocket of sticks. Which parent swooped in with a squirming rodent's dangling tail? Nestlings raised open beaks in infantile expectation of a meal. Poking and pouncing on the mouse, they learned to pierce into life and tear into flesh. John witnessed the fledglings set off into the wilderness to fend for themselves. The fleeting moments of a brief two months in the nest gave perspective to the peaceful safe community they'd created in Alderbrook. What might lie ahead for this new country testing a democratic constitution? What might lie ahead for his growing family and

Betsy? By the grace of God, they'd made themselves a safe haven, but how long would it last?

Chapter 23: Onward on the North Shore

Dad was dying. It was increasingly clear. The first choppy turbulence was leaving his home and moving his art, prints and slides. He had moved to an apartment with emergency buttons to press and chords to pull. He was seeing the strain his recoveries caused his cheering family and friends. We didn't recognize that he was not the same witty, capable and steady Dad. We could see there was going to be family turbulence ahead with disagreements about reproductions and the distribution of his artworks.

Years of our family spinning, on a tall pole that Dad balanced, with nine strong ideas of how to care for his art: sell it, preserve it, show it, give it, share it, copy it, store it, ignore it, hide it. How much to control and how much to let go? How much should we cheer our Dad to fight back from his last stroke? How much do we let go of his process of dying? "You cannot save his life." I was advised but dreaded confronting the spiraling apart of our family that Dad held together as a quiet reminder of Irene and Mac's patterns.

"What do you want?" I asked Dad.

"I want to distribute the rest of my artwork to all of you," Dad said.

"Then it's time for lawyers," I said.

Frank was the trustee of the Children's Trust. Dad and I met at his estate lawyer's conference room overlooking the water towers of Streeterville. Dad walked around the conference table to sit beside me. Frank and Andrew, Dad's estate-designated trustees, opposed Dad's decision to distribute his art and its copyright, with their thought that his life's work was more valuable as a combined body. His longtime lawyer sat at the end of the table. The meeting's cost was the value of decades of our family's possible peace. Our parents' wills said to distribute equally.

"Distribute immediately, today, assign copyright to each child," Dad's attorney directed from the end of the table. For years, Dad's art had been gifted annually to his family, children and grandchildren, in a trust with one brother as Trustee. Each painting was cataloged with a title, number, when it was painted, and where it was published. There were several years more of art to be distributed within the tax laws. The third issue was that Dad had photographed slides of his extensive collection for online digital sales.

"I'm not going to listen to the lawyers," Frank said while leaving the law office. Our mother's blanket of calm prevailed over her family's wishes: I want to hang Dad's art in my house; I want to show mine to museums; I want to frame his art for my child; I want to see what I get; I want to exhibit in libraries; I want to send mine to schools; I want to sell mine to the Library of Congress; I want someone else to sell mine; I want to know what I have.

Two brothers had an ongoing disagreement punctuated with comments so peculiar I relegated it to mourning their father's health. My impending trusteeship would reduce their vote to one-third. That concern was nourished by our grief over Dad's declining health. It became clear to me that my agreement with my mother was to watch over her children, not to keep her family together. And my agreement with Dad was to distribute equally his art to his children, an impossible task as each artwork is unique.

"I'm ready to go, let me go," Dad said. He was moving into a new bewilderment. A loneliness for *here* that couldn't be filled, a place we couldn't enter. Hadn't all the grandchildren grown up already? There was a fear of the unraveling of the tension he kept spinning on a thin pole that could bind us together or spiral us to the furthest corners of our rivalry. Who did he love more? Dad's gifting of his life's work was conscious and random. He chose to impose on his children that we work together by dividing subjects into nine packages with the same number, but variances of worth. Dad separated paintings of Vatican II into packages for one year's distribution. The Chicago Symphony Orchestra tours of Europe and Japan he equally distributed another year. He allowed each of his nine to feel fate cared for them. When the packages were too heavy for him, he asked me for help lifting.

"Which twin was born first?" he asked at each round.

"Patrick's middle name is Quinten, he's fifth, the younger twin," I said each round.

The tension in his shaking hand reverberated throughout the room, the family, the generations. Tension reverberated in the newly painted walls of his three-room apartment. Tension stared down from the fire sprinklers above. Each of his children's names was written, in his hand, on an art-filled brown package to gift his art, oldest to youngest, then again, a dozen more times. My arms shook with the weight. I carried one heavy package after the other for to him to assign to a child. His choice. His wish. His gift. At Christmas, each child accepted the packages he gave them. *As you wish.*

There was an ephemeral moment of his children hanging his artwork on the wall behind him when he was told he wouldn't be going back to his apartment. Like the Father's Day cards, it was notes from his family that he was being watched over. The nurses had a congratulatory tone for the paintings he could not see or remember so he smiled. All he could remember was that the frames should be buffed clean of fingerprints. He woke to two foggy shadows joined at their grey-haired-heads leaning over a spiral notebook that told the others of his medications. They were speaking quietly while reading his pulse, weight and diet. "My condition is fine," he said, fighting back from his last stroke and resting in supportive living with the hopes of getting back to his apartment.

Was our love and care from what we could give, or from what we wanted to receive from our father? Who knew the right amount to visit, or cling, or take, or ask. Who knew how much to demand, offer, assist, remind or take over? Ours was a slow up and down. We had time, this way, to adjust to his ever-present peril of death. As if anyone is ready for the reality. We shared his scary strokes. Many times of knowing this might be the last one, the last time we would see the artist's hand active, with only a tremor exerted from concentrated effort. It was a constant tug of not being there enough, not knowing enough stories, not bringing enough news to encourage him. What happened to my smile?

On my way to visit him one day, the magnificence of a Cooper's Hawk, trapped in my fencing for our urban chickens, gave me pause. Its claws clung to the chicken-wire, baring vulnerable brown-spotted down on a creamy underbelly. The wings flapped ferociously upside down. The hawk's inverted herringbone markings showed between open wings bent by the enclosure. Lifeless prey, a house sparrow, lay in the remaining bird feed. My presence invaded the Cooper's vulnerability into a flapping unknown fear. When I stepped away, the hawk found the courage to gracefully glide from its cooped entrapment. I could feel that Dad felt trapped in life. He would choose his moment of release.

The tectonic plates of my world jolted when the call came Saturday morning: "Your father has MRSA." He had protected me from a world so completely I had no idea what was in store for me. Frank and Andrew emailed everyone, "please come and get what you have given Dad". I was selling my minivan so I picked up my dining table, the encaustics he had given me and the sculptures I had given him. Then another email from Frank and Elizabeth stating no family member could enter his apartment alone while he was hospitalized. Thunderous, chorusing arguments from all of us were revived and roiled with the building storm. Heat of spiraling rivalry, greed and jealousy fueled the hurricane-force nature of a great spirit releasing life's grip. We reverted to our childhood family structure: "Whom did he love more?" was our paramount rivalry. "Who got more art?" "Who got what art?" was the actualization of who Dad loved more. "Be careful how you treat each other now," I told my children.

Dad's vitality altered over the years, the spiral of his energy, what he created, started to churn like a maelstrom slowly building around us as we spun at a pole's distance. Each of us was connected through him with our complicated sixty years of family life. Dad had been our hub in the three-ring circus of working at home to feed, clothe, drive and guide his children. We vied for loyalty and favors. Dad's waning vigor masterfully kept the right amount of vim to level our spin. "We will hang together or hang separately," Dad told Andrew. "No more prints."

The constant mystery in life of how loved ones get along was revealed within the nine families of six or nine each, making forty-seven people in total. Some constants were our holiday dinners, graduations and religious ceremonies. We were coming together to act as one with Dad's passing. We were coming together with our mother's patterns of shared instincts. We would decide what traditions to honor and which to abandon.

"Let me go, I'm ready," Dad said while he hovered between sub-consciousness and a week beyond what the doctors thought was probable. Six days before, the hospital Reiki master said, "Many family members are gathered to welcome him; they are circled around waiting." Settling the accounts of the soul may have long plagued this ex-Army Air Force navigator who denied his children pistols chewed from peanut butter sandwiches. He never carried a gun into enemy territory. He never had the intention to kill. Wait, what relatives were waiting for him? Jean and I have photographs of what they looked like, but what were they like?

While Dad floated between us and sleep, Andrew and I made arrangements at the funeral home. "Name of your mother's mother?" was asked. I answered, "Irene Agatha Rogers Leahy." "Name of your father's mother?" A long pause… "Elizabeth Margaret Franklin McMahon," I answered, thrilled to know her name before my father's burial.

"I could never had answered that," Andrew said.

The January evening that Dad passed away, his youngest son was visiting him and his youngest grandchild, Brie, celebrated her Confirmation that afternoon. With only one last moment, you can still change the world. He chose his time to pass away. He empowered the youngest of two generations in his choice. Swirling fluidity rose in a tornadic spiral.

At Dad's death, seven o' nine became the third trustee to balance the arguing. Dad had protected me from what I didn't know could exist. Tectonic plates fiercely split and creviced, ice carved from the mountain of a man who called himself a stone on the beach. Dad, our peddling unicyclist, wobbling color, toppled into the shifting tectonics with the delicately balanced pie-plate of nine mourning children. We, the pie, dipped and righted itself, then spun out of control. An emotionally charged maelstrom tumbled us with hurricane chaos. And that was with the art already gifted by our father. We all took a long pause of four months before the final distribution of Dad's last one thousand artworks. Frank went to Florida for a month.

To make sense of the chaos and rising anxiety, I developed a plan to distribute Dad's remaining artwork with copyrights. Andrew and I numbered the back of the Estate-owned art that was piled, face down, in a stack. With each drawing, we were awed by the mastery "The Man Who Drew the News" had accomplished. One single line said so much about how a set of glasses rested on a nose. Andrew and I made art every day, which enhanced our wonder at Dad's expression of graphite on paper we viewed in Dad's quiet living room that he'd made. A new numbering system indicated how the Trust distributed art.

The following weeks, I made a document to list the number for a copyright transfer sheet to be signed the day of distribution. As a sibling took a painting off the pile, they would list it on their copyright transfer, and on an excel sheet with a description of the artwork. The list gave each of us a record to search for images. From that list of numbers, the trustees could transfer copyright from the Trust to each sibling, assuming the trustees would sign the document. This system could become a fair and transparent distribution if brothers and sisters came to collect their art, the numbers stayed in order, no art was missing, and trustees transferred copyright with their signature. The copyright transfer could all take place on an April date scheduled. "Just put the pencil on the paper and made a strong statement," Dad had said. And "There is no good deed left unpunished."

Chapter 24: Orphaned

Recently orphaned, I slipped into a pew near the fan of an overheated chapel that was filled to standing room only for my father's memorial service. Mixing together friends and family, neighbors and cousins who hovered in the aisle, I stumbled away to gather my thoughts while my printed eulogy saved my seat in the second pew. With a sister on one side and my kids and husband on the other, I faced forward to a flower-lined altar as the scent of lilies wafted through the brimming crowd. Though my brothers and sisters had come together to plan this rite of passage we were at a major turning point in my life. The church began to calm, then quiet as a formally cloaked pastor walked across the altar to light candles, then to the back of the church for the procession. Cut grass aroma accompanied our singing "On Eagle's Wings" as an altar boy carried a crucifix through the back door and Father McNulty lifted a bible overhead past the front rows of my electrically charged nine siblings and their families of three to five settled in for a shared reverence. We discussed, agreed, disagreed and let-go in our many choices and offerings for this Mass: who would sing Ave Maria, who would give a eulogy, bagpipes to lead from church to burial site. These were puzzle-pieced into a Mass to express our love for Dad. Nephews passed programs down long pews.

My eulogy absorbed my sweating palms as I opened our service in Dad's Memorial program. What caused me to think I could read about his life history and our complex relationship? Would I be able to read my writing to those who knew him longer? The audience had not occurred to me as I brazenly wrote a sub-Cliff notes version of his life. My words were too brief to even symbolize him. All I could do was skip a stone over the surface of his life and hope it touched the right stories for an impression of who he was to us.

In the patterns of a full Mass, the program had readings from both the bible and gospel, the Apostles Creed and the pastor's homily set the tone. My eulogy would be read before the blessing of the host and communion. By the time of the pastor's homily and a brother and sister's readings, I was shaken to my core with the loss of a mysterious father who stoically braced himself against the rising and falling of our family's tides. I leaned to my sister for support. "I'm not sure I can do this reading."

"Then don't," she replied. A plume arose of all the rivalries that swirled from those two words. "Who cares?" columned up from those two words. Their enclosing us ensured one does not rise above, fall below or stray. I stood in defiance of all of them who needed to herd us all together for their sense of belonging. Stepping past my sister, the short but eternally long walk to the lectern felt like a march. As I turned to the room of Dad's life in faces and rustling grey, blue and black, I spoke from all the silenced suffered. I spoke through their need to corral and steer and cajole and confine me. I spoke my words as a gift about my quiet father who feared how we would fare with what he had made.

"On August 9, 1929, the east bound Graf Zeppelin, nearly 800 feet long and 110 feet high, cast its shadow over eight-year-old Mac McMahon in Santa Monica, California. It had been untethered from New Jersey and headed over Manhattan where the Empire State Building was being built. It flew over Yankee Stadium, where Babe Ruth hit his 500th home run. It traversed Wall Street, where the market was at an all-time high. The zeppelin circumvented the globe over a defeated Nazi Party where Edith Frank cared for her baby, Anne." I looked up to pause. "It was lifted by a four-million-person cheer of 'Bonzai!' and a Japanese typhoon before it soared along the coast of California. The boy, my father, would have seen it. He might have understood the magnitude of this world-touring blimp as a promising young Artist Reporter.

"Our dad shared his way of showing us the world throughout our childhood. He taught us the constellations to find our way home. With Sunday kite-flying over the lake, he taught us about the lift of the wind in relation to the angle of the string. When our balsa wood planes crashed, Dad delivered the right joke to turn our tears to chuckles. Our father soared thousands of feet above us, channeling his vision through a pencil tip into one bold, courageous, assured line, then another. He showed us a world in turbulence and the beauty of nature in pen on paper.

"We are awed by his list of accomplishments, humbled by the man of few words with pinpoint clarity. Each of us is honored to share our lives with him. His balance of family, friends and work pivoted on his solitary making of art with a world vision. His drive came from deep within. His love was profound, both simple and complex. Dad likened himself to a stone on the beach that the waves washed over. In his final years, he suffered a few tsunamis, in the form of TIAs and strokes. But the waves have washed away again this week to leave him like the stone on the beach. I will always remember his love-filled eyes expressing a spirit that will live *Onward*!" Echoing silence followed.

I sat in my pew as my loose silk shawl slipped off my shoulders. My sister looked straight ahead as if I had defied her. My husband nodded. Communion began. No one in the family caught my gaze with approval. They had all been asked to read, but didn't. Was it that I had not represented Dad well? Was it that I was one of the youngest and skipped over them to become his trustee?

A few words were spoken about the burial immediately after and lunch following at *Lovell's*. The bagpipes started up, overpowering *Man of la Mancha*'s theme song as we filed out in two lines. Stifled by my impending task, I ducked into a limousine as though hiding from what lay ahead, what I perceived happened and my unwelcome presence. The limo did not move. Childhood neighbors opened the door to say hello and that people were looking for me. Surrounded by my family in this bubble, I did not climb out to chat with dear friends. The drive to the cemetery slowly started and we sat back to take a deep breath. Bagpipes greeted us at the burial ground where his hole was opened between Gram and Mom's. He had requested no military taps or flag at his burial. A simple prayer, "Our Father who art in heaven, hallowed be Thy name. Thy Kingdom come, thy will be done, on earth as it is in heaven…" A shovel of dirt thudded on his lowered casket and we were led by bagpipes away to our funeral recession to lunch next to St. Patrick's church.

Poised in a curl over my elbows on knees at the edge of a chair, still panting from a sun salutation, I stared into the patterns of an oriental rug, granting myself a few more moments until an aching distress triggered my rising to action. Even my rug is someone's bone of contention. I tiptoed down the hall to check my email passing Dad's drawing of Mom traveling in Europe, his paintings of a flock of egrets in a leafless canopy and the framed silk map of 1945 Germany. I passed my three sleeping children's bedrooms into a glass room on the second floor as an April dawn rose over Chicago's Westside. Between canopies of a Maple and Pussy Willow that softened the ambulance sirens along Austin Boulevard hung a watercolor self-portrait of Dad. He watched over my email responses. Virginia Creeper climbed the windows reflected in my desktop screen. I swiveled in a chair as I scrolled through spam wishing I had a cup of coffee. An email from Frank announced that most of our siblings could attend April 21 for distribution of Dad's art.

My system of documenting the estate-gifted art was assembled in nine binders next to my desktop. The art was organized in Dad's apartment with the documents in the same order of distribution. We would all leave distribution day with furniture, rugs and over one hundred works of Dad's art and hope for peace. What had seven o' nine done to deserve a daily reproving email? On the April distribution weekend, I woke in a sweat of fear as if about to walk into an electric fence. In Dad's apartment, the mood shifted from tense hugs of greeting to an acrid mood of distrust as we breathed dusty-smelling heat and someone's dirty socks. The sprinkling system still glared down. Stand by the door if you need to leave in a hurry. Frank and Andrew had built an alliance that was focused on the slides of the art and declared they were Andrew's. They are not arguing as much as before? Andrew over-filled his cart with crates of slides and hustled them to his car first.

The binders were distributed and the categories described of art stacked on the floor, against the living room walls, encaustics leaned against the studio walls, boxes of reproductions were piled in Dad's bedroom sans slides. Dad's drawing table had a collection of weavings, pottery, souvenirs and Father's Day gift knick-knacks. "Anyone who gave Dad a gift could take that with them," Frank proclaimed. We picked numbers out of a hat to determine selection order. As a painting was lifted, a number was written on the page, written in the binder and the art placed in a pile. *The system is working!* Every few categories, Frank declared a change in the order which sent all of us scurrying to find the correct page. Pick your battles. For two days, we selected artwork in order, then chose an artifact, rugs, photographs, books or pottery. Car loads and one U-Haul drove away sedated with memorabilia, art of varying value and stuff to sort through later. It felt like being overstuffed after a Thanksgiving meal as we stiffly, wearily hugged goodbye. "This was the most transparent distribution we have had yet," Hugh said.

Frank and Andrew unified by not signing the copyright transfer documents that weekend though they watched each number written on the page in ink. In early 2012, we were trying to finalize Dad's estate. His paintings had been divided among the children equally, but there was contention about unaccounted-for print sales. Eventually, things came to a head between Andrew and I, co-Trustees. I felt the family should be notified that rights to sell their digital art images were going overseas. Things got worse over the week, until Andrew finally called it quits. "You are no longer a family member," he said. "We are not coming for Christmas anymore." He hung up.

That night, I called my kids for dinner just as Daniel walked in the back door. After lighting the candle, saying grace, *"Bless us oh Lord and these thy gifts..."* and the funniest things at school I said, "The cousins will not be at Christmas this year."

"What happened?", "Why not?", "Who is coming for Christmas then?", "No cousins?" I tried to summarize the confusing story ending with their married cousins were now splitting holidays with in-laws.

"We've been ghosted," Mahon said, raised his pumping arms to dance in his seat. "Ghost busterrrrred!" Sophia and Brie danced in their chairs. Daniel blew out the candle and they danced about the room. "Ghosted!…. Ghost busted….I ain't afraid of no ghosts…"

Brushing my teeth in the morning cast back a sister's straight edge smile that could easily be a nod of approval that Mom might have winked. The presence of a fogginess of connection surrounded me down the hall of their gifts of paintings, drawings and weavings. The bend of my shoulder caught in a wardrobe mirror was the same aging bend of a brother's stooped shoulder. When I picked up dishes to rinse at the sink it was Dad's gesture that now wiped the glass. Stepping past the front door's gold-leafed mirror I caught a glimpse of a sister teeing off. It was the way I turned on the step. Tilting a hat at the front door mirror another sister's blue eyes looked back, though our Aunt's voice directed the tilt.

Though our Christmas dinner table still filled with family and friends, I imagined having Christmas dinner with the 1800's Adirondack family and my brothers and sisters. John, the youngest brother, could be seated between John and Johnny McKillip, Mary and Jean on either side of Mary Jean from Antrim, The Elizabeth's, the Hugh's and Patrick's would have place cards next to each other. I would sit with Margaret McKillip Franklin and Daniel would be at the end of the table next to her brother, Dannie. While summoning I might as well have a Margaret's side table for five generations and an Irene's table of four generations. I wondered if the conversation would flow as if we knew each other all along? We would sip wine from Gramma Mac's amber depression glasses and eat from the same recipes passed along. We would all begin the meal with "Bless us oh Lord and these they gifts…" We would give thanks to Margaret McKillip who dreamed of her great-great-granddaughters?

Our phantom family spiked with news of a baby being born or a great nephew in middle school as if air poked a vertiginous cloud then the ever-wispy horizontal flow streamed our absence together. Our mist burned with heat, cooled with chill, dissipated and reformed and congealed to a substance to navigate. The presence of our flow directed my motion into the world melded as a grey silvery sheet of dense mist that surfed the brick garden walk, lifted and descended in the breeze until events of my day dissipated the spectral spirit.

Peace came from writing with my mother's cloisonné pen. It's not that the cloisonné pen was worn from writing. More so that my middle right finger was getting deformed from the callouses at the knuckle. A bulbous callous on the inside of the end joint hit up against my forefinger in an unnerving way like I need to flick something off. Like a beetle protruded. At a glance, my right hand looked like arthritis was setting in, but the callous did not have pain, just a growth from rubbing against the pen. The second knuckle of my thumb extended out in an enflamed protrusion exaggerating a cramped gesture. "Sky's the limit!" Mom echoed.

The cloisonné pen shone brighter than ever as if polished in its veins of silver by a gentile butler in a grand lord's estate. The melted particles became iridescent like mica particles caught the light and reflected it back. Prisms of rays shot out further than my fingers, hand, elbow and shoulders. More peculiar than its polished glean was that the pen hadn't run out of ink. Here were hundreds of pages of writing and revisions and the cartridge still allowed a steady flow of dark ink as smooth as liquid gold. The ink was neither blue or black, but a warm, dense chocolate-brown color.

My children graduated from elementary, high school and college while my Rolodex became outdated with family addresses. Our communication was diminished to checking for new return addresses on graduation and Christmas card envelopes. And finally, I searched online for condolences, wedding gifts and holidays cards. Annually, the women individually and together requested Frank and Andrew distribute the trust bank account. It reminded me that Frank had been slow to distribute Mom's estate too. I flew the coop to my Irish Catholic family in the 1800s Adirondack Mountains.

Part IV: Full Circle

Chapter 25: Westward

Then Margaret heard a faint faraway hum. Rumblings in the rails reverberated through the station platform. Her heart pounded hard. A whistle pierced the quiet. Margaret felt the love between her husband and father. James vowed he would honor his father-in-law by caring for Margaret with all his heart and soul. John lightly tapped his hand on James's shoulder to acknowledge the trust he had in his new son-in-law.

The engine's front windows gleaned in the sunlight. Black smoke rolled along the car's back. A sudden streak of white shot up through the smoke with a screaming whistle. A long wild screaming! The train swelled monstrously big, shaking everything around them with noise. With red eyes, Margaret breathed, and wiped her nose. Thick steel wheels screeched, cars bumped and crashed at the interlocking links. It heaves with mighty breath. I have to get inside that beast, Margaret thought. Her body fluttered. The monstrous steel giant roared its mighty churning wheels and screeched to an impatient halt beside the platform.

She said tearful goodbyes to her family and followed James up into the carriage. Adrenaline quickened the step of the newlyweds as they walked between rows of velvet seats. The wall of the car was all windows. Inside was as bright as outside. The soft seat was springy as she sat. She and James giggled and bounced. Her fingertips stroked the velvet. A tear welled up as she recalled petting the moss with her mother, then more so she hardly saw John and Bethie as they waved good bye.

As they settled still into their moving train car, the odor of bodies packed together and exotic food spices on the train benches was overwhelming. Polish, Italian, German, Irish and English accents filled the evening air. The speed of passing fields and lakes kept pace to the rhythmic chatter of the wheels on the still settling rails. Cuddled close to surround their belongings, keeping each other warm, they rested their weary, overworked arms and backs.

James and Margaret first felt the enormity of their decision. The panache of their travels to the big city was deflated in recognizing the reality of wooden benches crowded with scraped-together folks giving purse-emptying fares. No one had enough, nor any extra. No one had anything to offer but a smile of charity in their need for companionship. James and Margaret had spent the couple of months since their wedding relying on their friends' and neighbors' need for harvesting help. The palms of James's hands were cut, healed and cut again from harvesting hops. Margaret's fingers were still healing from the slicing of fruit. That companionship, with stories and memories shared, along with the grand send-off at the station, had left them looking at each other, lonely in their togetherness.

For the first time, they felt swept up in the tide of swirling unknown migrants. They rubbed a salve of honey, pine sap and wax into their palms and fingertips. They whispered old jokes, reminded each other of their family obligations left behind, kissed, hugged and cuddled in their striving for peace within. Then, they dozed off over their bags as Margaret clutched the bills, coins and packets of fruit and vegetable seeds sewn into the seams of her traveling dress.

"Everyone off, this train is not going forward until tomorrow morning!" They were abruptly awakened, necks stiffly crooked. It was pitch black, and they were still delirious at being jolted awake from their deep sleep.

"E-e-e-veryone off! This train is experiencing looo-coo-cmoo-tive engine maaaalfunction. Announcements will be made tomorrow morning on the platform ticket-booth for your next train connection. This Chicago Grand Trunk Railway train has been postponed until tomorrow! Everybody off! Last stop for this Grand Trunk Railway train here in Saint Thomas, Ontario!"

Still drowsy, they put on their hats and coats, looped bag straps over their shoulders and greeted the moonless dark. The smell of rural farm life greeted them as they stepped off the last metal-grate step of Vermont's Grand Truck Railway Train onto the sloping gravel of the train bed.

"Can you believe we've come this far, James, to smell the inside of a barn in St. Thomas, Ontario"? Margaret sniffed the hay, manure and acrid urine of large animals nearby. "Where and how are we going to spend the night?"

"Margaret, if you're willing, I see a freight train door open a bit up the track. We need to rest, to hear the announcement of the train time and keep out of the elements. At least the smell will remind us of home."

"James, I'm not sure. If we run into trouble, I've enough bills for an overnight in a hotel. If it works, O.K. Why not try... It's a nice night. And we have all these bags to rest on..." The reek of oil filled their noses. They strained to see what the freight train might hold, which car might have space. Their feet slipped on sloping gravel. Three cars were locked, followed by two open boxcars filled with canvas rolls stacked to the ceiling, Then, a partially opened door before them had a light inside. James reached for the grab bar and swung his bags up. Margaret's forehead clipped the iron edging as she passed her satchels up. The smell of rust mixed with blood as she climbed. James was balanced on the edge clinging to the grab bar, trying to get a leg over the ledge. Wood splinters cut under his right-hand fingernails. James's right foot was over the edge of the ledge—he pulled up and gave Margaret a hand. Her right knee was now over the ledge, then, another knee. Her shoe caught in a hem and ripped her fine stitching. They pulled their way up to standing. Burlap wrapped canvasses leaned along one wall of the freight car, and the newlyweds set their things along the wall and leaned into them to protect their gifts and possessions. Their stomachs twisted with hunger and thirst. There was a bit more apple bread and some dried grapes left, and a bit of water in their gourd. Within an hour, they were both sound asleep over their belongings.

Screeching brakes woke them. Their train car shuttered to a lurching start, then stopped.

"Watch out!" Margaret shouted as she and James were knocked into the wall of the boxcar, buffeted by their satchels. Suitcases slid and tumbled to jab their ribs and legs.

"Let's get out of here! Before the train takes off!" They gathered their belongings and rushed to the partially opened door. The train jerked forward then a high-pitched, bellowing animal scream, like a fluted pipe, filled the air. Then silence. Men were yelling and calling. They heard "He's over. Back 'er up!" "Get off 'im!" amidst a hollow wail.

"What's that sound, James?" Margaret looked frightened of what she couldn't see.

"It's some kind of animal, I think. It's louder than an ox, and higher pitched." James said. An ear-splitting trumpeting tapered to a purring, sputtering sound that churned like an ailing engine. Then a loud trumpeting again. Early morning light filtered through the partially opened door. Reverberations between the metal train cars calmed, and they stood to feel for bodily injury. The locomotive then revved up and reversed backwards! Margaret and James were jolted to the metal floor. The train tipped. The sound of crates of china and glass shuffled, slid, then shattered against the sides of the car, along with Margaret and James. The train car strained its connections, derailed and suddenly fell sideways. A flash of sunlight flooded through the car's sliding door, now on the top, giving a view of wispy clouds swiping a blue sky. In the distance, a symphony of trumpeting overlapped with the echoes of trumpeting.

"Climb along the sides, Margaret. We can get out on top, maybe unseen," James hoarsely called from the bottom of the sideways train car.

"I don't know if I can move," Margaret groaned. "I hit the side hard—my hip is locked."

James had climbed the pile of crates, grabbed hold of the door edge, and pulled himself up and out. He went to look for a rope to help Margaret. In the meantime, Margaret felt an excruciating pain. *The human shouts after the silenced animal filled her with a sorrow for having left home. The aloneness blended with the fear of how she would start over in a large city.* Then she saw a Baleek cup intact. In front of her a crate of Baleek china cups and saucers had cracked open in the fall. In her desire to hold onto their dream of a new life with a family, Margaret searched through the chipped ivory-colored shards to find three sets in mint condition. They were carefully wrapped in clothing and tucked in her bag. Our family will happen, she consoled herself. A rope dropped down and James dropped back into the car to tie it under Margaret's arms. He and another man above hoisted her while Margaret grabbed the metal door and pulled herself out to the morning sunlight. James climbed on top of the crates and canvas rolls with the suitcases and shoulder bags tied over his shoulders. He used the last of his strength to pull himself up out of the train car. Margaret sat on top of the car, mesmerized by the scene.

Along miles of train track were brightly painted *P.T. Barnum and J.A. Bailey's Circus, Greatest Show on Earth*. Gold framed and crowned train cars were decorated in gold leafed patterns along the top. Margaret gazed wondrously at what seemed to be a mile of red-and-gold trains on each of three tracks. Beyond the ticket gate were llamas, polar bears and cages of cats, lions, spider monkeys and zebras. She saw black and white horses, mounds of hay and two giraffes. A hill-sized elephant was on its side under the train car just before theirs. It was the most enormous beast she has ever seen, maybe 13 feet from head to foot and textured like dried mud in an empty creek bed.

Maybe twenty other elephants' ears were caught and prodded with bull hooks to move crates and boxes. Their trainers called and shouted *"Hey! Derri! Heye! Steh, Ragu, Steh!"* The steps were like a dance, choreographed between the trainer and wrinkled wise-eyed beasts. The elephants' massive mounded frames heaved like mountains and moved on short tree-trunk legs. An elephant's trunk seemed to be an animal all its own. It moved like a giant snake that hooked around handles or poles and lifted people and bales of hay. Its tip was more of a dexterous appendage with a graceful thumb that opened and grasped small objects with minute skills several feet from its eyes. Margaret Franklin forgot to breathe with the amazement.

"A circus," James said again quietly, staring in disbelief.

Margaret recognized the words but not their meaning. She could only stare at the menagerie in front of her. The color, the gold lettering, the shouts and most of all the loud, agonizing sputter of the enormous elephant releasing its life completely captured her focus. Margaret had never seen so much unharnessed chaos and sporadic motion. James joined her to revel in the collaboration of man and animal working together.

"An elephant is dying?" James attempted to understand by saying the words. What nightmare had he brought to the blossom of their marriage? Was he really able to fulfill the vow he'd made to his father-in-law to keep Margaret safe?

"Come on, Margaret, we've got to get out of here before they see us!" James held her elbow to redirect her attention to climbing off the top of the toppled train. Contrary to their plan to see everything, the young couple slept most of the way to Chicago, though Margaret's wrenched hip and James's sore back screamed pain with each jolt of the train. Sleep gave them temporary comfort. The young couple arrived in Chicago and were greeted by tugboats and railyards belching smoke. Rows of industrial smoke replaced the mountains of spruce they left behind. The stockyard stank, and privy vaults infected the water wells in many backyards. James encountered a new set of unknowns, like signs handwritten: *no Irish need apply* or labor bosses who shouted "No Paddy here!" Danny only had room for Margaret so James slept where he could and hoofed the wooden sidewalks through blocks of buildings still charred from the Great Fire. The Teamster job James had been promised was gone by the time he and Margaret arrived.

Chapter 26: Grafted Vines and West Town, Chicago

The leaders of Chicago were rebuilding the center of the city and letting West Town be slowly rebuilt by migrants and immigrants. James put his name in again, attended the meetings and worked day jobs until a Teamster job came through. He and Margaret moved into a one room apartment. Through the winter her hip caused chronic pain that she blamed on her pregnancy. In the spring, Margaret planted seeds from Alderbrook to sell herbs and vegetables until the empty lot was replaced with a wooden apartment building. Evelyn Franklin was born a Chicago, Illinois resident.

James picked up his young family with the delivery truck and pointed out an almost finished museum with long porches and arching doors facing a waterway at 53rd street. He explained, "this is the most controversial of all the pavilions—the Woman's Building. It mirrors the men's leaderships by having an all-white women's board lead by Bertha Palmer. Their goal is to show that women can produce outstanding art and will exhibit their great works of art here." They entered a palace built solidly of limestone stone at 57th Street and the outer drive to protect the largest collection of artwork Chicago had ever seen. James was excited to give his bride and family a sneak preview of the recently hung exhibit. The inventions and Woman's Pavilion reminded James of an Alderbrook which had been teeming with new businesses opening every week. Chicago was a boomtown of new ideas.

James and his daughter Bessie shared a fascination for whatever was invented after they had visited the World Fair. The new Brownie camera Eastman Kodak introduced or the Epsicle that was later named the Popsicle.

Cones for ice cream were first made in Evanston. They sat together on the couch reading the paper about the new inventions of 1900. A fellow named Marconi had sent a wireless transmission across the Atlantic Ocean from England to Newfoundland. It took all of four weeks for a letter to cross the Atlantic by boat. Margaret tried to imagine a message sent over the Atlantic in less than an hour! Bessie first learned to read sitting on James's lap seeing Ford Motor Company and Model T assembly lines in the paper. James and Margaret closely followed the two brothers who wanted to fly. Orville and Wilbur Wright made a kind of bicycle with wings called "Kitty Hawk" and were able to fly for twelve seconds above the ground. One night after kindergarten, James presented Bessie with an eight-pack of Crayola crayons in a yellow and green box. Bessie used her crayons to draw a colored bike with wings for her mother.

Margaret preferred to share art and theatre with her girls. She brought them to the only playground in Chicago at Jean Adams Hull House. While she watched them, she met other mothers in West Town who formed a regular time to share local gossip, recipes and news of Chicago. The children attended kindergarten, art and piano lessons while Margaret and her friends listened to concerts and lectures. At Jane Addams Hull House, the girls were introduced to music, singing, children's books and painting. Margaret's independent nature had been nurtured, which encouraged her to instill the teachings of Jane Addams in her little women. She taught them that women should generate aspirations and search out opportunities to realize their self-worth. She did this with a clear definition that they should follow their heart and be their own person.

Margaret's favorite outing was Hull House's woman's tea. The formality allowed civility in her days of caring for children in a city rising from a marshy prairie. At Hull House, she found a place like her father's front porch and her mother's back porch. At Hull House, Margaret talked about home-making challenges, where to purchase groceries, which doctor and dentist was honest. The Hull House lectures satisfied her longing for education and to make friends while adjusting to city life.

"Hurry girls, we've only an hour before the Magic Lantern Show,"

Margaret said as she gently helped them buckle their patent-leather shoes. Rubber boots were slipped over their shoes, with the wide opening flapped to the outside for a band to loop over a button. She was looking forward to her Christmas tea with her friends while the girls watched a projected performance. With camel-hair coats, scarves and knitted muffs for their little hands, the foursome stood for their ritual gaze into the mirror to recite "Parsnips, persimmons and Papa'" to correct their pout and create a small smile before encountering the muddy, snow-covered wooden sidewalks. Margaret taught them half-smiles on young Victorian ladies made for a very good entrance.

They caught the Roosevelt Road trolley at Western Avenue for the short ride to Hull House on Halsted. Though Margaret was eager to chat with her friends over tea and muffins, she paused a moment to see the amazing animated images illuminated from a double projector Magic Lantern Show. She recognized the tiny gas flame in the tin box and the hand-printed and tinted glass images in the wooden frames, the Wrigley's chewing gum advertisement and the rhythmic clapping and Christmas carols to engage the children for sound effects. One older boy was handed a tambourine, and Eva was given a dried gourd to shake. Margaret settled her children in kindergarten chairs and smoothed their best Sunday dresses with her still gloved hand.

What made Margaret pause during the *Little Match Stick Girl* story was the fluid animation the artist created between the two projectors in unison with the melancholy of the piano and a vocalist. The Little Match Stick girl, hand-painted on a glass slide, walked barefoot in the snow, which the artist showed by spinning a crystal in front of one projector. She looked hungry and cold as the next projector replaced that image with a weakened girl sitting along a wall and lighting a match for warmth. A soft aria was sung with repetitive low piano key strokes. A piece of glass was slid in to show the match lit. Another painted glass was slid over that scene with an image superimposed of a table filled with food and a cooked goose to imagine the hungry girl's thoughts. The projectors went dark, then returned to the girl lighting another match. A Christmas tree with lights and plenty of gifts slid over the tragic scene as a twinkle of high notes countered the drone of the repetitive low-octave piano chords. The projector went dark, and the bright twinkling of a star-studded night danced in the silence. A flash of bright light was followed by the Little Match Stick Girl lighting all of the matches.

"Please, Grandma, take me with you," the match girl called out. One tear sparkled from Margaret's cheek in the reflecting light. A spirit rose through the scene like smoke. Margaret looked back to see the projectionist squeezing a drop of food coloring into a tiny circular tank of water the size of a slide. As the spirit image faded the grandmother was carrying the little girl up to inviting clouds surrounded by winged angels. The last slide was the expired girl sitting along the wall surrounded by townsfolk who hadn't bought her matches with The Little Matchstick Girl saying, "Do not worry about me, I have no want, I have no hunger, I have no thirst."

Margaret watched her girls mesmerized by the movement and story. At the pause, they looked at each other with a new understanding. As the slides moved on to the Hans Brinker story, Margaret gathered her emotions, patted her cheek dry with a gloved hand and tiptoed out of the room to her Christmas Tea with friends. She glanced back to see Eva, Flo and Bessie looking at each other in amazement with a kind-of "we could do this" look in their eyes. They were already conversing about combining their drawing classes, acting and music into a collaborative storytelling. But, what story would they tell?

From the back door, ten-year-old Bessie entered with vim and vigor, and a Chicago autumn breeze. Their third-floor kitchen served as a living, washing, dining and cooking room for her family of seven. The treasure balanced in her arms was a flat, brown-paper package. She caught her breath from the climb up the stairs, inhaling the familiar smoky, mildewed smell the molding emitted. The soured laundry spilling over the basket by the tubs blended with the faint sweet scent of scalding milk on the stovetop. Two long, narrow windows, smoked dark with coal soot, flanked the wall near the rear door. A squat coal range rested in a coral-colored brick recess with a slate floor.

Bessie had been discouraged from drawing on the wallpaper and directed by her mother to sketch on this slate floor with chalk and chards of coal. A wet rag wiped clean any unruly chalk line. Above, the stove fire let off a plume of smoke beneath a pot of milk. The stove also heated an adjoining water boiler next to the two soapstone washtubs with hinged wooden covers. The night before, Margaret had removed the partition between the two to make one long bathtub. The dank wooden covers had banged on Bessie's head while the rough floor of the tub rubbed her bottom sore and the faucet whacked her back during her weekly soap-and-soak. The laundry stood in place tonight, readied to occupy the divided tubs with a hot soapy wash, then cold clear rinse.

"Hi, Bessie, we're making clabber." Her mother turned cheerfully to greet her second-oldest daughter.

"Mom, I think the milk is warm enough, it's about to boil over," Eva said.

"Please take it off the stove," Margaret said from her kitchen stool. "Then cool it by the tub. Florence, take down yesterday's clabber from the shelf and a clean spoon from the basket."

"We have only a bit left," Florence said.

"We only need a little bit."

"I'll come back after I set down my package," Bessie said as she walked past the steaming pot of milk. Margaret noted the air of confidence her daughter brought in.

Bessie cradled the package in her arms through the short hall where two bedrooms faced each other into a grander space. The family kept the front parlor for special evenings when company was welcomed. Here, after-dinner stories were told, quiet conversations between Margaret and James took place while the children slept. Street noises were muted to a comforting background hum of activity in this room that overlooked a tree-lined Edgemont Avenue. Thirteen layers of grayed wallpaper covered the high walls. The top layer was dark brown with once-yellow stripes. Where the wall paper had peeled back in a few low spots, a plaster wall on wooden lathe was visible. A side table stood between the two tall windows at the end of the room, which was shuttered with wood to shed light on a cloth-covered chesterfield. Bessie set down the package on the side table. Mr. O'Connor had given her wrapping paper to protect three sheets of drawing paper and two broken pencils. Her mind swam with the images she wanted to capture on the precious paper. Passing the piano, she returned to the kitchen.

They found joy from the miracle of the piano that had been left there by the previous owners who could not afford to move it to their new home. This upright was made of black polished wood with a cut-out veneer and a candle-holder on either side. The stool in front had faded rose fabric adorned with brocade. On the music stand was William Wright's "The Pet Birds" compositions. Eva played "The Robin's Waltz" over and over again, giving a rhythm to the pervasive street sounds of automobile motors and horns. The piano teacher came on Tuesdays and taught all the children. Eva enjoyed playing parlor music and practiced often. Bessie played some piano, but preferred to draw. She liked some of her drawings on the slate, but had to erase her work each day to make room for the next sketch. As she became more independent, she would stop by the stationery store to talk with Mr. O'Connor. He saved broken pencils or paper with bent edges for Bessie. Often she brought Mr. O'Connor a drawing that he pinned behind the cash register. The pencils she shaved sharp with a kitchen knife.

"Florence, you can stir in the rest of the starter," Margaret said. "Bessie, we'll need the cheesecloth next to the stove to tie over the top of the jar. There, well done." The jar was stored to ferment in the ambient warmth of the room. Margaret shooed her children to their reading and math practice while starting to fill the tubs for laundry.

"Mom, I've finished my homework for tonight will you tell a story?" Florence looked up. "One about flowers."

"When I was about your age, I wandered to a favorite ledge of McKillip Mountain that overlooks a meadow. The spring daffodils covered this meadow like a blanket of yellow along the brook. A nine-point stag grazed amidst the grasses between the jocund flowers, occasionally looking up in the grandest fashion to inhale the sweet air." Flo was carried back to this place with her.

"I was high on the cliff with puffy gray clouds about me, and it seemed I was one of them, one of the clouds looking down on this glorious sight. As a heavy cloud caught the spring breeze, it burst and rained on the flowers, emptying itself onto their radiance. The rain made the cloud lighten its gray shadow. And the sun shone through. Then, the wind scattered the cloud into wisps. Remembering this brilliance of the sunlight setting aglow the yellow field of jonquils, with sparkles of a fresh rain, lets me rest easy at night. Now, take that vision to bed with you, Florence, and rest knowing the sun will always shine tomorrow."

"Bless us, O Lord and these Thy gifts, which we are about to receive through Christ our Lord, Amen." The Franklin family of six were saying grace before their Saturday night supper. They sat in their West Town kitchen with interlaced fingers around a wooden table with spindle-backed chairs. With the expectation of a new baby, they all knew their lives would change, but none of them had the foresight to know how few meals they would have like this one. This nucleus of a family would be abruptly altered and reconfigured into another definition. It's not as if Margaret had not given her children a hug and kiss each time they stepped out of the door, or went off to sleep. Loss of a child was a way of life in 1902. James led grace, "And thank you for beautiful suffragists; Evelyn, Elizabeth, Florence, and our strapping young Founders; George, James Emmet, John Jay and our new hope still baking in the oven, Benjamin."

"Or Mary," Margaret said. James looked with pride at his six children ages five through fifteen. "Amen," they all said, barely noticing their names as they were announced at every Saturday dinner.

Margaret started the clatter of passing plates filled with liver and onions, boiled potatoes and green beans. Cautious Eva asked, "Will there be enough?" Her brow knitted above the bridge of her nose. Margaret shifted in her chair with a wince of pain. Eva took on too much of the parents' concerns. Neither James nor Margaret worried as much as their eldest daughter. "We have enough for you and Bessie to have seconds," Margaret said. "You both will be fasting until after Mass tomorrow, so please fill up."

Bessie sat up a bit straighter in her chair as she was now confirmed as a Soldier of Christ in the Catholic Church and allowed to fast with the adults through Sunday Mass. If Eva had acquired an air of caution and concern, Bessie was about the next moment, invention and idea. To be allowed to decide a name for herself was soul-fortifying. To decide to be Catholic was her new passion. Bessie had chosen Margaret for the guiding saint who would watch over her through life.

"Please pass the potatoes," Flo requested with a flourish of elegance. She chose to treat every moment as if she were auditioning for the stage. James lit up with Flo's eager humor and grace. "Here you are, our little princess," James said with a wink. Flo was a satellite orbiting around with star quality and the absolute pride and joy of Margaret and James. If Margaret was having a low day, Florence would run up to her with big round eyes and dimpled smile. Flo's hands on her mother's knees could bring back the promise of any day. With her thoughtful ethereal ambiance, Flo seemed to be a visitor from a better place than Edgemont Avenue, Chicago, Illinois.

In late winter, James had tapped the sugar maples, and the freedom of hunting and farming was still in his nature and yearnings. His longing emerged during bedtime stories with the girls that night. "Do not bore holes closer than two feet directly over or under a former tap hole or closer than six inches from the side of an old tap hole," he'd explain to his weary-eyed children on their way to sleep. "Drill the tap hole with a slight upward angle so the sap flows out readily. Use a sharp drill bit to minimize shredding wood in the tap hole."

They tried to ask, "What's a 'tap' Dad?" or "What's a maple tree?" He'd continue on as if it was more important to remember by telling, than engage his children—too young, too urban, too tired. "Tap the Sugar Maple trees on warm days, with snow still on the ground, when the temperature is above freezing. Hammer the spout in tight enough so that it can't be pulled out by hand. But don't drive it in so hard that you split the tree. And boil the sap to syrup with Silver Maple wood because it burns hot. The boiling of the sap filled our home with humidity that warmed the rooms like a summer day." The little women went to sleep not knowing if there were different names for Maple trees like they had different names in the Franklin family.

Sunday morning, as they prepared for church, Eva set out the boiled eggs for the younger boys. Bessie had to catch her breath and hurry to the back porch steps to keep from sharing their light breakfast. She was allowed a glass of boiled milk to calm her growling stomach. Mass, in mysterious Latin, carried on in what seemed to be interminably long for this young woman. "We believe in God, The Father Almighty, the maker of Heaven and Earth…And in Jesus Christ his only begotten Son…" the entire congregation recited one sentence each, from the twelve Apostles' stories, and their shared belief. The smell of the burning incense nearly brought up the warm, ammonia tasting milk. Bessie knew she was accomplishing the fast. She allowed herself to lean back against the pew during the long kneel before Communion. She made the Sign of the Cross: her forefinger touched her forehead, her heart, her left, then her right shoulders, while the priest consecrated the Host. "In the name of the Father, the Son and the Holy Ghost. Amen."

Bessie's light chestnut hair met the sun of the day after the long Mass. She was a slip of a girl with a confident mixture of tomboy and bookworm, which was a mercifully kind arrangement for a West Town girl. The spiritual side of her was feeling its way as with any young girl whose mind was active, and whose mother was unusually busy. When there was no time for reading, Bessie made a habit of clipping articles to share with her Dad about new business innovations. She clipped pictures for her drawings, a line along the neck of a woman in an advertisement that might catch her eye, or the way a horse's leg lifted in a prance. She kept these images to inform her drawings under her mattress.

"Bessie, Eva, the baby is coming!" Margaret whispered in a strained voice from her bedroom. "Call the midwife!" Eva stayed with their mother while Bessie ran for the neighborhood midwife. "It's time, the baby is coming!" she called through the opened door. Eva calmed Margaret with gentle conversation and wiped her brow. The midwife arrived and directed the girls on errands. They raced away, eager to be relieved of their mother's discomfort. The most beautiful baby boy, Benjamin, entered their life. Eva cared for Ben while Margaret rested.

Chapter 27: The Heartwood

Margaret didn't bounce back after her youngest child was born. She barely had the strength to feed Benjamin, let alone keep up with the boys. Fevers rose and fell. Margaret's reoccurring hip injury flared up with sciatica and kept her immobile. Her nightly prayers were for the girls to finish high school. Margaret could not stop to rest. James spent too much time at Teamster meetings, listening for the street politics, grasping at the change in the air, until he, too, was bedridden more often than not. His logging accident was exacerbated by climbing the steps, or walking more than a block. His feet throbbed. Whiskey dulled the back pain that radiated through his legs. Margaret's fevers persisted as Benjamin learned to sit up, then crawl. She rested more afternoons than not, and had to turn down job offers. Eva and Bessie did not ask questions, but stepped up. James aggravated his chronic back problems when he drove the truck. The few hours he was home were in bed resting.

Eva stayed home from school to care for Benjamin, tend to meals and put on her best dress and spit polished her Sunday shoes to teach piano students after school, while Flo watched the baby. Eva arranged an alarm clock and wound a metronome. The students sat off to the side on a bench while she instructed finger position, chords and rhythms to the soothing clicking. The students were allowed to come on other days to practice for fifteen minutes a day. They all knew to bring some bread, some stew or a piece of pie. The progression seemed natural. School teachers sent Eva's homework home with Bessie to keep up in class. Bessie learned at school for both of them. They'd worked late into the night on schoolwork, then awoke early the next morning to make breakfast for the family. One day, James did not get up to go to work and Eva cared for him as well. Bessie had to earn groceries.

Bessie had many admirers among the boys, who always saw her well dressed, straightforward and capable of more than less-serious girls. Jack O'Connor and Bess used to walk to his father's stationery store after school. She asked if there were any errands to run and made more and more deliveries for the stationery store for a few nickels. She headed out with a strong singular step in her fourteen-year-old pace. Mr. O'Connor enjoyed this spunky young woman. She showed him her "It's a Piece of Paper" writing assignment about how paper was made from the pulp of leftover rags. He showed it to his Jack, a paper salesman.

"Are you two still friends?"

"That was a long time ago Dad," Jack said.

"I want you to take Bessie to see the paper presses at the Museum of Science and Industry." Mr. O'Conner knew his son had the potential to become a good salesman, but his interest needed nurturing.

Jack balked, "I can't do that, Dad. There's a lot you can make me do, but I can't go with Bess." Bessie was in the artists' group at school. Jack was more comfortable with the sports guys who ran track.

"She might make a good salesperson to ease some of your territory." His father looked hard at him. Jack couldn't imagine a girl doing his job, but knew he needed help. It was awkward, yet it was Jack who asked Bessie if she'd like to see a mill turn rags into paper.

Jack and Bessie went to the Museum of Science and Industry to see the paper-making machine. It had been built for the 1893 Chicago World's Fair that she had a ping of memory visiting the Woman's Pavilion. They talked about paper with lunchboxes in hand. Jack described as they watched, fascinated, while a pair of soiled and greasy old blue overalls were dusted and cleaned and put through this acid vat. In that acid tub, the rags grew whiter and pulpier with each churn. The pulp was fed into a great crushing roller that pressed the moisture out of them, flattened the pulp to the proper thinness, and spewed it out, miraculously, in the form of rolls of crisp, white paper. As Bess watched the stained and spotted overalls of some possible railroad engineer, she wondered, how they came to be spotted, faded or torn, and finally, worn out? How did the rag man get them? How did he deliver them to the mill? What was talked about in the room where the girls sorted the rags into big gray bins?

"A penny for your thoughts"? Jack looked at the intensity of her eyes. She looked at a penny in his palm.

"All this relentless machinery. The acid burns on the hands of the men at the vats. Look at their shoes with holes burned through." Bessie was mesmerized. "The paper is so white and crisp. Think of the way we tear it up, crumple it, throw it away. Just a piece of paper, don't you see what I mean. It's a piece of paper to write a shopping list on."

Bessie recalled her grandfather saying, "This paper, which had been made from old rags, pulp." Pulp that used to be made from wood. It was rolled flat to capture drawings and the ink of newspapers. Jack O'Connor was infatuated by her perceptions, quickness of imagination and depth of thought. Who ever thought about paper being so complex or full of stories and history? Bess opened a new understanding of the importance of paper in a single afternoon. Who was this young woman?

He tried to describe her perceptions while selling to his clients. He'd pause to recreate the image a bit too often, and a bit too long. He mixed up the descriptive words and received cockeyed looks, but his sales skills improved over time. Bessie went on sales appointments with him. Not only was she fascinated with the paper but also the carbon tissue and typewriter ribbon. These materials could duplicate my artwork with different projector slides. Bessie could make a drawing, then slip carbon paper under it and retrace it onto another sheet of paper to animate the image. One carbon-paper sheet could make enough copies for an energized horse to canter across a field of wavy grass. She stapled the stack on the edge and flipped the books to animate the pages, making the hose run.

Bessie could not absorb Jack O'Connor into her life due to caring for her family. Without explaining, she gently declined his offers for an evening dance or stop at the soda shop. She could not confide, even in him, about the situation at home, because she did not understand it herself. Her mother slipped into longer and longer night sleeps and lengthier naps waking only to attend to the baby. By the end of the week, Bessie and Eva could assemble a dollar or two for sautéed liver and onions that they continued to cook for Saturday night supper. Margaret's tenderness to James hardened when she saw how hard her girls worked for the family that got in the way of their schoolwork. As the young women grew into the promise of this family, the parents shrunk away. James seldom rose from bed so the parish pastor arrived at their home to baptize William Benjamin Franklin over a bowl in the living room. Bessie took her world head-on by managing the rent, the accounting and groceries while adding some sales work into her deliveries. She tried to calm Eva's panic over their

mother's health. Eva cooked, watched over their brothers and continued piano lessons. Eva calmed Bessie's fears. Before the baby was a year old, Margaret passed away.

Then, Bessie and Eva learned, with their bedridden father's instruction, about family burial plots and tombstones etched with their mother's full Christian name, Margaret McKillip Franklin 1857-1903. "Come on, Florence." Bess took her hands and pulled her to standing. Uncle Henry and

Aunts Molly and Rose brought their father, Nicholas, Uncle Henry Fox and two Franklin uncles to gather for her memorial. The conversation strong-handedly turned to which family could take which of the six children.

"My children will stay together," James said. "We will BE together as a family."

But not so long after his wife's passing, James felt overwhelmed. All he could see was his loss. His injuries and risks caused their loss. All they had hoped and strove for, lost. All they optimistically had left the Adirondacks for, lost. Without Margaret, James could not summon the will to overcome his pain. He attempted to cheer on his three girls, who supported each other to care of the younger boys. Patiently, Flo brought her father the best cut of meat, largest broccoli florets and hottest cup of tea. "If you aren't the Fountain Girl!" James sang, "…and beware of the of Miss Willard's spring in a cup o' spittal, it'll put you under or leave ya' brittle, Hey Hey Ho boys…" He snoozed again.

Now, when her father told stories about a waterfall in Alderbrook near the cypress stand, Bessie couldn't listen. Who needs a waterfall when fresh water from the well was needed? She moved with an intuitive feeling that life is now. Life is the instant. Their needs inserted themselves into her very nerves and the marrow of her tired spine. Water must be carried up the stairs and boiled, food must be bought, cooked and eaten, the laundry must be washed and dried, and sleep must be slept. Bessie had only the next step in mind. Each person she spoke with was a lifeline of information, but there was not enough of her to give to anyone. Jack glided away.

In one of Bessie's hurried moments, when the laundry was behind, she slipped into one of her mother's old dresses, pulled the belt to the last hole and matched it with a pair of shoes. She went out to see about errands at the stationery store. It was impossible not to notice the effect on the neighbors in the building. Men on the street looked at Bessie differently. The stationery salesmen took her more seriously when she picked up a delivery or made a sale. Bessie washed all of Margaret's dresses that night and wore a different one each day. Mr. O'Connor knew when to be old-fashioned and when to be modern. It was Bessie who spotted each new item that entered the store:

a pen, a small stapler, copy paper or the latest typewriter. Mr. O'Connor also sold pins, needles, soap and thread, but Bessie frequented the store for the colored pens, copying film and construction paper. Mr. O'Connor was good at his business and successful enough to try new ideas. He made friends with the paper and typewriter salesmen, who often stopped to share business, gossip, and the latest innovation. She tried to look small behind the counter to listen.

Once a week their father rose from bed to attend the Teamster's meeting though he was no longer assigned work. He hadn't returned from the night before and the boys were sent out to look for him. While a student was hesitantly playing a parlor tune a thunderous knuckle-to-wood interrupted. Eva motioned for the student to continue and noted the visitor's solemn demeanor. She closed the door behind her. "He didn't make it through the night," said the Teamster abruptly. He quietly handed her an envelope. "The boys have taken up a collection for you children." Bessie climbed the steps to see the stranger at the door. Henry Fox invited Eva and baby Benjamin to live at his house. Bessie and Flo kept watch on the two boys in the apartment with familiar patterns. They ate their biggest meal at school. Every Sunday, a Woman's Guild from Our Lady of Sorrows Basilica delivered a dinner. Eva returned to teaching piano lessons.

Bess and Flo were used to scolding their brothers and making ends meet financially. *Bess* emerged with a new fortitude and strength, while *Bessie* receded into vague memories of a dearly loved child. In her parents' bedroom, Margaret's want-for-a-legacy was preserved in her three Baleek china cups and saucers, which sat stoically on the top of her cherished bureau. Bess sat down on the floor before the bureau and opened the bottom drawer, looking for another belt and some stockings. Under the clothing she found a curious wrapped package of clippings. She loosened the cotton cord, carefully unwrapped 1880's advertisements clipped from Parisian woman's fashion magazines. One was folded into an origami fortune telling square with four finger pockets: "He's coming back, he's not"; "He is decorated as a captain, he is not; He is a civil war hero, he is not" were written on the corners. "Black is the uniform of man," "the man is the foil of the woman and should never outshine her." "Walk in public as if to never draw attention, but have subtle accessories to establish your place in society." She read on. "There are two ways to be affluent, by birth or by dress." "Affordable fashions before were only accessible to the wealthy but now they are available and affordable through your local department store." "Up and coming middle class." Inside were family photos and letters from Great Uncle Hugh in Antrim to her Grandfather John in Alderbrook arranging his and Patrick's immigration. Newspaper clippings of Jumbo the elephant being crushed by a freight train in St. Thomas Canada. *Avoid trains.* A postcard of bicycles with large front wheels photographed at the Columbian Exposition. Bess sat back on her heels thinking deeply of this library of hopeful dreams her mother must have had as she traveled with her new husband to unknown Chicago. A deep breath helped her to comprehend the unrealized aspiration of what the city might have allowed her mother to become. Then, the reality of the loss of her oldest son. Orphaned children. The dream of the grand and fabulous life Margaret had imagined, Bess breathed in from these saved clippings that settled into the marrow of her bones. Bess knew she would make them happen.

Flo and Bess settled into seats on the bus and placed their hats on their laps. Bess opened the newspaper. The banner headline said "Teddy Roosevelt says Americans could learn democracy from the Austro-Hungarian Empire?"

"What is that about?" Flo asked. "It says here the Empire had a tolerance for the various cultures, languages and customs of various peoples while establishing a general structure to the Balkans and Middle East. Heir apparent Archduke Franz Ferdinand has been assassinated." This shifting of the world Imperial Order couldn't allow anyone's imagination to conjure the upcoming decades of turmoil, carnage and catastrophe that industrial wars could bring. The map of Europe and the Middle East would be torn apart and with it, imperial ties around the globe. Bess and her sister tilted floppy-brimmed hats to step off the bus for their weekly Saturday at the race track.

"Bessie," only Flo still called her that, "who is that handsome, brash man over there?" In a sea of woman's hats and men's fedoras, a tall dapper man stood out with his wide brimmed straw hat.

"Come stand in this line for a ticket, Flo, the race is about to begin. Now, who did you think looks good in the paddock?" Bess guided and respected her younger sister, who had a winning way with her horse picks. "I've seen him here before. It seems he always wins—must have a way with horses?"

"Bessie, let's go see his bets!"

Florence had already gone to stand in line behind the man they came to know as William McMahon. He was a charismatic thirty-eight-year-old gentleman with a boundless imagination. He was always developing the next scheme, networking with the next business venture and seemed to know his horses. The three of them hit it off right away and made quite a picture on Saturdays, ebulliently huddled into their racing forms. As the months progressed, Bess and Flo looked over mostly women's hats to find William. The young men of the Midwest trained on weekends for entering the Great War. They trained in groups and boarded boats to be transported overseas. Propeller planes dotted the skies. Trains rumbled them away.

Bess was twenty-eight and it was 1914. William saw in her a levelheaded, sharp businesswoman who understood the chance of doubling her salary. He was swashbuckling, charming, handsome and ten years older. A tall man in a large hat. His charismatic and affable nature had an urgency radiating from him that caused people to gravitate to him. It seemed everything was going to go his way. Bess admired his easy and confident way with people, as well as his ambition in the stock market. William had begun his adulthood as a pre-teen with only an air of destiny and seventeen cents in his pocket. The oldest in his immigrant family of one brother and four sisters, he'd started working young. His first job was in the stables along Canal Street. The day of the horse and carriage was passing. Look how the transactions for grain and hay and the variance of prices paid each week. The fluctuation fueled his interest in grain options, and he began following the market. In his twenties, William created contacts in the stock market, aspiring to be a trader. He often used his salary to purchase a lead on corn or wheat to turn a profit. If the day of the horse for transportation was passing, it was only beginning at the racetrack. He frequented the horse races to boost to his weekly wage, counting only his wins.

Chapter 28: Espaliered

Bess woke up tired one early January morning, still groggy from a deep sleep and dialed in the radio. She tried to remember why she felt worn out and scooped ground coffee while still in her nightgown "...and one teaspoon for the pot," Bess said with the same intonation her mother had lilted. Eva was joining her and Flo at their West Town apartment this morning. "News Alert!" the disc jockey had interrupted. "Teddy Roosevelt suddenly passed away in his Sagamore Hill home." By 1:45, the roaring, boisterous, hideous and magnificent steel giant of Chicago, had come to a mourning standstill. Clear music came through the static. She sipped her coffee, ruminated over how President Roosevelt had changed the path of the Franklin and McKillip families by turning the Adirondacks into a State Park. If it had been a federal park like Yellowstone, the economy would have been buoyed to support the Alderbrook families. A generation later, she couldn't imagine living anywhere but Chicago, though maybe she and William could marry at St. Rose of Lima Church? She should have been giddy with the expectations of her summer wedding to William, yet uncertainty was pervasive. William realized his hopes of being a stock exchange trader. But devastating inflation kept him treading to stay above water. At four o'clock, William would pick up Bess for picnics along the lakefront or a city park.

Last night he told a frightening story about a colleague who left work as he turned purple. The Spanish Flu had infiltrated every aspect of their courtship, with bans on the theatre, movie houses, restaurants, and schools—all shut. Weekly horse-track visits halted. Lingering kisses had become quick pecks on the cheek. After months of only women in corseted dresses, headbands over bobs promenading, soldiers returned from the Great War. Sparks momentarily appeared in a girl's eyes. The pandemic flowed from Great Lakes Naval Base and decimated family, friends, officemates. Women crossed streets as a vet walked towards them. Vets weren't hired, not invited. William walked confidently to Bess's West Town apartment rather than take the train. He covered his mouth and nose with a handkerchief clutched in his gloved hand. Streetcars kept their front doors open. Churches, libraries and concert halls closed their doors. Bess questioned every scheduled sales appointment arranged outside of shops. Increased orders of postcards and notecard deliveries were left at the back door. Bess kept her mind active with the women's movement Right to Vote campaign.

Everywhere, people wandered deliriously, babbling and chanting with fevers in the streets. William passed mothers with ill children calling out for doctors who couldn't keep up with the demand. Bess and William kept to themselves, dined with picnics and danced in parks with a comfortable joy of being together. At a peak, thousands of new cases of Spanish influenza with fevers and delirium were reported each week, then, that many each day. The careful ones survived. Bess followed Carl Sandburg's reporting in the *Chicago Daily News:* "drink plenty of fluids, wear and bleach gloves, pin a veil on your hat brim." She and William were determined to be survivors. Bess focused on the two and a half million Chicagoans who did survive. Children were still being born with their elderly grandparents tucking them in at night. It took time for Bess and William to change habits, visit ill family and neighbors and compare the growing list of lost friends over a hot toddy at night. Her passion was the Women's 19th Amendment to the Constitution.

July 1st brought saloon life to a halt with Prohibition. The night before, the biggest carnival night in Chicago's history erupted from the city's social oppression. They enjoyed the camaraderie of a wild city hitting a wall. They met up with some of Bess's activist friends in Bughouse Square and William's trader friends on Rush Street, spending a raucous celebration outdoors. The Dill Pickle Clubs' Bughouse Square debates were in full oratory battle over the next step, a woman's right for equal pay. May the best debater remain standing, William thought. May the winner be for equal pay, Bess hoped. They celebrated the 19th amendment passing for women voting and their imminent wedding day.

That afternoon, Bess and William planned a picnic in Lincoln Park. She unpacked a tablecloth, put out olives, cheese and crackers. William uncorked a bottle of wine. "If the Mayor is getting out of town, he may know something we don't," he reasoned. Mayor "Big Bill" Thompson hosted his loyal supporters, nearly every major leader of Chicago, in Cheyenne, Wyoming for a long weekend to celebrate his win. They should be negotiating a strike of the transit system. "Maybe one official should stay around?" William said.

"Then Alderbrook might be a good place for our wedding. We can't enter a church in Chicago," Bess said. "It can't get any hotter. There is no 'cooler by the lake' forecast for today," Bess sighed aching for some relief from the heat. She was safely home by noon as the temperature reached 96 degrees.

Race riots flared up on the South Side. Five black boys floated on a raft in the current near a mostly white beach at 29th Street. A stone was thrown; a boy on the raft died. Skirmishes erupted into a bubbling cauldron of chaos along Cottage Grove between 29th and 35th. This led to a week of riots, looting, arson and brutal murders. Hundreds of whites and many more blacks were injured, mostly black businesses looted. Some blacks were brutally killed. Baseball bats hit bodies.

"I don't know what's worse, the deflation of cotton or our political rift in Chicago. The governor has got to do something about it." William folded the newspaper after reading about the contentious relations between Governor Lowden and Mayor Thompson. "They have caused the market to dip." Bess closely read Carl Sandburg's literary voice in articles of futile deaths following the Southside arson. To compound the racial chaos, all public transportation halted with a transit strike. Truckers transported workers to offices in open-bed trucks. Bess thought about how her father would have enjoyed being there, piling walking commuters onto his Ford truck. Every car was filled to capacity. Somewhere between the flu and the riots, black people took risks to walk long distances to and from their jobs. Many jobs went undone. Even this was better than the fear of what was in the South. Carl Sandberg's articles switched from covering the flu to the horrendous news of the Southside unraveling for the safety of black people throughout Bronzeville.

Bess received a letter from the McKillips in Alderbrook. "The family is looking forward to our arrival and has the church reserved," she read to redirect the conversation. "They have the homestead fixed up for our honeymoon suite. The delay was infant triplets died from the flu." The invitations were mailed for August 19, 1919, at St. Rose of Lima Church, reception to follow at Hugh McKillip's Hall.

Florence, Eva, Daniel and the giddy couple took the Grand Trunk railroad to Alderbrook. Turbulence was behind them. Marriage ahead. Bess wanted her savings for a legacy of fine furniture, china and rugs. So it was not wasted on a large wedding, she thought and may have said. The Chicago relatives were met at Burlington's train station in Thomas Franklin's straight eight-cylinder Hupmobile. They ferried to Au Sable Chasm, then down the Au Sable River Valley to cousins Honora and Thomas Franklin's milk-cow farm in North Jay. After the wedding the happy couple stayed twenty forested miles away with Uncle Eddie. Bluejays darted through first growth forests that lined the river valley. Sweet nectar rose to protect third generation growth of once-leveled forests. Bess breathed in the pine and fir, spruce, and birch while rumbling beside the river in her cousin's Hupmobile. A clutch of quails crossing the dirt road caused a pause. Her parents married here when the vibrant community was at the height of its promise. She and William suffered through moaning about the family's struggles during the pandemic.

Embraced in the McKillips family at Catholic Corners and the extended Franklin family near Au Sable Forks, the couple could barely find a moment to think, let alone talk. Relatives drove Ford trucks and automobiles from Black Brook, Union Falls, Goldsmith and Jay to St. Rose of Lima for a candlelit ceremony in Alderbrook. A few cousin's daughters sprinkled Queen Anne's Lace petals in the aisle ahead of Bess in a standing-room-filled church. Larkspur bouquets and candles graced the altar. Uncle Eddie McKillip and his family welcomed and organized the arrangements with his neighbor, Father O'Donnell. Flo and Eva were Bess's bridesmaids. Uncle Eddie escorted Bess down the aisle to give her hand in marriage to William Francis McMahon. The married couple were driven in a horse-drawn carriage down Alderbrook Road, the mile-long long driveway to John's first homestead and Eddie McKillip's home, beside the brook. All the Chicago McKillips were sorry to leave, yet also recognized there was no opportunity in Alderbrook. Those who chose to stay were isolated without the vibrant growing community the founders created.

"Let's consider a move to Oak Park," Bess said.

"Oak Park is a shorter travel to work," William replied. Fifteen trains stopped in Oak Park each morning and night with westward workers. Two-story homes were being built with porches, ice-delivery hatches and carriage barns. Electric streetcars crossed the village north to south. Heated sidewalks, gas lamps, two flat rentals ringed a village circling Frank Lloyd Wright's masterpieces. Bess and William decided they would move to Oak Park after their wedding where they would start their family. Their new Village of Oak Park offered a library, stellar high school, and theater to explore. One-and-a-half-square-mile Oak Park had black families in the Northeast corner, Germans along Harlem, Irish Catholics along Austin, Protestants on Oak Park Avenue and Jews on Lake Street. The Oak Park Art League started the year Mac slid into the world.

Bess rode the Madison Avenue streetcar to deliver typewriter ribbons to Peritz Brothers Stationery in Austin. She was always on the happier side of life, except when she saw a crank-started Studebacker which triggered pangs of jealousy. At this point, she'd appreciate a Model T Roadster. Bess calmed her automobile desires as she felt the new life in her womb, a natural occurrence, yet its own miracle. Already her blood was starting to make milk. She felt special. She had many new beginnings in the past few years, but this one glowed from within. Bess had been setting up the nursery of their Oak Park home with drawings and prints from the Art Institute. As soon as her infant's eyes focused, he or she would see Henri Matisse,

Picasso and Toulouse-Lautrec drawings. The third bedroom in the house, her office, had framed cartoons from *The New Yorker*. Unemployment topped 20 percent, yet she felt on top of the world with her work and William's promise as a trader.

How could she explain to William how she had changed? How could he be part of all she was feeling? Had he changed too? Bess worked harder than ever to be ready for juggling life as a new mother. Here, I'll get off on Humphrey. It's a quieter walk. On the three-block walk, a soft swirl of breeze loosened a fall maple seed into a helicopter spin. Bess wondered as she watched the single blade spiraling in the wind, lifting and falling, until it spiraled between the Orr and McDonald homes. The weight of the seed took a nosedive into the earth amidst the bridal-wreath bushes. She felt a strong kick from her womb. Then another, then… the baby was coming! She was eight blocks from home but Bess's Aunt Ann had married Uncle Henry Fox who lived a few blocks south.

She made her way to the house and announced that the baby was coming.

"Come in Bess, I'll ring William," Mrs. Proteau calmly welcomed her. The smell of fresh baked bread wafted through the room, then overwhelmed Bess with nausea. She was soon being driven in the Proteau's crank-started Buick to the hospital a few blocks away. She was in the automobile of her dreams, and all she could focus on was conquering her labor pains.

Mrs. Proteau parked in the emergency room lot and walked with Bess leaning on her. Bess handed Mrs. Proteau her purse while a nurse rushed out with a wheel chair and whisked Bess behind a curtained area. Mrs. Proteau called William again as well as Eva and Flo, filled out the forms and stepped into see how Bess's delivery was progressing. Soon William rushed into through the emergency room door. The nurse told him the doctor would let them know as soon as the baby was born.

"It's a boy!" the doctor said to Mrs. Proteau and William. A healthy, big boy. Still breathing heavily, she was handed a round-faced, crying baby boy bundled tightly in soft white cotton. At that moment Bess, with William by her side, saw their whole life completely altered to a place she always meant it to be. William was hit as if by a tidal wave of emotion he was not prepared to grasp. "Well, I'd better get back to work for this little fellow," he said.

The radio gackled in the kitchen. "WTAY Your Jazz station from Oak Park Arms." Then, Louis Armstrong's jazz riff. Jazz was sweeping the world and Bess couldn't get enough of it. William's current favorite was Duke Ellington's "Creole Love Call." Bess looked out over the grassy next lot, slated to be renamed Fox Park in a few months. A bright chestnut-suited brown thrasher darted past the window then perched to sing. A scarlet tanager added gorgeous notes from the tip of a branch. Then came the staccato percussion of a red-headed woodpecker in its striking blazing red-head and rich black wings. Bess silenced the radio to catch the canaries and whitethroats, then a catbird who was imitating a mockingbird. She had already read the *Oak Leaves* headlines while watching over Mac as he crawled across the Oriental rug. She rinsed William's cup and plate and refilled hers. He'd taken the electric street car for the Stock Exchange over an hour ago. The Borden's is almost empty, she thought and jotted a reminder under the last item on her list. "Stop by Peritz Stationery—fill the carbon paper order."

"Mama," Bess heard and turned in a flash. "Say it again," she said as she picked Mac up. She kissed him and cooed, "My handsome young Mac." She kissed him again. "You are so adorable!"

Bess smoothed the socks over his feet, then sat him up and lowered the shirt over his ears and nose. She gently pushed his arm through a coat sleeve, then another, as boots sounded on the front steps. She saw the mailman through the front window and glanced at the clock. She then sat Mac in her lap and straightened his knees to put his feet through the legs of his wool pants. The door-slot lid opened with a squeak, a rustling of mail, then the clatter of metal-on-metal as the lid dropped. Bess flipped through the postcards, mail, a *McCall's* magazine with a Zane Gray short story, and a *Chicago Tribune* from the mail basket. Mac fussed from his high chair. "The River Forest Woman's Club has a lecture by Josephine Blackstone," Eva had written on a postcard. "She's lecturing May 17th about saving park land in Oak Park. Want to go?" Bess flipped the card over to Eva's family photo in front of their River Forest home.

Bess took out a postcard with the Star of Bethlehem poking through the late spring snow photo, and responded right away. "Yes, and Grace Wilbur Trout is talking from my automobile caravan for National Women's Voting rights on June 2 at the 19th Century Club. I've been invited by my neighbor Bridget, I'm sure you're welcome. P.S. June 15th is the dedication of Fox Park. Bring the boys, I'll make sandwiches." Mac started to cry as she placed the penny stamp on the card with Eva's address for the afternoon postal pickup.

She tied Mac's outdoor shoes, and he began to whimper. A bead of sweat dripped from under his bundled blue woolen coat and matching snow-pants. The symphony of birdsongs beckoned from the prairie next door. She carried Mac out the kitchen back-door into the blast of an early spring breeze and sweet high notes of shy veeries and vespers of thrushes. Bess went down the wet wooden back steps as orioles trilled and canaries flitted by. Notes of repeated melodies by wrens and meadowlarks. Catbirds added a cat's mew. A bluebird was perched on the edge of its nest built on a post reflecting the sky on its wings and the warming earth on its breast. It sang to her as if it understood her caring for Mac. Bess stepped daintily through the delicate white Dutchman's breeches and blue and yellow violets into the tall grasses with shooting stars. Pink phlox and tiny wild orchids poked through the turkeyfoot grass.

All around them was the background hum of hammering and sawing of Oak Park's spectacular new homes. Bess nodded at the house going up across the street with pride and set her baby boy down. Bess and her son often made their own space near the Mertensia with the little bit of sweet nectar pulled from the stem of its bluebell flower. In the flattened grass, they nibbled crackers or watched a spider build a web. She spread a blanket over grasses, under the three burr oaks as he gazed up into the wintery branches swaying in the soft but cold wind. A crowned and brownish cardinal dropped a stick it had plucked for a nest. Here in the midst of a booming town of prosperous neighbors, Bess grinned at her bright blue-eyed baby who, with a frozen mist coming from his perfect nose, reached for the stick. She watched him pick it up in his chubby hands. He poked it into the dirt and scratched a furrowed line. He tasted the stick. He hit the stick into his pant leg. It hurt him. She didn't take the stick away. He rolled the stick, then turn it over and turned it back. He drew back in pain when the stick hit his other hand. He fussed. His hand was red where it had hit. Bess poured a little water on the red spot and picked him up. She never said no to little Mac. Everything he did was just so and there was no need to correct him. The most she might say to him was "I don't think so," or "maybe later, honey." Bess often noted and sometimes said how content and happy she was. "All right Mac, everything will be fine now," she spoke to his tears. A red-winged blackbird darted by and perched on a cattail. When the blanket was taken up, the turkeyfoot grasses bounced back tall; the space remained only in their collective memory. No one else would ever find it. She was happy.

Mac crawled, walked and ran on these floors, outgrew the Jack-in-the-Box and maze of letters on tracks cut in an oval board. He laughed when carried on his Dad's shoulders to Sunday school, but his father had a scratchy face and was big and handled him roughly. Bess could see that their son was a bit scared of his father who was loud and spoke firmly. But Bess knew he thought about shadows and light streaming through the dew drops, how the wind felt and made the leaves move, how water flowed. With the stock market at an all time high, the happy couple decided to test their luck in sunny California. They sold their home, packed her china and moved to Santa Monica where Mac would start first grade.

Chapter 29: Under the Avocado Tree

"Look what I found today—gold! Bess, Mac, I've got to show you!" William stormed in the arched wooden front door in Santa Monica. William dug into his pocket, extracting a rock in the outstretched palm of his hand. It was small to medium sized, rough and covered with dirt. He held it with care. William showed Mac a large nugget of gold in the palm of his hand with the pride of a boy who had just won a cat's eye in marbles.

"This is what it's all about, Mac, gold! This is why we moved to California!" Eight-year-old Mac saw the crumbles of dirt rubbed into his father's palm and the lumpy rock. He tried to grasp its importance beyond his father's excitement. William had landed a gold-speculating job in Los Angeles after the oil began to flow. Bess and Mac followed him to Santa Monica, a welcome release from the strict judgmental confines of the Midwest. Even here, the temperance folks had stamped out both alcohol consumption and gambling, as well as dancing. Mac watched William shave in the shared bathroom, then loop around the wide part of a tie and thread it through that loop to tighten a slip knot neatly over the top shirt-button. Bess's rinsed stocking and garters hung from the towel rack next to the sink. Mac had started first grade with new tied black saddle-shoes. Bess unpacked the china from the Brinks shipment.

Prohibition created a pressure in the Los Angeles area. Folks were bursting with nowhere to go but church on Sundays, and Tijuana offered unlimited indulgences in just a short trip south. The young family found themselves driving in this chain of traffic. "Tijuana has the longest bar in the world, 241 feet," William said. Tijuana kept bargain-basement prices that enticed U.S. visitors to live the life, from lobster to high-grade alcohol. They were drawn for the thoroughbred horse racing. The Tijuana Racecourse was dilapidated, inventive, had moveable gates and photo finishes.

"Annnnnd she off!" the race-calling voice echoed through the park from the public-address speaker system. United States farms had been selling off their horses, abandoning the sport or heading to Tijuana. There, racing was lawless and wild and Bess and William loved it. The horses captured their attention. With William's earnings reaching an all-time high in the stock market, William, Bess and Mac took their chances to make a Saturday bonus on the track. When William wasn't following the horses, he was following the stories of self-made Charles Howard. Mr. Howard had made a fortune selling Fords in L.A. after his bicycle business collapsed. At the track, William closely watched Charles Howard, who was now racing his horses in Tijuana beside his bride, Marcela. Tired, Mac curled up in the back seat to sleep as Bess and William followed the ocean to Santa Monica. California was working out for William.

Bess washed the dishes after their avocado-on-toast-with-lemon juice-and-a-dash-of-salt-lunch. She looked out her kitchen window at her young son curled over his drawing under the avocado tree. He erased and tried the line again, then erased some more. He was drawing a new skinny black mouse called Mickey, a mischief-maker and the talk of his first-grade class. As she glanced out to Mac's drawing, he jolted his head up in fear, then wonder. He leaned back over his drawing and quickly drew the looming, terrifying enormity of a monster in the sky. To capture its ferocity of gobbling the sun, swirling lines trailed behind like writhing tendrils. He and the tree were engulfed in the Zepplin's phantom shadow. Mac drew the specter descending on a frightened, skinny Mickey. Bess had just clipped an article to mail to Eva of a Zeppelin's course as it traversed the globe and along the California Coast.

"On August 9th, 1929," Bess read, "the Graf Zeppelin was untethered from New Jersey and headed to Manhattan where the Empire State Building was being built. Where Babe Ruth had hit his 500th home run. The Zepplin flew past the Wall Street that was at an all-time high. The Zepplin banked right and circumvented the globe over the recently defeated Nazi Party in Munich's *Hafbrauhaus*. A fringe politician promised to feed the hungry

Germans. After the Zeppelin traversed the earth, it was lifted by a typhoon, after four million Japanese cheered 'Bonzai!' from Japan before it soared over the Pacific Ocean and along this coast of California."

"Mom, look what just flew over! Mom look what I saw! What is it?" Mac ran in with his drawing of a mouse and a Zeppelin. He and his mother hovered over the article and map,

"You drew the Zeppelin with vigor, Mac," Bess said. "You discovered it and needed to tell about it. It's drawn with speed and accuracy and tells me its moving in air. She knelt to his level. "The little mouse is a bit persnickety like you want to get it just right. Maybe you would rather draw your own vision? Draw what is new. Make your art from the excitement you live and experience."

That October, Bess read the newspaper cover story. Her hands trembled as she peeled a spiraling red skin off an apple. "The stock market has plummeted, marking the end of six years of unparalleled prosperity. Stock prices have crashed and banks have called in loans." Within the next month, $30 billion in stock value disappeared. California was hit the hardest. Over the radio, President Hoover said that the worst effects of the crash upon employment would pass in the next sixty days. In November, Mac and Bess moved the antique furniture, rugs and china back to chilly, ever-changing Oak Park to stay with her cousin, Henry Fox, on Austin Blvd. and Jackson. William remained behind to get work in the oil fields beyond the Santa Monica mountains. William moved near the Santa Anita track in the St. Andrew Apartments.

Bess moved a few blocks north to an apartment on Washington. Her McKillip cousins, the Proteaus, lived across the alley in their large apartment building on Austin and Washington with a new brick bump-out after their ninth child was born. She reconnected with her business contacts and added new skills she learned from William of trading stocks. To build her portfolio she bought low, of the bedrock of a rebounding economy, with her hopes for a high. Bess's brothers and sisters lived within a few blocks, with Eva in neighboring River Forest. There were unannounced visitors, whose hushed conversations and raised brows hinted at her audacity to move without William. Bess, all powdery and pink, with lovely lipstick and jewelry, noticed their silent, judging glances. Mameh Cheney and Frank Lloyd Wright's affair had left the community regaining its equilibrium and people reacted rigidly. Bess replaced family drives along the Pacific with drives along Chicago's Lake Michigan in her brand new Roadmaster. She and Mac visited an open house at the Edgewater Beach Apartments where there were tennis courts, golf course, and pools, both indoor and out. Her portfolio performed with the economic recovery and she channeled herself to live the life her mother imagined. William contributed from his entrepreneurial victories.

Lake Michigan's lapping waves splashed against the east passage above the apartments as Bess and Mac moved to the newly finished pink Edgewater Beach Apartments on Lake Michigan. Mac attended St. Ita's elementary school a few blocks west. As he entered a new school, he knew to smile at the girls if they looked at him, then look away. They might talk to him later, and he'd quietly smile or talk like they'd been talking all along. He intuitively knew teachers would like him better if the girls were on his side. With the choice of Latin or French he went with French because that class had more girls. The boys noticed the girls liked him, so they tested him with clenched fists and chin clips. Boxing was taught in Catholic gym class, making Mac equipped to show them what he knew. Soon, Mac was on the teams and teachers' favorite.

The doorman of the Edgewater Beach taught Mac to fold his tongue in half, curl it under and let out a loud reverberating whistle down the long hallways of the pink hotel. He and his friends would wander the lobby for sightings of President Franklin Delano Roosevelt and General Dwight D. Eisenhower or Nat King Cole and Bette Davis. "Guess who's coming this weekend?" Mac told his friends, "Marilyn Monroe." They roared with hoots when they saw flyers that announced Charlie Chaplin, Judy Garland and Frank Sinatra performances. The boys would watch the stars board the seaplane from the pier to head into Chicago. This was all before the outer drive was landfilled to extend to Lincoln Park. Mac and Bess listened to WEBH, the hotel's radio station, which broadcasted big bands like

Benny Goodman, Glenn Miller, and Bess's favorite, Tommy Dorsey. Just as the Edgewater's 1200-foot private beach was widened, William wrote to announce he'd found a job in California's Ventura oil field. Bess wrote back to look for a house near Good Shepherd Parish in Beverly Hills. Mac's classmate was moving there. Bess packed and shipped china, Oriental rugs, glassware and furniture to California with Brinks for Mac's middle school. President Roosevelt's voice on the radio, full of leadership, care and compassion, offered Mac a consistent role model in the shifting sands from Chicago's to California's beaches.

Chapter 30: …Or Bust

Florence, Bess and her twelve-year-old son boarded the bus for a deliberately slow ride along Route 66. It began from Buckingham Fountain through a bit of Kansas, a lot of Texas, New Mexico, Arizona, and ended at Santa Monica Beach, California. The route had just been finished with Al Capone's cash and Bess wanted to see it all. Mac had a stack of *New Yorkers*, paper, pencils and pens for the long bus-ride. Bess brought her accounting.

"I always sit in the outside seat in the front row to be able to see out the big front window of the bus," Bess said. "Then, I can see everything between here and California. I can't wait for the sunshine and fresh avocados." Eternally optimistic, she would always find the silver lining in any cloud. If others thought they'd rather take the train, which cost three times as much, she settled for the slower bus ride and wish it were slower yet.

"Santa Monica Pier or Bust!" the driver called out. Was it the tone, the deepness of the voice or the mention of the pier? Bess daydreamed of being held in William's arms in a dance on the pier. Their hats occasionally bump as they swirled through the room, his right hand on her hip, her left hand on his lower back, their other hands laced together as they moved through the jazz music. The pier's otherworldly glamour drew them there often. Back then, their gaiety had floated on a sea of undulating business investments and a seemingly calm Pacific Ocean.

"Mom, what does 'or Bust' mean?" Mac looked up from his cartoon perusing.

"It has to do with pioneer days, when settlers went west, hoping their wagons and oxen would survive the travels." Mac was flipping through cartoons, reinterpreting their style in his notebook. He showed his mother one cartoon which had a jalopy with a family parked on the side of Route 66 with a handwritten sign: "California or Bust." The caption below said "Go West Young Man."

"Mom, what does this mean?" Mac asked.

Bess explained how all the farmers migrated to California because they'd lost their land to the drought. Mac leaned his head against the windows as Bess and Flo chatted about the Beverly Hills house William had chosen for them.

"I so want to be in the movies Bessie!" Florence lifted her head with a flare.

"Give it a try Flo, you're as good as any actress I've seen in the pictures. Let's get some rest so we don't miss seeing the West." The two settled their heads against the cushioned seats for the night's ride to Oklahoma. "Achoo!!" Mac sneezed from the seat next to his mother. The bus had stopped in the middle of the night, presumably for gas. Mac was brushing a pollen-like dust from his sleeve, sneezing powder in the air. Bess's eyes opened; a cloud of dust fell from her eyelids and forehead. She coughed and saw little lines of dust on the window ledges. A howling wind made a dry rushing sound as it lifted the dry fields and fluffed up the road in front of the headlights. *Al and Suzy's* cafe sign blinked through a dense fog of dust that didn't settle to the earth, but swirled in the movement of the air.

"Everyone off! We're at Al and Susy's Cafe for the night. I can't see the road in front of us for the dust storm," the driver announced. Bess reached into her purse for a handkerchief, which she put over her nose and mouth as she roused Mac from a deep sleep. The night was black with the emulsion of dust swirling in the hot air.

They stepped into the hot, stinging air, ducking from the strong winds that whipped through the brim of their clutched hats. Mac watched the dust erupt in puffs around each footstep. If he stepped harder the dust would float up to his knees, then rise higher, rather than settle. They were the first off the bus and to be seated in the window table of the cafe. No view could be seen but the headlights of the bus and silhouetted passengers groggily rushing out of the storm. The dust blew in with the passengers through the opening and closing door and settled again on the tables and coats, blanketing every surface with a film.

"Welcome, everyone, you are welcome to sit. Coffee is available for five cents and soup for 25 cents," announced Susy, the hair-curled and powder-faced patroness of the café. Al came out from the kitchen. "Welcome you all, please have yourself rest—no need to order anything, you are welcome as our guests." Susy looked over at him through her eyebrows.

"We're in what has gotten to be a regular dust storm. Hard to know when one dies before the next begins again," Al said as he wiped his wet hands on his stained, once-white apron. Those that came in first got seats and maybe a table, a few shared their tables, then the rest stood. At the slot machine and one or two fed nickels while the others watched.

"Bessie, I want to try the slot machine." Florence motioned to the crowd.

"No one ever wins at those, they're fixed somehow," Bess told her. "Just wait and see if anyone wins tonight." And they sat looking inward. The wind, racing its clouds of dust through the cracks of the cafe door, deafened the conversation. Bess slept a bit in the dark of the early morning, but only remembered being awake with the quiet of the calmed storm. Her eyes were dry from the haze, and she felt a constant sneeze in her nose.

"Florence, look!" she shook her sister awake. The sky was still dark. A distant redness grew up as a glow in the eastern sky. A fuzzy sphere of the rising sun attempted to shine through the miasma floating both up and down. From the swirl of dust passing in front of the red sphere of the rising sun rolled a sedan-type truck filled high with household objects and people of all ages. As it came closer, Bess said, "The front is a Hudson Super-Six sedan, but the back is a sight." The front end had been cut off in the middle and a truck bed welded to the Hudson. Wooden boards were built up high on the sides filled with belongings. Mattresses, wooden boxes of clothes, and four poles held a tarp that blocked the sun and rain. It sprouted from the truck bed still emerging from the dust cloud. Two children, a young couple, two elders and middle-aged brothers balanced on top of the load. The truck pulled up to the window, completely blocking the glowing sun.

The brothers and their mother, in a loose Mother Hubbard dress, left the cab.

Through the window, Bess, in her Mother-in-Law silk, looked into the mother's eyes. Within an instant, they connected. The mother's hazel eyes spoke of tragedy and pain overcome to mount a place of high calm and understanding. This woman knew, accepted and welcomed her place as leader of the family, a place earned that could not be taken. By not recognizing hurt or fear, but by her very act of denying those, she buffered her family. Hurt and fear could not reach or be acknowledged by her husband or children if it was not first felt by her. Bess recognized her stalwart look as one she'd acquired along the way. She now understood herself for the first time. They had both learned that calm was a better place to be than joy or sorrow. From this great and humble place, these two women had a calm stoic beauty. They stood against all differences with a remote and faultless sense of judgment. The steady and sure walk out of the dusty cloud showed a priestess who knew if she shook, the whole family shook, and if she wavered, the whole family could fall into an abyss. This woman looked into Bess's eyes and, without a nod, deferred to the matriarch she recognized Bess had become.

"Where you heading?" Susy asked the extended family coming through the door.

"Don't know?" the older man replied. "We have got to go 'cause they took the tractor to my granpappy's home. Only the metal barn can't be plowed under. His pump's gone dry." Banks had left the farmers in the dust, perplexed and scratching plans with sticks into the earth. Their next step, to survive, had to be taken by each family. They didn't know where that step might lead.

Suzy poured two cups of coffee into mugs. A dime was set down, where the family sat beside Bess' table. Flo, Bess and Mac listened.

"Ma, they keep saying it's the bank, but the bank is made up of folks, ain't it?" the tall thin man with the shaggy beard asked quietly. His sunburned face was dark in expression and his brow furrowed deeply as he tried to figure out a way to feed his family. Sun-whipped eyes set deep into his sharp-angled cheekbones smoldered in the pain of his loss of direction and work. His wife and children walked cautiously beside the heartbroken man hoping his anger would consume his despair. They'd already seen gentlemen aching with hurt so bad that they'd turned on their children and wives. "It'd be our land, Pa," she said. "We were born on it, and every year we broke it, worked it, buried our parents in it. It makes ownership to do that year after year."

"My grandpa killed Indians for it, my pa' killed snakes for it, now the cotton's sapped it of an' strength to keep us fed. The bankers are worst than the Indians and snakes," he said.

At that moment, Bess saw only the cars. She held a bus ticket that caused her to leave her brothers and sister to be with her husband in Beverly Hills. She had left her husband to be surrounded by her friends and family in Chicago. This woman had nothing but a cut off truck with all her possessions piled behind, but she kept her family together. What Bess had worked for, since she was a child, was from the same cloth she just heard in the local vernacular: We're going to stick together. A few hours later, the bus was back on the road. Sitting in the front seat again, with her son at her side, Bess watched the light of day illuminate Route 66 as a path of people in flight. Refugees from floods, dust and shrinking land migrated by horse and wagon, automobile and foot. In a three-day-dust-storm, 350 million tons of soil blew off the land of the West and Southwest and was deposited as far east as Boston and New York, where streetlights were illuminated during the day to shed a glow through the dust.

This long concrete path wound over red and gray soil from the Mississippi River to Oklahoma City. After Texas, they would cross the Great Divide and down into the New Mexico desert. Mac drew the fences made of willow as the bus was going by fast. The fence was two strands of barbed wire on crooked willow poles. Where there was a crotch at the right height, the wire lay there. When there was no crotch, a rusted baling wire lashed it to the badly trimmed post. Behind the wire fencing, the dust-covered corn attempted to grow, mostly beaten down by wind, heat and drought. He started again. Mac sketched the whole scene, then filled in the details as he spotted them. Bess learned the Buicks, Nashes, DeSotos. Plymouths, Chryslers, Rocknes and Stars came in a parade of rolling, rusty junk. "Flo, is that really an Apperson?"

"Bess, those haven't been made for at least ten years." Bess glanced again at Mac's drawing. The fence worked. He gesture-sketched in dried corn stalks behind the wire fence. The sun burned down on the green corn that grew darker green to protect itself before fading to light ochre. The surface of the earth crusted over, becoming as pale as the cloudless, musty sky. The leaves of the young corn lost their strength for want of water and tilted downward. Mac saw as he drew the bent stalk, it was like the bent-over posture of the farmer who had walked into the cafe. He drew another stalk, worn out like its caretaker, then another and another. The drawn field of corn became an army of worn-out hungry-looking farmers bowed over from their weary spines. Brown lines on the leaves widened and moved in to the central ribs. On occasion, the sky attempted to form a high wispy cloud that gave no rain. Dry stream beds taunted the farmers. The sun seemed sharp and brutal in this world that paper and pencil attempted to capture. Mac wanted to show his father what they saw. The inventiveness in the drawing came from an inner, non-coercive order created by the trust between Mac and his mother. She allowed him the confidence to experiment by not interfering, while offering protection and continuity.

"Mom, look!" The two watched a rumbling tractor in the field. Close-up, the wind whisked under the stones, carrying with it clouds of dust, old leaves and straw, marking its course with drifts and depressions of the land. The diesel tractor crawled the field, laying tracks after picking and overturning everything in its path. It thundered through the wispy cotton while raising a huge cloud of dust and fuel exhaust. It droned through fences and houses, over the goose-necked pump, purposely ignoring hills, streams and gulches. The driver was goggled by his own hunger and need for work, driven by the faceless banks behind him. The feet of that bank owner and the paid tractor driver never touched this earth. But a driver sat on an iron seat pressing an iron pedal three feet above the ground and five feet below the cloud of dust. The diesel tractor ruled the land now, surgically removing the roots of life of Oklahoma, Texas and Missouri.

"Bessie, I'm going to check out the jazz I hear from the speakeasy out back." Florence wandered off while they waited for a dinner of meatloaf and potatoes at a Texas roadside cafe with *Joe and Minnie's Eats* on the sign over the door. I'm not hungry from all the sitting we're doing." Flo pranced out the side door following the music. Bess let Mac put a nickel in the slot machine. *We have cash to risk*. She said, "It's only money."

"Bessie, LIVE jazz music is coming from a speakeasy—they have tapped beer!" Flo rushed back all flushed, smoky smelling and perspiring from dancing in the crowd. Mac looked up calmly, then held his drawing at arm's length and squinted to see it differently. He set it down and smudged more of the graphite dots into dried ears of corn.

"Flo, look—Joe and Minnie only got five cents from us," Bess pointed. As the bus was backing up, they saw the owner step over to the slot machine and put in nickels until the lemons lined-up and the machine emptied nickels into his apron. Scraps of discarded farm equipment, household items, flat tires littered both sides of Route 66. It seemed what was once precious had become a burden, then extra and finally, not even worth it.

Just before the Arizona Mountains, a family who had built a trailer from junk wood waited by the road with their possessions. What were they waiting for? Hope or faith? Jalopies were every fifth car rolling along filled with an extended family or families and their crates and boxes. Belongings were left on the side of the road or in broken-down cars. Mac felt his mother shiver and looked over. The ominous sign for Route 666, the Devil's Highway, gave Bess the quivers because of its treacherous, deadly reputation. A tortuous, wild, and strange road angled off and up the rugged eastern seam of Arizona through the Petrified Forest, across the Zuni River, across the Apache National Forest, and into the mountain mining towns. One hundred miles of twists and curves and altitude ranges from twenty-nine hundred feet to more than eleven thousand feet sent more than its share of travelers crashing off cliffs. She hummed a bit of Nat King Cole's song "drivers get their kicks on Route 66," then added with a smile, "they take their risks on Route 666." Gently rising over the mountains in

Arizona to plateau before descending into lower mountains, their bus leisurely wound into California. Long caravans of overloaded jalopies with steaming radiators and anxious drivers listening to their engines streamed along the highway.

Bess came to fancy the Packards, Chryslers and Buicks over the Pontiacs and LaSalles. The highway had become their home and the constant motion, the flow of their conversation. Pauses at cafes gave a flavor of the country they traversed. The stops slowed the progress so that they could taste the air. California had well- established Mexicans who allowed the settlers onto their land, until the settlers registered as actual owners. The Mexicans moved on. New owners opened grocery stores. They employed the Chinese, Japanese and Mexicans who lived on rice and beans from their grocery to grow and harvest their oranges and grapefruit. The settlers thought of themselves as honest folk from the Midwest. They were forming groups of neighbors as they traveled. Arriving in caravans of thin children and starved adults. With the influx of new workers, crops changed to rows of lettuce, artichokes, potatoes and cauliflower. Crops to stoop, crawl and clean the bugs as the farm owner forgot how earth smelled. The feel under their feet was of metal machinery, not soil. The workers were paid in store credit. They didn't unpack from their travels, but camped out of their trucks in Hoovervilles. Migrating from crop to crop throughout this fertile valley and bay of the Pacific Ocean kept families employed. First 20,000 then 50,000 then 200,000 migrants flooded into Southern California. Each wanted a small plot they could grow their saved seeds. Many ended up willing to trade their car for a full meal. Amidst the swarm of the hungry came the bus from Chicago. Mac was now drawing the jalopies on Route 66 and the bundles of mattresses, pots and pans on the truck beds. Bess couldn't stop looking at the clusters of families, tired cars and campsites in ditches in Hoovervilles along the side of the road. She saw the mother with the hazel eyes over each campfire making a stew, if lucky, to feed a family of twelve.

Chapter 31: The Edges of Stone

Sunday ambles at Santa Monica Pier beside the placid water and drought-like sunshine were treasured days. William and Mac, Bess and Flo moseyed along the pier in broad brimmed hats, flowing dresses and twill slacks. An airplane waved an advertisement that beckoned visitors to the *Rex*, a fancy logging ship three miles offshore.

"Rex is a high falutin' off-track horse-racing boat," William informed his wife and sister-in-law. "I've heard of the ship while in Ventura." Taxis transported Californians three miles offshore twenty-four-seven, beyond the boundaries of the laws of prohibition. International law prevailed out there.

"Let's go Bess! Let's try our luck on the horses!" Flo said.

William was excited to go out on a boat on such a beautiful day. "Sail the high seas! What'd ya say we head offshore!" swashbuckling William said with a wave of his hat. Bess was pleased to see her cheery sister delighted with the day. Flo had been so disappointed auditioning for acting roles. Bess held the shoulder of her only son. She wanted a moment to talk with Mac, and this offered her the opportunity.

"How about an ice cream cone on the pier, Mac?" Bess said. Then, to her sister and husband, "We'll walk."

"Brilliant, then," William said and charged off holding Flo's hand. As soon as they left, Bess was a bit bothered by the abrupt change of plans and gazed at them prancing to the shore. In her white dress flowing with the easterly breeze, Flo pranced with William to the pier. As the water taxi set off over serene water, Florence and William sang WWI sea songs and turned to wave.

"Mac, this stone is just an object," Bess leaned over to pick up a smooth granite stone and put it in her son's hand. "The water can coat it to a shiny brilliance, but it will dry to matte. The sand will cover it, but not stick. The waves roll in and over it, receding away, leaving the stone where it lay."

"It's a rock, Mom." He didn't know why she was talking like that. He noticed the rock had a remarkable quality.

"To know its name, granite, is not enough. Sniff it. Imagine its origin. Touch it with the tip of your tongue, check its roughness or hardness, listen as it drops in the water." This was not like Bess but she sensed her quiet son was upset and let her instincts flow with an unusual philosophical insight. The stone tasted salty, a sea-thing. He grimaced.

"It's a rock," Mac said deadpan.

"This stone has a resistance and a response that changes with the time of day or season, through light and shadow," she said. "It has a propensity that caused us to pick this one."

"Why are we talking about a rock!" The two continued walking down the beach beside the lapping, quiet waves, their shoes in her hand and his trousers rolled to mid-calf.

"This stone has edges worn by the forces of life. It remains itself through it all."

"What is the point? Why are you talking about this rock, can't we talk about something else?" Why did Mom want to talk about a rock? His friends were in Chicago. A new California buddy, Tony, had blown off half his hand with an M-80 on the Fourth. That was something to talk about! They'd taken the bus along Route 66 with the long, frightening masses of famished Midwestern kids making their way from dusty farms for food in California. That was worth talking about! This rock was not worth talking about! They reached a pool of seawater, separated from the ocean and held still by a drift of sand. An offshore gust gave the surface an erratic motion. Bess opened her palm for the stone calmly. Then she dropped the stone into the pool. It made a hole in the water which rippled.

"See, the ripples expand. They rebound off the edge and cross back. You send out messages with your actions like this stone's action. That action rebounds right back to you—watch what energy you send out." Ripples of wind intersected the expanding rings. She picked up the dripping stone and placed it in Mac's hand.

"Mom! Cut it out about the rock. I don't get why we have to talk about it." The lifeguard siren sounded.

"Now that's a new sound since we lived here in '29," Bess noted as he picked up the rock. Panic swelled… abruptly, she grabbed Mac's shoulder. "Come on! We've got to get back." The wet stone dropped in his pocket. The weight of it pulled on his hip. It thumped as he walked. He reached in and rubbed it between his fore-finger and thumb, feeling the sun's warmth, the wet coolness, emanating from it still. "Your father and Flo are out there! Something is wrong! Let's go!" How did she know? A flock of white gulls flapped away.

Was it only a moment… Was it an hour, an afternoon or a day? … Flo and her white dress filled with the sea was being carried up the beach by his father. Is she dead? Bess hurried down the beach in stocking feet and caught Flo's hand. It was cold already. Where is an ambulance? A lifeguard? The colors of the face, which hadn't seemed right, were becoming increasingly wrong. Yellow around the eyes. Pale lavender creeped up near Flo's lips. She was still in her white summer frock, soaked to her skin with the memory of her laughter. Her strong boned, toughened adult face, with concerns and wants, melted into her child's face that Bess used to scrub with a washcloth before bed. "Remember behind the ears," their mother used to say. Tears welled up. Bess's head filled with phlegm and pain. Can this be undone. Can we start this day over? Flo is dead. I'll be more cautious if we can start again. A gaping hole burnt through her forged demeanor as Bess turned to the silent father and staring son—"Boat Accident! Florence died in a boat accident." Mac reached into the weight of the wet stone in his pocket. He rubbed the cool wet surface between his forefinger and thumb. It slipped in his grasp. This stone has edges worn by the forces of life.

The linden trees lining the street flung down a shadow denser than a velvet curtain on Mac's way home from school. His grades tumbled from Bs to Cs. Bess let him decide if he wanted to go to school each day. She found herself balancing on the point of a pin that caused her to shift with any motion or breeze. Planning Flo's memorial service kept her from sinking below functioning at all. Eva did not ask questions when she came to California to attend the burial. William did not enter her home but rented an apartment at Wiltshire's place. Her horse-playing husband now lived half way between them and the Santa Anita Racetrack in Wiltshire's St. Andrew Apartments when he wasn't in Ventura.

Bess felt half of her had died. Between Bess and William, there were promises forgotten. Over the decades their love ebbed and flowed. He didn't save her sister. I should forgive him, she thought. William gave her space. They called once a week about Mac. Bess accepted him for who he was. She recognized his strengths, his failings. Maybe I still love him? She needed her family. Mac recalled his father's words from their car ride: "Just keep up your art, I'll be watching your progress." Mac rubbed the stone in his pocket. Bess became shakier as she tried to regain her balance without Florence, then packed their bags to move to Chicago. Brinks came to pick up the loosely packed china. After the long bus ride back on Route 66, she and Mac watched farmers plant shelter belts to slow the wind and capture the dirt through Texas and Missouri. They stayed with Henry Fox and his sister, Maggie, in Oak Park. She fended off the opprobrium of a single woman with a son in a tight knit community. Bess had no tolerance for judgments passed in Saint's Rest and knew she'd move to Edgewater.

Inseparable in loss, Mac and Bess settled in at the Edgewater Beach hotel on Lake Michigan's shore. The consistent and varied rhythm of the ever-present waves reset her heartbeat and calmed her soul. Their combined solitude gave them a reassurance over the summer as the rhythmic waves lapped on the shore. Mac and his Saint Ita's school friends met after Mass.

She was a bit relieved when he asked to get ice cream with them and looked forward to a quiet day in her apartment. Bess sat in a sunny corner, her desk arranged to write letters. All left untouched. At the moment, she was content to sit in silence and listen to the waves lapping the shore. She looked down to the lines of gray water ripple to frothy lines on the sandy beach. Or, she found comfort in her patterned Oriental rug, the textured plaster walls and the high cornices meeting gracefully in the corner. Checking the list of items as they were unpacked gave her a peaceful quiet calm. But now each glass, china plate and collectible was set in its place in her mahogany carved furniture. She dozed in the chair, then made a cup of coffee and watched the rippling water again.

Mac and his friends walked along Sheridan Road. A bundle of Sunday newspapers bounced off a truck into the gutter at their feet. They stopped, went silent, looked at each other, and grabbed the papers, ran to the el-stop corner. As riders slowed to enter the door, the boys called out, "Papers!" Ten cents a paper. The friends divided their earnings, bought ice cream at the drug store and had enough for el rides to the loop and back. They ran up the el aisle to the front window to press their faces close to the glass. It frosted with quickened breath. The speed of the train built. Mac's exhilaration of flying over the rumble of fast metal wheels on tracks engulfed another afternoon. They flew over the city.

Mac loved the el—the speed and loud rattling above the rooftops. He loved the sound of rushing past skyscrapers, over water tanks and above cars. They would ride the el to Evanston or Wilmette. They rode to Cubs games to watch Gabby Hartnet catch from the el platform. They jumped on the train again and paused in the Loop. When they weren't riding the el, tennis lessons or the swimming pool at the Edgewater Beach brought them together.

In the fall, Mac began the long commute each morning by el and bus to Fenwick in Oak Park. He sat in the front seat while reading *The New Yorker* cartoons on his way to and from high school. The radio was tuned to FDR, the calming male voice in their home, soothing the country as it shook on a rumbling economy. On Saturdays, Bess's horse racing outings to see friends started up slowly as she drove along Sheridan Road. Most thought it was an improvement.

Besides the French club, dance committee, football and boxing teams, Mac was the frosh cartoonist of Fenwick's yearbook. Mac was thrilled with the heady mix of anonymity and authority over his own sense of self. He welcomed the validation to become himself. While mastering his long-legged stride, he sold stocks to family and friends for stamp money to mail out his cartoons. If the cartoon was published, he shared the profit with his contributors. And so, he began the delicate balance between the creative spirit and commerce. He accepted the talent he'd been given and his mother constantly encouraged him. Mac knew that making art and giving his drawings exponentially enhanced them by communicating ideas. The giving created the void to conjure more art. He built his connection to community through art. It was a continuous squandering of all created perishables: make, distribute and make to fill the vacuum. He was finding balance between illusions of grandeur and gaining respect. He needed to learn to not exploit the essence of what he made. A monetary value was already being imposed on his talent. He needed to learn grace in the financial bet with others investing. He adapted to teetering out there while editors decided if his cartoons were published.

"It helps if you have success when you are young," his boxing trainer coached. The fine balance of soliciting risky investments from friends who invested in his stamps and solitarily creating his drawing lyrical graphite magic he found was the difference of making it or not. He was working towards cartooning with *The New Yorker* when life threw him a twist. It was on a September day in 1938 with his cousin Jack when they were celebrating their shared birthday at the Esquire ice cream shop. Mac nibbled on a macaroon cookie and wondered out loud about what it would be like to fly, just as a tall woman behind him ordered a hot fudge sundae with peanuts.

Epilogue

As we had inherited and were unified by the changes of the 1960s while we watched them happen, Dad gave us his lifetime of art so that we would work together. Eventually his estate closed to each of our gain. The reportorial art Dad gave me hummed and throbbed from the walls, fluttered from the brown paper packages to be told as a story. While my children packed to live in the east, the west, Asia, South America and Australia I reminded them to listen to an angel if one advised from their shoulder. As our nest emptied and the paintings lined up to inform my narrative arc, Mom's columns and articles answered some of the questions I failed to ask. Branches of my family retreated into their lives, yet came together during Covid to watch out for each other. My splinter of our story tells of an adventurous Irene and Mac who recognized injustice and a way to nudge the world in a more just direction. Their creativity came from a purpose beyond themselves that instilled a tireless energy for making things better than they found them. It was not hard to discover that their life

"Hawk and Dove" by Margot McMahon

force evolved from generations of seeking equality. May this story tie my children to their past and to each other as they continue on their path of purpose that is larger than themselves for a lifetime of nudging in the right direction. I look forward to experience what happens next.

Acknowledgments

It took a village of readers and fellow writers to help me complete this story. My family: Daniel, Brendan, Irene and Aubrey gave the time, tolerated the struggle, and had believed at some point I would throw in the towel. My family's mixture of first, middles and confirmation names helped to reduce repetition. Scott Jacobs, Gail Duberchin, Eileen Pollack, Nadine Kenney Johnston, Marilyn Walton, Heather Buchanan, Rachael Herron, Fred Shafer and John Knight guided me through the weeds. My book groups, Everscholars, Ragdale Foundation residents, neighbors and friends may find our conversations or readings in the threads. For the shelves and shelves of books that I turned to when words alluded me, Mom and Dad for exemplifying and providing remarkable lives, I thank you.

About the Author

Margot McMahon, daughter of artist-reporter Franklin McMahon, has received several writing awards and authored non-fiction books for adults and young adults including *The Fifth Season,* the recipient of the 2020 Mate E. Palmer First Place Book Award. An internationally-awarded sculptor, Margot lives in Chicago with her husband and visiting three grown children.

If Trees Could Talk is the second book of Margot's family saga. The first book, *Mac & Irene: A WWII Saga,* is based on the true story of Franklin "Mac" McMahon, Emmy and Peabody Award-winning artist-reporter and filmmaker. In WWII, McMahon was a U.S. Army Air Corps B-17 navigator who survived the Stalag 13 POW camp to return home to Chicago and his sweetheart Irene. McMahon later served as the courtroom artist for the Emmet Till Trial and the infamous Chicago "conspiracy" Trial of 1969/70. McMahon was also a U.S. Presidential artist.